MENTOR ME

INSTRUCTION AND ADVICE FOR ASPIRING WRITERS

HEIDI STOCK, EDITOR

ISBN-13: 978-0-9958990-3-2

www.aspiringcanadianwriters.org

The creator and editor of this book, Heidi Stock, wishes to acknowledge and
thank all contributors.

All images provided by contributors are property of the photographer or
subject and may not be reproduced or shared without express permission.

Many thanks for the editing services provided by Sherry Hinman,
www.thewriteangle.ca, and cover design, book design, and final proofreading
services provided by Gillian Katsoulis, www.gillianryanpublishing.com.

CONTENTS

FOREWORD

Mentor Me: Instruction and Advice for Aspiring Writers has five sections: Creative Coaching; Poetry; Songwriting; Screenwriting; and Musical Theatre.

This structure follows my own personal and creative path and the evolution of mentoring opportunities in poetry, songwriting, and screenwriting, created through Aspiring Canadian Writers Contests Inc., which I founded in 2012.

Each section contains instruction and advice, with interviews and essays written by acclaimed writers and industry experts. These are followed by a concluding piece called *Mentor Me: An Inside View*, which guides you through the creation of first and final drafts of a poem, song, or script, and can also give you a sense of what one-on-one mentoring sessions might be like for you.

~ Heidi ~

Photo credit: Magenta Photo Studio

Heidi Stock, Founder
Aspiring Canadian Writers Contests
www.aspiringcanadianwriters.org

CREATIVE COACHING

Interviews with Mentors and Creative Coaches

Interview with Patricia Pearson

about loss and grief, mental health and creative expression, and her interest in mentoring

Photo credit: Russell Monk

Patricia Pearson is an award-winning journalist and novelist, whose work has appeared in *The New Yorker*, the *New York Times*, *Huffington Post* and *Businessweek*, among other publications. She is the author of five books and was a long-time member of *USA Today*'s Op-Ed Board of Contributors. She also directed the research for the 2009 History Channel documentary, *The Science of the Soul*.

Pearson is known for upending conventional wisdom—her first book, *When She Was Bad*, which questioned our simplistic understanding of violent women, won the Arthur Ellis Award for Best Non-Fiction Crime Book of 1997. Her most recent book, *A Brief History of Anxiety (Yours & Mine)*, challenged the notion that mood disorders are purely brain-based, with no relationship to culture and personal circumstance.

~~~

Heidi: With age, I've found that my reaction to death has been an urgency to take action on dreams, new or old, or sometimes not yet discovered. After 9/11, I got moving on an entrepreneurial project. Ten years later, when four extended family members died over the course of a year, I committed myself fully to my path. The loss of close family members—your father and your sister—gave life to a new creation, your book, *Opening Heaven's Door: What the Dying May Be Trying to Tell Us About Where They're Going.* **How did this book come to be?**

Patricia: Well, my first impulse after my father and sister died, was to make some sense of the grace of their dying. I was braced for the sorrow of death, but I didn't anticipate the mystery. As a writer, I was in the unusual position of being able to explore what I'd witnessed and felt.

Heidi: Although most of us won't personally experience near death experiences (NDEs), because we won't be in the scenarios in which they occur (e.g., in life or death situations on the operating table, the battlefield, tragic accidents), I have personally heard many stories from individuals (family, friends, co-workers) who dreamed of their loved one at the time of death, without knowledge of their passing until the following day. In each account, the dream was comforting, and I wondered if they were open to sharing their story because it was a dream. If I was dismissive or indifferent to their experience—there was minimal risk of embarrassment. It was "just a dream." It wasn't their personal account of "seeing the light." **Did you find hesitation among those people who provided testimonials for your book? Or did you find a desire to share?**

Patricia: I, myself, hesitated. It took me a few years before I even put pen to page on the subject. When I talked to other people—told them what I was researching—they would often preface what they said by confiding, "I've never told anyone this, but ..." It was actually amazing to discover how many people were having extraordinary experiences around death and keeping quiet.

Heidi: In writing *Opening Heaven's Door*, from the time of concept to publication, did you anticipate resistance from a segment of the population, even though your approach was that of a journalist, researching and presenting facts, truths and beliefs from many perspectives: science, medicine, health care and world religions? On your Twitter account, you describe yourself as a "deeply alarmed soul."

Patricia: The Twitter reference was actually from my earlier book, on the history of anxiety. I did anticipate resistance, but what surprised me was how little there was in face-to-face conversation. Many people, including other journalists, are eager to explore this area but don't want to be written off as silly or credulous. What helps is to explain that these are genuine experiences that are felt very profoundly, just as love and anger and anxiety are real emotional states. What it all points to is another matter. But we don't rush to explain away love by insisting it is just an endorphin cascade in the brain.

Heidi: In recent years, in popular culture in the West, there has been a strong appetite for what is not human—vampires, zombies, aliens, robots. One of our greatest scientific minds, Stephen Hawking, has cautioned us about artificial intelligence ("killer robots"), and yet we are still fascinated by what is not human. Why

does there seem to be less openness to the possibility of NDEs in the West?

Patricia: I'm not sure there is less openness to NDEs—as witness the bestseller status of Dr. Eben Alexander's book, *Proof of Heaven*. I think there is less awareness of what is actually entailed in the experience and how powerful and reality-shattering it is. We make pop culture references to "the tunnel and the light," but those sound like minor visual glitches or brief hallucinations. In fact, those who have NDEs are entirely immersed in an ocean of light that possesses qualities of sentient intelligence and love. They are *blown away* by what they encounter. This is what is missing from popular understanding. Mostly, I think that is a failure of media. Journalists have been far too incurious and skeptical about spiritual experiences and tend to avoid interviewing people who've had them. When my own book came out, newspapers that had always reviewed my work on other subjects just completely ignored me.

Heidi: You have researched and written books on serious, complex, controversial topics like NDEs in *Opening Heaven's Door*, and also on anxiety in *A Brief History of Anxiety (Yours & Mine)*, but you have a playful spirit and wit, evident in your bio on your official website and publicly recognized when you became a finalist for the Leacock Memorial Medal for Humour for your bestselling comic novel, *Playing House*. **How has your gift of humour affected your life personally and professionally, as well as your approach to writing *Opening Heaven's Door* and the public response to it?**

Patricia: I think humour is a powerful tool for communicating painful subjects. It's an icebreaker, really. If you use it properly, it is a way to put your readers at ease with what you want to discuss. It also signals to them that you don't take yourself too seriously or aren't trying to be self-important. That being said, it is still difficult for female writers and speakers to use humour without being stereotyped as fundamentally unserious. I've had to live with that. We still inhabit a world where women are allowed to be funny or smart—but not both.

Heidi: In *Opening Heaven's Door,* you also discuss Western mysticism and the spiritual connection of the artist. I came to writing, first to poetry, through a spiritual experience resulting from traditional prayer and meditation—in particular, my concern for a dying loved one. Catherine Graham, our inaugural poetry contest judge and mentor, has shared that grief (the loss of her mother and her father during her undergraduate years) led to journal writing, which later became poetry. **Please talk a bit about the concept of *synesthesia* and your view on what mystics and artists have to offer to our understanding and interpretation of the connection between the physical and spiritual world.**

Patricia: Artistry is the capacity to weave patterns, to make connections that alter understanding by showing hidden meaning. To do so, you have to have a kind of unbounded perception, which is why artistic talent, sensitivity and mental illness often group together genetically. Spiritual intuition or perception also seems to occur in this cluster of traits. There is quite a bit of very intriguing new research on the fact that people with psychic abilities, or those who have NDEs, also experience synesthesia. This is, essentially, a neurological condition of crossed senses: people with synesthesia "hear" colours, or "see" musical notes. They process sensory information in an unbounded, cross-associative way. So, it may be that a human attunement to non-ordinary reality takes place—or possibly can only take place— in this neurological state. That may be where shamanic trance and drumming, and even hallucinogens, have played a role historically.

Heidi: Your experiences and the loss of your father and sister led to *Opening Heaven's Door* and a new path as a life coach. What is an integral professional coach, and why does this type of coaching appeal to you?

Patricia: I've always been interested in engaging in counselling and mentoring and find myself doing it quite a lot, informally. But I've recently trained as an integral coach, which is someone who works with people to help them grow and develop. In a way, it's like a cross between a therapist and a personal trainer. There's a great deal of wisdom in the integral method. For one thing, it doesn't assume that one approach fits all. You're trained to meet people where they live and see out of their eyes. You don't label them or tell them "you should" do this thing or that. It honours human complexity, which has always been important to me in my writing.

Interview with Laurie Wagner

Photo and biography courtesy of Laurie Wagner

Laurie Wagner has been publishing books and essays and teaching writing for the last 25 years. She is a process guru and has a genius for holding space, helping people unzip what's inside of them and get ink on the page. A creative brainstormer, she specializes in out-of-the-box ways to tell your stories.

Her Wild Writing classes are the cornerstone of her live work, but she also teaches on the internet. She is the author of *Living Happily Ever After: Couples Talk about Long Term Love* and *Expectations: 30 Women Talk About Becoming a Mother.*

Check out her blog at 27powers.org.

~~~

Heidi: "Tell true stories," you say on your website. "The stories are just below the surface, waiting for us to slow down so we can open up, pay attention and begin to write." **Please share the connection between slowing down, being aware, and the ability to write, as well as the value to the writer of telling his or her true stories.**

11

Laurie: The value of slowing down is that stories are moving through us all the time, or rather, moments that trigger stories are always moving through us, hovering around—if we're paying attention. You can go to the supermarket and find a story as you squeeze lemons or avocados for ripeness. Your mother did this—you remember shopping with your mother or making a pie with your mother. Now *you're* the mother. A story about making pie is a story about becoming the mother, you know? We could probably go to the grocery store and make a list of five stories that each of us could tell just being around food: stories of family meals, stories of cooking and tradition, stories of food as it relates to our bodies. We think we're just going to the market, but we're actually moving into story central if we're paying attention.

You ask about the value of telling true stories. What I've come to understand over the years is that there's a psychic alignment that comes from telling the truth. You've heard the phrase, "the truth will set you free"; well, it's true on the page as well because when you lay down the right word—the most honest word—you will experience a kind of relief because you're naming things as they are and you're not hiding. You are resting in the truth, and when you do this it has the effect of calming you down. Think about when a chiropractor aligns your spine—she does this so that there's no stress or pain as you sit or stand or move. It's the same when you use honest language to tell your stories—true words fall into place and there's a calm, honest, energetic fit to them.

Heidi: You also share on your website, "I got over my fear of not measuring up to what the 'market' wants, decades ago. Interestingly, that's when I got my first book deal." What advice do you have for aspiring writers who are discouraged about their "progress" and fearful that their work will never be published?

Laurie: As wonderful as getting published is, if you're too focused on that, you're focused on the wrong thing—but especially if you're a newer writer. Newer writers need to write—a lot. Newer writers need to build a relationship with themselves on the page. They need to deepen their ideas and share that work with friends or in classes, get feedback and take the work to a deeper place. When I took a break from the market and from selling my work a number of years ago, I did it because I was focused on writing pieces I thought the market wanted, but I wasn't in touch with the kinds of stories that mattered most to me. I also hadn't really developed my voice and my style. Trying to get the market to pay attention to me when I didn't even know who I was as a writer seemed to pull me off course; I needed to pull away from the market to find myself.

That said, it's wonderful to see your stories published. My counsel to writers who want to see a byline is to write as much as possible and to share that work with friends and in classes, and eventually, if you're lucky, someone will want to publish your work. But do spend more time writing than thinking about publishing. And start small. A lot of times people don't get published because they've set their sights too high—they want to publish in *The New Yorker* or some super prestigious literary magazine. What about starting more modest, like publishing something on a blog, or publishing something on a small, online magazine in your community or in your local paper. Don't think about the money—it's not about the money. It's about you making work that means something to you and finding a way to share it with the world—even if it's just a small corner of the world.

Heidi: In addition to being a writing coach, you are a professional Co-Active Coach®, trained by the Coaches Training Institute, www.coactive.com. How does this training influence and assist you in your role as a writing instructor?

Laurie: What I learned as a coach is the value of letting people struggle and suffer and not be happy all the time. Through struggle comes epiphany and deeper understanding. When I'm teaching, I'm often in the presence of writers who are working through some really tough things, and becoming a coach helped me to learn how to be okay with people being unhappy. I needed to learn how to trust that unhappiness to take them to the next place.

Heidi: How can we make writing part of our day-to-day lives, and what are the benefits of regularly nurturing our creativity?

Laurie: It's easy to make writing a daily part of your life. You can do morning pages, the 15-minute writing practice that Julia Cameron talks about in her book, *The Artist's Way*. That's a beautiful and easy way to land on the page each day. Don't worry about whether it's any good or not—that's not the point. For me, when I'm spending the first 15 minutes of the day writing, I'm stirring my creative pot; I'm placing creativity and words and thoughts ahead of everything else, and honestly, this makes me happy. When I'm really on my game, I'm waking up at 6 a.m., making a cup of tea and sitting right down to write. That's the most creative thing I can do for myself because when it's early, my brain hasn't turned on and I'm not that smart yet. Smart is great for editing, but it's not great for creativity and getting ink on the page. When it's early, I'm still in that fuzzy, creative wonderland that's part dream–part waking, and my words and my ideas are much more interesting and fresh. Starting the day like that makes everything else livable—honestly. Being in a relationship with my creativity first thing in the morning transforms the mundane aspects of being alive.

Interview with Chris Kay Fraser

Writing Coach, Facilitator, and Firefly Creative Writing Founder

Photo and biography courtesy of Chris Kay Fraser

Chris's history with Firefly goes right back to the very start, when it was just an idea flickering in her imagination. With an abiding love for words, people and community, Chris did a Master's degree at the University of Toronto in Adult Education and Community Development, focusing on the potential for writing groups to create positive personal transformation and community cohesion. While still adrift in academia, Chris followed her deepest dream and tacked some colourful flyers around her neighbourhood to see if anyone would sign up for a memoir-writing workshop in her home. To her extreme delight, they did.

Chris has been coaching and facilitating for 10 years and brings that comfort, experience and ease into her workshops and coaching relationships. Masterful at creating warm personal connections and helping people feel at home in their stories, Chris is an in-demand coach and facilitator.

www.fireflycreativewriting.com

~~~

Heidi: Tell us about the beginnings of Firefly Creative Writing and your mission or goals.

Chris: Firefly started in a trailer in the woods.

I wasn't doing too well—I was in my mid-20s and feeling that big shaky uncertainty that I think a lot of us feel at that stage. I was finishing an academic degree that left my heart empty. I loved creativity, but I felt small and insufficient in the writing and photography classes I'd been taking. I wanted to "work in the arts" but I had no idea what that meant, so I was starting to think I should follow family tradition and stick with academia.

In a last-ditch attempt to take this creativity thing seriously, I signed up for a week-long filmmaking class at a little hippy film school in an old logging camp on one of the woodsy islands west of Vancouver. About two dozen of us slept in bunk beds and spent our days helping each other make weird little movies. It was the first time I'd been in a creative environment with zero competition. Whatever we wanted to make, we'd just figure out how. We collaborated and colluded and stayed up all night editing each other's scripts or holding boom mikes into the forest to capture frog sounds. There was no possibility of failing, no right or wrong—just helping hands and the breathless feeling of our own creative potential.

The computers were in these little trailers, and I remember one night at 3 or 4 in the morning, deep in the throes of editing, sticking my head out the window to get a gulp of fresh air. I looked up, saw the bright stars shining between the treetops and realized that I was happy for the first time in ages.

So that was my template. I'd found my breath again. I'd learned how to make movies, but I'd also learned how to trust myself, to use my voice, to believe in my right to be heard. I learned that creativity isn't a hierarchy, that there's room for everyone, and that when we help each other we can do incredible things.

Afterward I did a Master's degree in Adult Education and Community Development, trying to turn that big breath of fresh air into something—a path, a plan. I had no idea what I was doing, but I knew it had to do with writing. Finally, I made some little flyers for a writing workshop in my living room, and here I am, nearly 10 years later, with a thriving small business, a wildly dedicated staff, writing workshops almost every night of the week, retreats, online classes and a phenomenally beautiful community of clients.

It's been a decade of slow growth and hard work, but with every class, every retreat, every interaction, I'm trying to recreate the feeling I had in the trailer that night—that everything is possible and not nearly as scary as I'd thought.

Heidi: I returned to creative writing at age 39 after a 20-year absence. When I found the Firefly Creative Writing website, I was intrigued (and relieved) to discover I'm not the only one to put creative self-expression on hold. I was moved by your website's welcome video in which you said, "We can spend years keeping our creative hearts underground." Please speak a bit about this and the challenge to be creative again later in life.

Chris: Oh, *absolutely*, Heidi. There's a huge (and very mistaken) idea out there that it can be "too late" to become a creative person. That's simply not true.

For us, writing is about the joy of expression, the freedom to be and find yourself and the beauty of being seen. None of that has an expiry date. We've had clients in their early teens and we've had clients in their early 90s, and you know what? They have the exact same blocks, same fears, same resistances.

17

I think that we all come to creative expression differently. A woman who starts telling her story at 50 after a cancer scare and a divorce will bring something completely different to the page from someone who gets started in a high school creative writing class. It will be rounder, fuller. She may not know it, but she's spent decades quietly preparing, marinating in the material of her life. I think it's really important to trust our timing and to understand that there's no such thing as wasted time.

There are hundreds of examples of this in the press. Charles Bukowski got started when he was 49. Those *Little House on the Prairie* books weren't published until Laura Ingalls Wilder was 64. (She must have had an amazing memory!) If you Google "writers who started late in life" you'll get a huge, inspiring list. Or you could skip the Googling and just get down to writing, because that, after all, is what it's all about.

Heidi: How can we nurture creativity in adults, especially those who believe they aren't creative? And going beyond creative writing or artistic expression, how can creativity of any kind be fostered?

Chris: I think it comes down to three important elements—safety, space and inspiration.

First of all, safety. If we're worried about being judged, we can't be authentic. It's such a shame that most of us discover writing within the school system. The school system has many merits, but imparting a deep sense of what creativity is and can be is a huge gap. We write; we are judged. We do this over and over. Most of us learn how to please our teachers and in doing so, lose touch with that deep, wild, raw, authentic voice that's inside of us.

We can reclaim it, of course, but we need to feel safe—radically safe— to be messy and uncertain and loose. It's scary. It's vulnerable. In our workshops, when someone shares something they just wrote that minute, we only talk about what we love. What was your favourite line? What skills did you see in this piece? What is this writer great at? Through taking that in, week after week, we learn how to build our strengths and our writing becomes more and more satisfying, then joyful, then completely wondrous.

I also want to say, there are some amazing teachers out there. Kudos to the amazing teachers! I don't want to vilify the whole system. It contains gems.

Okay, now space. Space is key! I hear from people all the time who are scheduled up the wazoo and they want to write. I encourage these people to slow down, even just a *tiny* bit. Sleep in one morning. Clear off a desk and spend an hour looking out the window. Find a café you love, order the most luxurious coffee drink and open your journal. We need to romance our stories and our creative voices out of us— to *woo* them. That starts with giving them a little room to be seen. At first, making time to write might look a lot like making time to nap. That's okay. Nap more. Then open your journal. Not ready? Take another nap.

That's ideal. But it's also possible to make beautiful things in tiny snippets of time. There's a poet here in Ontario, Susan Holbrook, who wrote a long and beautiful poem while breastfeeding her son. She committed to simply write one line when he nursed on the left, then one line when he switched to the right. Slowly and thoughtfully, the poem emerged.

The last important piece is inspiration. In order to produce beauty, we need to consume beauty. In order to exhale, we need to inhale. When people come to us and say, "I'm blocked, I'm empty, I don't know what's wrong with me," we often ask when the last time was that they were truly inspired. This doesn't mean you need to read voraciously; it just means you need to let in the things you love. If you adore flowers, get to a garden. If you love architecture, go to a neighbourhood you don't know and take in the houses. If it's all about heavy metal, blast it in your kitchen and dance your heart out. Feed yourself. Then see what happens.

INTERVIEW WITH ALLYSON LATTA

Photo and biography courtesy of Allyson Latta

Allyson Latta has edited bestselling adult and young-adult fiction and creative non-fiction books by some of Canada's most respected authors. Many have won national and international awards, including the Scotiabank Giller Prize, Rogers Writers' Trust Fiction Prize, the Governor General's Literary Awards, and the Commonwealth Writers' Prize. She holds degrees in psychology and journalism, and she has worked as writer and editor for newspapers and magazines and in university media relations. She was also a freelance writer in Canada and Japan. Allyson taught memoir writing for more than 10 years, for Ryerson University and University of Toronto, and currently leads workshops on writing and editing in Canada, the U.S. and abroad. She has been interviewed on public television about memoir. Her website is Memories into Story.

~~~

Heidi: Memories into Story: Life Writing is the name of your writing course at the University of Toronto School of Continuing Studies (SCS) and also of your website at <u>www.allysonlatta.ca</u>. What are some of the challenges writers face putting their memories into story?

Allyson: I called the University of Toronto SCS courses (intro and advanced) Memories into Story because, in a nutshell, they're intended to help writers take memories, which are in their head and might otherwise remain so, and record them to be shared and appreciated. The curriculum applies whether students want to write for themselves or for family (children, grandchildren, etc.) or hope to publish and reach a wider readership.

Among the biggest challenges is convincing early writers that their stories are worth sharing. "My life hasn't been that interesting" is a common lament, until students discover how fascinated they are by their classmates' stories and have had positive response to their own shared writing. Mark Twain said, "There was never yet an uninteresting life. Such a thing is an impossibility. Inside of the dullest exterior there is a drama, a comedy, and a tragedy."

Writers also find it challenging and worry (too early in the process) about how to reduce a whole life into a story, which in fact isn't the point of memoir. A memoir isn't an autobiography (about an entire life from birth to old age), nor is it necessarily chronological. It frames a single memory, or a series of related memories, and explores its significance to the writer's life. But my approach is to encourage students to write whatever they remember, in no particular order, for a period of time—say, six months, a year, or longer—before considering which stories to share. Many published writers have expressed in different ways the idea that we may have to write to find out what we really want to say.

Honesty and vulnerability, too, are difficult to achieve for writers. It often takes many drafts and much mental and emotional digging, not to mention courage, to create a story that resonates with readers, a story that shares the secrets of the writer's heart. If those secrets are, in some form or another, similar to ours as readers—we human beings are not so very different, after all—we will respond. That's how the magical connection between writer and reader happens.

21

Heidi: Just from my own personal perspective, I found the experience of the workshop process in memoir class when compared to poetry class different. Poems have the soul of the poet in them but are well masked with mystery and tend not to be literal. Memoir is writing about your own life and opening up your memories and experiences to an audience who, weeks before, were strangers.

Allyson: It seems to me that all writing—prose and poetry—is in essence personal. Many novelists I've worked with as editor have revealed, either to me or publicly, what settings or characters or even storylines derive from their past. And on the receiving end, most readers are intrigued with which parts of stories are fact and which are made up. Some writers complain about this questioning, saying a work should be accepted for what it is, not what went into it, but such curiosity seems natural to me. Are we any different when we view any work of creativity? We're curious about what lies behind it, about its connection to the artist's own life.

That said, yes, in a memoir class, students are often timid at first, wondering how much to reveal personally and how their stories will be viewed. I respect their feelings, and in the peer-critiquing component, I encourage them to comment on the "narrator" and how the story is told, rather than to talk about the narrator and writer as "you."

Heidi: As a literary editor, you routinely read memoirs of well-known authors. What are some common features of a captivating memoir?

Allyson: Almost without exception, captivating memoirs are character driven. The reader must find the story's narrator, even if flawed (and the most interesting narrators often are!), intriguing. The reader must want to keep turning pages, take the journey and discover how it changes the narrator. The best memoirs read like good novels, making use of techniques like scene, description, metaphor and believable dialogue. And they are honest and vulnerable. They don't have to be about an experience the reader has had, but the emotions explored—fear, pride, sense of loss, joy, shame and more—must resonate with the reader's own experience. The ending of a memoir should leave the reader with what I call a "gift"—some emotion or way of thinking about human nature or the world that the reader can keep and hold, mull over some more—something that makes reading to the last page worthwhile.

Heidi: You run annual writing retreats at remote locations. By taking the "class" out of the "classroom," how do retreats enhance and enrich the writing experience?

Allyson: For my first offshore teaching experience, I was invited to lead workshops at Los Parronales Writers' Retreat in Santiago, Chile. It was a fabulous couple of weeks of travel (including visiting Pablo Neruda's home in Isla Negra) and discussion about writing. I was gratified and humbled to see how participants' confidence and storytelling "sense" improved even in that time. Since then, I've organized more than a dozen of my own retreats for small groups in Canada and abroad (including in the U.S., Grenada and Costa Rica). My fall 2016 retreat was in British Columbia's scenic Okanagan Valley.

Of course, any writer serious about improving, serious about being published in some form, needs to learn to plant seat in chair and write anywhere. We can't all live in quaint cottages with views of the sea, nor have most writers who've written enduring memoirs or novels or poetry done so (well, okay, Neruda did). That said, there is something wonderful about going "away" to write—shaking up one's routine, looking around with new eyes at one's surroundings in a foreign place and carving out a special time to write and to commune with other writers. I find that shake-up really helps emerging writers to hone the art of paying attention—but the challenge is to take that experience and, once home again, build on it.

I try to leave participants with more than a good time and short-term "inspiration." My workshops are instructional and focus on specific aspects of writing, providing tips on craft and tools I hope writers will practise well after the retreat. I know they won't remember and apply everything we discuss, but if they come back with even a few nuggets, their writing as they go forward will benefit. Something as seemingly simple as realizing what it means to read like a writer can make a huge difference. I also encourage them to submit short works to journals and contests and to join or form their own writing groups. Writing tends to be a very solitary act, and by its nature it needs to be, but in my experience, writers progress more quickly if they have trusted others—the key word being *trusted*—to read and respond to their writing on a regular basis. Not to mention that having writing deadlines—whether once a week or once a month—never hurts!

Heidi: What recommendations do you have for aspiring writers to encourage daily writing and to combat writer's block?

Allyson: I don't believe there's any such thing as writer's block. To paraphrase something one wag said, "Is there plumber's block or surgeon's block? Thankfully, no." Writing is a creative endeavour, but if you're serious about it, you must treat it the same way you would treat a job, or even a hobby at which you wish to excel. If you're learning tennis, you don't sit around waiting for the tennis muse to appear. Nor as a writer can you afford to wait for a muse to seize your writing hand. Inspiration grows out of the act itself. I tell students, "Memories beget memories." (I may have stolen that from someone!) And writing ideas beget more writing ideas.

Sit down and free-write regularly, at least three times a week, even if just for 20 minutes. Set a timer. (Write longer, if you're on a roll!) Over time, ideas will blossom and skills will improve. I guarantee it. Don't use writer's "block" as an excuse. Just take a writer's "break." If you're stumped in the short term over a particular piece of writing, take a walk, clear your mind for an hour, or read something wonderful by a writer you love and whose work will stoke you up again and increase your determination to create something of your own that makes the same connection with readers. Then get back to your writing chair.

Interview with Kelly McNelis

Photo and biography courtesy of Kelly McNelis

Kelly McNelis is the founder of Women For One, an online community of women who are ready and willing to make life happen. She travels the world as a speaker, teacher, and facilitator of workshops, helping others tap into lives powered by truth. With over 20 years of experience as a nonprofit and small-business consultant, Kelly is excited to empower generations of women around the world to become Women For One Truthtellers as they build relationships, community, and the support they need to achieve their wildest dreams. She finds her own daily inspiration in spending time with her husband and children in their home outside of Seattle. Her first book, *The Messy Truth*, (Hierophant Publishing) is due out in spring 2017.

~~~

Initiative: From Concept to Being

Heidi: The online community, Women For One, began with one person and grew to thousands — all because you followed the voice

of your intuition. **Tell us about the beginnings of Women For One and the importance of following intuition.**

Kelly: Women For One is a locally founded international organization that empowers and uplifts women worldwide. As a global community, we are committed to women of all races, all cultures, all socioeconomic backgrounds, and all walks of life. After experiencing a long divorce, as well as the death of a dear friend and blending a family of eight, I realized that I wanted to write and give back to the world with the lessons I had learned. I also wanted to create a global tribe of like-minded women who could learn from each other and share their own life lessons.

Following my intuition in this process was vital, because it led to bigger and better things for me and my organization. I could never have predicted where Women For One would go or that it would end up being a global community of hundreds of thousands of women. But listening to my heart and following it made all the difference. I learned that in order to know who I was, I had to tap into that inner voice. I believe that if we listen to our gut, it enables us to discover our personal genius, which helps each of us tap into the greatest joy imaginable.

Heidi: **To bring an idea to life, you need not only the sense of urgency that intuition creates but also the courage to act. How did you find the courage to create the Women For One online community and the motivation to support conferences and become an approved blogger for Oprah's** *The Life You Want Weekend* **2014 tour in Seattle? Do you have any advice or tips for living courageously?**

Kelly: I'm a big-picture woman, so if I'd gotten stuck in the details of how I was going to build my community and what I needed to do to get from point A to point B, I would never have started! When I'm up against a challenge, I always look at the bigger picture. I see it as opening up to bigger and more expansive questions about how I wish to live and how I want to express my passion. Sometimes "obstacles" can be great fodder for thinking in new ways—for asking myself what needs to be done in order to bring my genius out into the world even more powerfully.

As far as living courageously goes, from my experience, every single one of us has the desire to shine, but often, our fears make us our own worst enemies. I know that self-victimization can be our greatest hindrance to achieving greatness and living lives that are worthy of us. Authenticity is also important. We need to know and respect who we are, and to believe in our desires if we ever wish to find peace, joy, and genuine power. Truth is paramount. Aligning with our own integrity is imperative. Doing what you love and truly living into your passion is really the best thing you can do to contribute to the world. When you do this, you naturally inspire others to do the same.

Storytelling: The Power of Telling the Truth

Heidi: The Women For One online community of writers are called Truthtellers. Please share Women For One's core values and how you have witnessed the healing power of truthtelling through Women For One.

Kelly: It is Women For One's mission to support women in sharing their truth and making life happen on their own terms. We raise awareness on a variety of issues—from poverty to sexual abuse to those magnificent women who are creating positive change right in their own backyards—so that all women can share their stories and inspire action that will transform the way we live, love, and learn. It is my hope that, in continuing to share women's truths and talents, Women For One will encourage everyone to take a stand on the issues that most impact our lives, while building a supportive community. I have seen so much transformation in women from all over the world; simply having a place where they can be themselves and share their hearts and souls has led to enormous healing. We are promoting

28

something that I believe is fundamental to most people: full self-expression, sharing of our truth, and creating authentic community. It not only transforms us from within when we heal the voices of shame and victimization—it also means that we send ripple effects through our own communities. Women For One begins with the individual, but it always spreads out to the global.

COMMUNITY: EVERYONE HAS A VOICE

Heidi: What drew me to the Women For One community is that everyone has a voice. Anyone can be a Truthteller. Truthtellers come from different backgrounds and don't need to be experienced or professional writers. Tell us about the importance of inclusion in the Women For One community and the positive outcome of hearing diverse stories or tales of truth.

Kelly: With a few exceptions, we accept the stories of almost every single person who submits to us. Our main criterion is that we want their submissions to be examples of truthtelling, which I refer to as "sharing from the heart." Our readers are thirsty for first-hand experiences of women's deepest life lessons. So while every person who submits to us (which includes some brave and wonderful men, might I add!) has wisdom to share, truthtelling isn't about getting up on a platform and preaching to other people or giving them advice on how to live their lives. It's about really demonstrating how your life story has affected you and how you are using it to empower yourself and dream new dreams.

We get stories from women of all different backgrounds in terms of age, ethnicity, socioeconomic status—you name it. One thing I have learned is that while our circumstances might be different, our struggles and triumphs are universal. As women, we yearn for the same things and find meaning and purpose in our work, our families and our communities. Fundamentally, our truthtelling stories show us how we are all connected; they show us the beauty and power of women doing something that is so basic to who we are: sharing and learning from each other.

I truly believe in the power of collaboration, connection, and community. When we as women can uplift and help each other to shine and be seen, we empower each other to be our very best.

Action: A Place to Make Life Happen

Heidi: Once Truthtellers own and share their stories, they gain the confidence and support to make their lives happen. What kind of opportunities does Women For One offer for skills or personal development to encourage and engage Truthtellers?

Kelly: I'm very excited that Women For One will be offering more opportunities for our global community of Truthtellers to dive even more deeply into their potential; we are rolling out new courses, tool kits, and other fun stuff right now.

I developed an online program entitled Truthteller: A Course for Boldly Claiming Your Story. It is Women For One's signature program, and the purpose is to help women develop their leadership and truthtelling skills by learning to be more present and to embrace the stories that have shaped us. Women in the course connect with each other in a community and do some really deep personal work that helps them to share the stories that have most informed their lives. For me, leadership (and especially what I think of as women's leadership) isn't about hiding behind a charismatic persona; it's about being totally transparent about who we are—the good, the bad, and the ugly. Those are the stories people want to know about—the ones that show us a woman's courage and that create important points of connection. Every single woman has a truth that can help other women discover their passion, genius, and capacity for building community. That's really what Truthteller is about.

Visit www.womenforone.com

Articles and Essays on Mentoring and Coaching

A New Year, a New You

by Heidi Stock

A New Year, a New You. Scratch that.

How about, *A New Year, the Old You?*

Wait a minute. Old you? That goes against the annual tradition of making New Year's resolutions. We want to move forward, not back, don't we? But if the old you is the original you—the you at the time of your birth, with your whole life ahead to discover and use your talents—then this is the you I'm chasing.

I used to make New Year's resolutions, but each year I'd write the same ones. So what did I resolve? How did I move forward? My intentions were good, but I'd lose focus, energy and discipline two months later. To me, my resolutions were just one more list in an already busy life filled with to-do lists. If self-improvement through my New Year's resolutions was a chore rather than a joy, good luck to me for tackling self-improvement among the day-to-day survival of existing tasks.

So let's get rid of chores and look at joy. *But how can I get everything done?* you may say. You are probably haunted by *I need to do this* or *I should do that.* So am I. I feel stressed if I don't complete my tasks or if my house is out of order. I thought that kind of chaos was a reflection on me. *They* think of me as organized and reliable. Now what will *they* think? Focusing on joy instead of chores was foreign to me. I liked work, achievement, and taking pride in accomplishment. I certainly

31

didn't think of this approach (joy versus chores), but it became my path to self-improvement or rather my return to myself—the original me, the newborn waiting to use her talents and express herself in the world.

As children, our natural talents and skills emerge, and if they are nurtured, we may be the lucky ones. We may be the ones who stay on the path, using our talents in our personal or professional lives in alignment with our purpose, and through our example, inspiring others to do the same.

I was inspired by Janice Cunning, who became my life coach or, as she calls herself, my *joy coach*. When I first approached Janice for coaching, I disregarded the term *joy*. I thought, well, maybe she wants to be a little different, calling herself a joy coach rather than a life coach. Maybe by *joy*, she means contentment or the feeling of achievement from completing a task or a project, because I don't have time for joy. Joy is for kids and I need to get things done in my life. But I wasn't getting things done and I needed a new perspective—a third party perspective from a coach or a mentor.

I approached Janice to coach my career. That fit with the person I was and my goals at the time, five years ago. Achieve, achieve and achieve some more. But coaching would have none of that. Instead, she taught the stifled me to breathe.

One aspect of Janice's coaching was about looking at joy, at childhood passions, and bringing those back to life. For me, my childhood passions included dance, music and self-expression. Many of us share these passions.

I returned to dance midlife. When I was a clumsy toddler, at three years old, my mother enrolled me in dance and, along the way, I found grace, confidence and discipline in ballet. The physical movement also encouraged the flow of language and I began to express myself through creative writing. But my teen years brought all these passions to a screeching halt. I went into survival and achievement mode. *I should get good grades. I should go to university. I should focus.* No time for fun. No time for joy. That's for kids. I need to think about my future.

It took me a long time to see that it doesn't have to be one or the other. Work and passion co-exist and can even fuel each other. I decided I would make time for dance, but not dance classes—that might get me into New Year's resolution failure mode again. I would dance for myself, by myself, freestyle, and at home, when I felt like it!

Once my body was free, my mind was free, and with this free flow, just as in childhood, I was able to write again. Today, I sponsor mentorship opportunities for other aspiring writers.

This was all a beautiful surprise, but really it shouldn't have been a surprise at all. It was all in my history and just needed to be reborn.

Originally published by WomenForOne* on January 18, 2016. womenforone. com/new-year-new/

* To read Heidi Stock's interview with WomenForOne founder, Kelly McNelis, see p.26; or Janice Cunning's essay, The Joys and Impact of Coaching, *see p.34.*

The Joys and Impact of Coaching

by Janice Cunning

Photo credit: Nizam Photography

Janice Cunning is a Certified Professional Co-Active Coach®
trained by the Coaches Training Institute (CTI), www.coactive.com.
She was previously a senior consultant at KCI, Canada's largest
fundraising consulting firm. Today, Janice combines her passions by
partnering with clients in the social profit sector to help them create
an inspired vision that transforms lives. She supports fundraisers and
fundraising teams to harness their passions, strengths and values.
This allows them to be leaders who make a difference in the world.

An active volunteer, Janice was a founding director of APRA Canada
and the second international member to serve on the international
APRA board. Recently, Janice served the coaching community as
vice-president and secretary for the International Coach Federation,
Toronto Chapter. When she isn't coaching, Janice can be found
dancing, ice skating, taking improv classes, reading or hanging out
with those she loves.

www.janicecunning.com

Biography courtesy of Janice Cunning

~~~

Think about a moment in your life when you accomplished something that you never thought you could do—when your vision of who you are suddenly shifted. As you reflect upon that moment you can discover so much about yourself. You can discover your unique values, dreams and strengths.

Coaching offers people the space to articulate their dreams. Coaches help uncover your unique values and what is most important for you to create a fulfilling life. They see your strengths even when you may not. They propel you forward. Action flows from your dreams and those actions lead to further learning and an expanded view of who you are.

In 2014, I had an experience that shifted my perspective of who I am and what I can accomplish. For as long as I could remember, I had a paralyzing fear of heights. I believed that this fear was something I would never overcome. Then I signed up for a leadership program that included participating in a ropes course. Knowing about the ropes course almost held me back from pursuing my dream of participating in this program. I honestly was not sure what a ropes course was because it was so far out of my comfort zone. I did, however, know that it would make me face my greatest fears.

The leadership program is offered by the Coaches Training Institute (CTI), which is where I did my coaching certification. At CTI, they teach in the framework of The Co-Active Model. To me, being co-active means focusing on both who I am being and what I am doing.

We so often focus on doing or, in other words, on accomplishing tasks, taking action and checking things off the list. In order for me to participate in a ropes course, however, I knew I would need to focus on who I was going to be that day.

When the day arrived, it was an amazing experience with huge successes and failures and great learning from those extremes. The pinnacle moment happened in the morning, when I broke through my fears and climbed higher than I ever thought possible. This happened because I was so connected to my true self in that moment and so clear on how the task connected to my values and a larger dream I had for myself. I had signed up for the program to challenge myself and to grow as a leader. I knew I wanted to be different and, therefore, I was willing to do something different.

The other key decision I made that day was that I would be completely vulnerable and turn to others for support and help. In the past, I had usually gone within myself when I was afraid. This time, I looked to my teammates for support. I opened my heart and cried and asked for help with such clarity. I knew exactly what I needed in that moment and I was brave enough to ask for it.

There were so many gifts that came from that experience and I still think about the learnings when I am faced with another experience that's new and out of my comfort zone.

To me, this period of reflection is where the real magic happens. We often take action and achieve success. What is even more powerful and fulfilling, though, is the ability to pause and explore that achievement.

Coaching allows you to see beyond the action. To see who you were in that moment. To realize that your abilities were greater than you had imagined. Exploring this new version of yourself is the key to moving toward your next dream.

The Power of Support Without Attachment

One of the most powerful gifts coaching offers is to provide support without attachment.

What I want for my clients is for them to live a life that is in alignment with their values. I want them to set goals with intention. What those goals are is not important to me. It does not matter if they are big or small.

Next, I want and encourage clients to grow and try new things. I will even challenge clients to take on very specific actions. What is crucial, however, and a key part of the coaching relationship, is for clients to always have the right to say no. In fact, I will often challenge clients to do something that I sense they will say no to. This allows them to ponder the idea and create their own next step. When someone gives you a big challenge it stretches you, and the next step you choose is likely to be bigger than you expected. What clients decide to do is not important to me. I simply want them to move forward, to try something and to learn from it.

This position of being unattached is one of the reasons that coaching is so powerful. We have people in our lives who support and love us. Of course you should share your dreams and goals with your family and friends. And if you tell them you want to quit your job and move to another country, they will be impacted by that decision. A coach, on the other hand, is simply committed to you and willing to let you explore in a safe and open space, so that you can discover and claim your dreams.

Ultimately, I want my clients to feel fulfilled—to feel they are living the life they are supposed to and having the impact on the world that they want to have.

Uncovering Values

People usually come to coaching at times of transition or because of a desire for change. For most of my clients, that transition relates to a promotion, a new job or a move. The desire for change can be specific, like wanting to discover a new career path. Sometimes it is not as clear. They simply feel stuck, unsure or unhappy. They know they want something to be different in their lives, but they may not be sure what that something is. What they all have in common is that they are ready to do something that will create a change in their lives.

So change is often the starting point and clients want to get into action. However, as we explored earlier, the idea of Co-Active coaching is that it incorporates a sense of both being and doing. The truth is, if we keep taking action from the same place then we create similar patterns for ourselves.

The journey to change begins when you reawaken to who you want to be, and that begins with claiming your core values.

I am passionate about helping people reconnect to their values because values are the guiding force that points them in the direction of their dreams. Until we really articulate what is important to us, we cannot take the steps that will lead us to our most meaningful goals.

In other words, I want my clients to articulate who they want to be before they do anything.

So what are core values? Your values represent who you are, what is most important to you, and how you want to express yourself in the world. Your values are there inside you and you express them every day. However, you may not have articulated them to yourself.

My core values are:

- Joy/playful/flow
- Passion/zest for life/dreams
- Purpose/impact/change
- Authenticity/true self/truth
- Connection/love/relationships

Joy especially resonates for me and represents my unique way of being in this world. It has become my personal brand. Joy has many layers. I can be living this value when I am laughing and playing. And I can be living this value when I am deep in a meaningful conversation. It has an energetic quality of dancing or ice skating—to be connected with my body and flowing and moving with ease. And it can be found in the stillness of meditation. I know I am living this value fully when I feel lightness and ease in my life.

When I begin working with clients, I ask them to spend some time articulating their unique core values.

You can explore your own unique values using this process as inspiration. Start by exploring the question, "What must I have in my life for it to be meaningful?" This is a powerful question that can be explored in so many ways—in thought, in writing, in pictures, or in conversation. Create a list of all the words and phrases that come to mind.

Make sure you explore fully each aspect of your life. For example, you might say, "I value my friends and family." Explore what values are represented in these relationships, such as connection, love, being yourself, trust and so on.

Next, think about times in your life when you felt you were at your best. Imagine yourself back in that situation and capture the values that you were living in that moment. You can repeat this by remembering times that touch on different aspects of your life, such as home, family, work and so on.

Think about times when you were stuck in your life or unhappy. These difficult moments occur when we are not living in alignment with our values. What values were being violated in those moments? Capture those values.

What do others say about you? Other people, especially those closest to us, often describe us in both positive and negative ways. From their observations, what values do you see emerge?

This exploration of your values will take some time and attention. Spend a few days creating a list of words and phrases that represent what is most important to you. Use your own words and be creative. Once you have a full list, choose the five or ten that are most important to you.

So now you have your core values. What's next?

When you really take the time to do this work, three important things happen:

- You feel motivated to take action.

   Your values can help you find a way to do things that you might be avoiding doing. Even when we are pursuing a dream, there will be difficult steps we have to take along the path. We can encounter things we are afraid of, things that we don't know how to do, or simply things that we don't like to do that much. Our values can help us to authentically find a way to complete a task or take a next step.

- You can quiet your negative voices.

   We all have those voices that keep us stuck in the status quo. They might say you aren't good enough or convince you that you don't want to move outside your comfort zone. Truly connecting with your values can help you move forward despite these voices.

- You have a more fulfilling life.

   Values serve as a compass and point you in the direction of what will be most fulfilling and meaningful to you. This isn't always easy. If you value honesty, then there will be times you need to speak your truth and risk offending others. If you value stillness, there will be times you have to say no to people, and there will be tasks to create that in your life. But in the end you will be living a life that truly reflects who you are and what you hold most valuable. And that is the ultimate goal.

There can also be times when it feels like your values are conflicting with each other. If you value impact, there may be times you need to be provocative—to be uncomfortable and push yourself to do things that you are not sure you can do. At the same time, you may value flow and want ease. So you have to be intentional and conscious of finding a way to hold both of these values simultaneously.

Now that you have a sense of your core values, it's time to dream your biggest dreams!

Exploring Your Dreams

There are so many ways to explore your dreams, and for each person there will be different access points.

Some people enjoy exploring their dreams by looking to past experiences, in particular from their childhood. The passions we pursued as children have a purity to them. We did not worry about what other people thought. We did not doubt our abilities. We did not have an aversion to trying and failing.

- What activities did you love to do as a child?
- What was your favourite toy?
- What was your favourite game?
- What did you want to be when you grew up?

The answers to these questions can give you insight into the things you love that might be missing in your life. If you loved to solve

41

puzzles as a child, could you look for opportunities at work to solve complex problems? If you loved to be outside running free, could you move your workouts from the gym to a park? If you always wanted to be a teacher, could you look for someone to mentor?

The important thing here is that taking the time to explore what you used to love can point you to try new things or return to favourite things. The child inside you is still alive and has a lot of wisdom to offer.

Another way to explore your dreams is to look forward. You can explore your dreams using visualizations that take you to your future. When we envision ourselves in the future, we can uncover the true essence of what we want and who we are. If we try to imagine our dreams in this moment, we can get caught up with concerns about how to make it happen. Or we can trigger our doubts and fears, bringing them to the surface. Taking ourselves well into the future allows us to claim our biggest dreams without our minds getting trapped trying to figure out how we could create them.

I often have people imagine themselves at the end of their career. It can be a powerful and transformative experience. Simply close your eyes and focus on your breath for a few minutes. Then allow yourself to imagine your retirement party. Pay attention to all the details of who is there, what is happening, how you feel and what people are saying to you.

When you complete this visualization, spend a few minutes journalling and asking yourself questions like:

- What accomplishments am I most proud of?
- What experiences meant the most to me?
- What are my strengths?
- Who am I?

The powerful thing about visualization is that you can return to it anytime you need to reconnect to your dreams, especially when doubts or stress appear.

The ways in which we can explore our dreams are endless. You can write a story about your desired future. You can create a vision board that reminds you of what you want to attract and create in your life. You can ask someone to listen to you talk about your dreams and have them be curious and help you bring them to life. What is important is that we each create time and space to engage in this wonderful activity of dreaming. Having a dream will make your life richer and more joyful.

As a coach, I am fortunate to support my clients as they claim their biggest dreams and take the action needed to make them happen.

One of the reasons that Heidi, this anthology's editor, has been able to create so many amazing things is that she realized that no dream or goal is farfetched. She truly believed in her dreams and looked for signs that pointed out where to go next. She followed the positive energy and was open to seeing what might emerge.*

Taking Action

When you truly claim your dream it can inspire you to begin to make it a reality. It can seem scary and you may doubt that you can achieve it.

While your values can help to inspire you, it is also helpful to think about your strengths and how you can use them as you move into action.

I love to ask people the question, "What do you contribute that is unique?" Often, it is difficult for someone to answer that question, and many of us feel that we are not unique. Or we feel that it is boastful to say what is unique about us. This is where coaching can really support people, by creating a safe space in which you can reflect upon and claim your strengths.

Often, what is even more powerful is having a coach acknowledge your greatest gifts. It is often easier for someone else to see our strengths because we may not recognize that what comes naturally to us is actually a powerful tool that we can use to be successful.

Knowing your talents and strengths can help you move forward and it can also point to where you might need help. Asking for help is an important part of achieving your dreams. What resources do you need and who might be able to offer them?

So now you are ready to take action. This is where, for most people, the scary part comes. If you are going to pursue your biggest dreams then you are going to have to move out of your comfort zone.

It is like you are going on a grand adventure and exploring new lands. Of course there will be excitement and fear mixed together. There will be confidence and hesitation. What you know at this point is that you can pack a bag that contains everything you need to push forward. This bag will contain your dreams, your values and your strengths. You will be able to reach into it and pull out whatever you need when you encounter an obstacle along the path.

Earlier, I told the story of my success on the ropes course at my leadership program. My comfort zone around heights expanded that day. About six months later, I was on a trip to Northern Ireland, where my cousins live. We had an opportunity to visit and cross the Carrick-a-Rede, a rope bridge that links the mainland with a small island. Now, I have been to Northern Ireland many times, and crossing the rope bridge had never been on my itinerary! This time when my cousin suggested it, I said, "Yes, let's go." The important part of this story is that I was still very afraid of crossing that rope bridge, but past experience told me I could do it and that I would be grateful to have the experience. And when I reached the other side, I was grateful and proud of myself.

This is the powerful thing about taking action. Our comfort zone expands and suddenly we are living a bigger life. And then we can imagine taking another step to expand even farther.

REFLECTION AND LEARNING

So taking action is a way to expand ourselves and our world. There is another important step. When you come to a new place on the path, you need to slow down so you can reflect upon what has happened. This is where the learning occurs. Think about what you did on this adventure and who you were during this exploration. What new information do you have about yourself? What new strengths did you discover? Where else in your life can you apply these new strengths?

Before each coaching session, I ask my clients to reflect upon their successes since we last spoke. What do they want to celebrate? This idea of celebrating sometimes gets lost in our fast-paced lives. It is not uncommon for people to simply want to move on to the next thing. Celebrating can seem trivial. I firmly believe that taking the time to honour our past achievements is what allows us to grow and expand our sense of who we are and what we can do. And there is nothing trivial about that, because your next great adventure awaits you.

* To read Heidi Stock's article, A New Year, a New You, *in which she discusses working with Janice, see page 31.*

Learnings from Life and Creative Coaching

by Heidi Stock

At the time I write this, I have never published a book. As you read this, I will be the creator and editor of one.

Five years ago, I wouldn't have imagined this, although a photographer who took shots for my business website at that time said, "This one's for your book cover." I remember pausing and taking in that comment, even though it didn't make sense—a book about what? I had started taking creative writing classes only a couple of years before. But it was exciting to even consider it for a moment.

It's very likely, or almost certain, that every time someone struck that pose, the photographer said, "This one's for your book cover" for a little reaction and a grin. It didn't matter. For me, that day, it was spoken as a possibility, and today it is a reality.

This brings me to possibilities becoming reality. For me, the following has worked: see it, say it, do it.

See It

Visualization can work. There are enough testimonials about the law of attraction and success stories in sports psychology, modern-day psychology and Eastern spirituality to support this.

The path for me has been finding or customizing a practice that works for me. For goals and dreams, I tried a vision board. It's a common and successful practice for a lot of people, but for some reason not for me; maybe because I'm a fairly visual person by nature, the images didn't match those in my imagination.

One New Year's Day, instead of creating a vision board, I decided to sit on the couch, close my eyes, and do a meditation—my own, simple meditation. I asked myself what the year ahead would bring. I spoke that one question—"What will 2010 bring?"—in my mind once, and then I shut up. I had a pen and notepad in hand, expecting eyes open, clear answers, and soon. That didn't happen. My head bobbed a bit; my shoulders dropped. My body relaxed as if massaged. After that point, I wasn't aware of my body, any bodily sensations or time passing. I imagine now that I kind of looked like a slumped over, exhausted toddler, fast asleep in a car seat.

There was auditory and visual silence, deepening blackness, and I was very comfortable in it. Images started to appear but not like I was used to in dreams. In my dreams, I'm the lead in a technicolour feature film and I have all my senses. This meditation was a plain, formal, slide show presentation, all black and white. White images appeared: first, a large plane flying to the right; then a large plane flying to the left; then a book; then a grand piano.

When it stopped, I opened my eyes, and I was incredibly relaxed. I jotted down the images on my notepad. It seemed to be against my analytical nature, but I wasn't overly concerned at this time about what they meant, maybe because I had sensed that the images appeared in sequence, in chronological order, and that I had understood the first images to be a trip south and the rest I'd figure out later. But I didn't head south that year and was surprised with the opportunity to go to Wimbledon in June 2010. The planes—distinctly large planes—going right (east over the Atlantic) and then left (west back to North America) were as significant as that trip to England was to my personal and creative growth.

The images of the book and the piano were more mysterious to me. I assume that the book represented encouragement to continue taking writing classes, but it may in fact have meant the compilation of *this* book, this anthology. The piano could have been interpreted in a

47

couple of ways, too, as the songwriting contest I would create in the future or a return to music for me.

It isn't important that all this took more than a year to unfold, nor is it important if I ever pinpoint the meaning of each image. It was enough to learn that writing and music were to be part of my future, so I continue to explore that today.

In later years, on other New Year's Days, I tried this self-imposed, self-constructed meditation again, and with the exception of one year, I came up empty except for the pleasant side effect of 20 minutes of relaxation. I can't explain whether this is because I was more focused during the first meditation or whether I was in much more need of direction back on New Year's Day 2010. Or, possibly, everything is still unfolding. I don't think it matters—the process of visualization and meditation can be as unique as each one of us. It can provide hints to our potential path and the motivation to journey on that path.

Say It

If you see it and then say it, that's a good start.

Sometimes we're surprised about what others say to us—"This one's for your book cover"—and sometimes we're surprised about what we say to others.

I saw Lesley Pike open at a Darius Rucker show in fall 2009. I didn't know her music at the time. I sat and listened, and by the end of her set, I was deeply moved (if not emotionally spent) and inspired by the rawness and authenticity in the delivery of her songs.

I wanted to thank Lesley for that connection she made with the audience that night. To do so, I would sign her online guestbook, putting my comments out there to the public, which back then was uncommon and uncomfortable for me. But on November 16, 2009, I wrote, "Thank you for the honesty and emotion of your music, which strikes a chord with the emotions that most of us lack the artistic talent or courage to express." There. I said it. I shared publicly that I admired artists like Lesley who have the courage to express themselves creatively.

Moving forward, in private thought or in quiet meditation, I asked for the courage to express myself creatively. Slowly, month by month, year by year, from 2009 to 2016, I was given the courage to express through poetry, prose and music and to share in workshops or in private mentoring sessions. Who knows if I have "talent" in any of these areas? It doesn't matter. I can't pray for a natural ability. It's either there or it's not. But I can work on my skills and the courage to share. Self-expression alone has its own benefits.

Do It

Skills development. I saw it, I said it, now I'm doing it.

Now, I've started to express myself through writing. The process is slow but it's rewarding. It started as journalling. Journalling turned into poems, poems into a little unpublished collection of 40 mostly bad or mediocre and a handful of fair or good poems. Then I explored prose writing, with some short stories and short film scripts, and then music. My creativity seems to be a buffet of this and that, but it is what it is. My journey may be more about the exploration of many and mastery of none, but I don't want to judge it. I just want to be grateful for it.

Getting back to the courage to share, I was comfortable developing my writing skills, at first, with private one-on-one mentoring with a published poet, Catherine Graham, who is also a creative writing instructor.

I emailed my manuscript of 40 poems to Catherine, and we discussed the handful of ones that had potential for development. It wasn't so much an edit as it was getting a sense of the voice and the tone and the rhythm of my poems and what poets and poems I should read, might enjoy, might learn from. And, I reiterate, the potential for development, not publication. That was an important lesson to learn.

I remember one mentoring session in which I asked Catherine to read my poems that might be "good enough" to be part of a chapbook of a writers' association, but none of them were—not one of them. And at 40 poems, my well was dry. Catherine spoke with me, honestly and sincerely, about the desire of new writers to publish. It's understandable that a new writer wants to share and be heard, but I shouldn't want to submit work that's not ready. I realized that I was impatient and I hadn't put in the work. I didn't take shortcuts elsewhere in life—in high school, I didn't skip class after class or flunk test after test and then expect to ace the final exam. Why the impatience now?

I think that some new writers like myself may experience impatience because we have finally taken that courageous step to express ourselves and we're waving a flag, saying, "Here I am." We now want to share, and without publication, we may feel ignored or not worthy. I want, I want, I want to be a published writer, an author. It's emotional, not logical. We all know that every skill in life requires commitment to development from the time we learn to walk and talk. (Note to self: keep that in mind when impatience tries to win.)

So with poems not yet ready, and with accepting that now is not the time, I tried learning in a peer environment by taking in-person workshops and receiving feedback from classmates. It went better than I'd expected. In time, my ego was able to handle it. Honesty does so much more good than harm. A pleasant surprise was how much I enjoyed my classmates' work and my awe in hearing how the quietest student, who'd been dead silent almost every class, hit us with her own masterpiece.

Accepting that development takes time but also, considering that it's a shame that a "masterpiece" won't be appreciated outside of the classroom for years or maybe ever, I started to think about the possibility of creating a poetry contest for aspiring writers, with the prize being mentorship. A contest for aspiring writers would satisfy their need for recognition and give them encouragement to continue. And winning mentoring rather than a cash prize would emphasize the value of skill development.

During my last few private mentoring sessions with Catherine Graham, I ran out of material. I was given writing exercises, but I was experiencing writer's block. I told her that I couldn't get my mind off the idea of a poetry contest for aspiring writers like me. Catherine confidently said that the creation of the contest appeared to be my passion and that I should follow my passion—that's what a writer does.

The many steps I took, from creating a poetry contest and a songwriting contest and then collaborating on a screenwriting contest over a four-year period, are too detailed and too specific to my journey to write about, even briefly, here. But the key learnings for me in working toward these new creative project goals are that I needed to invest in a cheerleader and coach (my life coach, Janice Cunning) to keep me on track, to remind me that this is all possible, and I needed expertise in the form of a legal team and judges and mentors for the contests.

The most amazing discovery was that the skills I developed in my professional work as a freelance fundraiser with a small business—research and writing, strategic thinking, matching people to projects, marketing, budgeting, accounting, business incorporation—all served me well in this endeavour. What a relief and an encouragement to do something so new when you realize that you already have some of the skills and experience to get it done. We all have skills acquired through education, work and most importantly, life that come in handy when we set out to do something new.

Read Janice Cunning's essay to learn about taking action (p.34).

Read Chris Kay Fraser's interview for a perspective on discovering or rediscovering creativity at any stage and age in life (p.15).

Read Catherine Graham's interview to learn about her own path from journalling to poetry (p.59).

It's Not What You Know

… it's *who* you know. I'm not going to deny that that's true. If you are connected to people of influence in your desired field, you are steps ahead. But what happens when you step into a new field, a new industry, without any connections? Do you run and hide? Or not even try? Those are temptations, just as they may have been for you on day one of kindergarten, but think of how bold you were back then. You entered that new field with a lot fewer life skills and survived!

I wrote earlier about starting a creative project—an annual poetry contest—out of the blue. If you look at a new project with apprehension, you can fall into the trap of seeing it all as new territory. I thought I was entering this project with no connections—no contacts in the arts—but when I really thought about it, that wasn't true. I had confided in Catherine Graham and she was supportive, so I asked her to be the contest's inaugural judge and mentor and she agreed. I had also mentioned the idea to another of my instructors, Allyson Latta, and she was supportive. She didn't say, "Who do you think you are?" or "You can't do it." Allyson became the contest's editorial advisor and put forward recommendations for three judges in later years: Shannon Bramer, Stuart Ross and George Elliott Clarke.

It's Not Who You Know

… it's who you *get* to know. I found this to be the truth for me. Networking is really about the interconnectedness of people. Allyson led me to Shannon, Stuart and George. One person leads to another.

With the songwriting contest, I would have said I had no music industry contacts, but then—pause and think again—I did. I was a member of the Songwriters Association of Canada, I had met Theo Tams (one of the future judges for the songwriting contest) at a charity event, and I had a touchpoint to Lesley Pike. When I invited Lesley to be a judge for the contest, I could refer back to the 2009 concert and my comment on her online guestbook.

Too busy creating the songwriting contest, I contacted my screenwriting instructor, Geneviève Appleton, to tell her that I had to drop out of her class because I had too much going on and I just couldn't keep up. But Geneviève and I kept in touch, and early in the new year, Geneviève emailed me and proposed an aspiring screenwriters contest for which she would be the mentor and judge alongside her recommended expert panel of colleagues. Her network and expertise would be paired with my skills and experience producing and running contests.

It's Not What You Know

… it's what you *give*. I've learned through the creation of these contests that prominent people you may not know will collaborate with you if they believe in your project and if they respect you. In hindsight, this is something I had already observed in the field of major gifts fundraising, also referred to as *relationship philanthropy* in Robert Ian Peacock's book, *Face Time: Relationship Philanthropy—A Resource for Canadian Major Gift Fundraising.*

Prominent industry people participated as judges and mentors in my contests and in interviews in this book because they believe in the project and the impact their expertise and advice has on contestants and readers of the book.

As far as respect, the individuals who join you on your creative project or adventure need to feel that there is consideration for their time commitment. For the judges and mentors involved in my contests, I respect their time by creating broad timelines to accommodate their schedules and value their role with financial compensation.

Don't Feed the Artists

Speaking of compensation, sometimes writers and artists aren't paid well for their time and expertise; sometimes they aren't paid at all. Not coming from an artist background, I found this odd. A skill is a skill. Time worked is time worked. Why weren't their skills and their work valued as much as mine or maybe yours? On top of skills, their creativity helps us see things in new ways and helps us get through the day. Doesn't that make the writer, the artist, even more valuable? I paid those who honoured my projects by participating as a judge or mentor. But what do you do if you can't compensate collaborators on a creative project with cash? I suppose you could put that project on hold for a while until you earn enough money to finance it and also make some short-term sacrifices on any little luxuries in your life. Or you could collectively finance it (with a team project or by using crowdfunding), you could exchange services (a traditional barter), or you could offer an honorarium.

Read Navin Ramaswaran's essay for advice on crowdfunding and collaborating with artists (p.315).

The New You Is the Old You

I believe in reflective thought, visualization, meditation, walking, being in nature, and prayer to inspire my creativity and just to relax and reconnect with myself. But that's my belief and my practice and what works for me. Everyone believes in something different. Do whatever works for you if you want to be creative or just want to be clear-thinking about a circumstance or a current challenge in your life.

I was surprised by the creative explosion I experienced over the past few years. But again, in hindsight, the foundation and the inclination for creativity were there in childhood. We're wildly creative as children, and creativity of any kind (artistic or otherwise) is part of being human.

Read more on re-engaging your creative side in my article, A New Year, a New You *(p.31).*

POETRY

INTERVIEWS WITH POETRY MENTORS AND CONTEST JUDGES

INTERVIEW WITH INAUGURAL JUDGE AND MENTOR, CATHERINE GRAHAM

Aspiring Canadian Poets Contest, 2012

Photo Credit: Prosopon Photography

Winner of the International Festival of Authors' Poetry NOW competition, Catherine Graham is the author of five acclaimed poetry collections. Her most recent collection, *Her Red Hair Rises with the Wings of Insects*, was a finalist for the Raymond Souster Poetry Award and the CAA Poetry Award. She teaches creative writing at the University of Toronto School of Continuing Studies, where she won an Excellence in Teaching Award.

Her work is anthologized in *The Field Day Anthology of Irish Writing, Vol IV & V*, and *The White Page/An Bhileog Bhan: Twentieth Century Irish Women Poets* and has appeared in such journals as *The Malahat Review, Poetry Daily, Poetry Ireland Review, Room Magazine, The Ulster Tatler, The Fiddlehead, Prairie Fire* and elsewhere. Her next collection is forthcoming in 2017.

Graham was the inaugural judge and mentor for the Aspiring Canadian Poets Contest.

www.catherinegraham.com.

Biography courtesy of Catherine Graham

~~~

In the Beginning, an Aspiring Writer

Heidi: When did you start writing poetry?

Catherine: I started writing poetry after the deaths of my parents. They died during my undergraduate years, while I was studying psychology at McMaster. After a long battle with cancer, my mother died on Christmas Day during my first year of university. My father died the September of my last year, in a late-night car accident. Despite the devastation, it was through grief that poetry found me.

A worried family friend suggested I see a therapist. The therapist suggested I write out my feelings to help cope with the grief. I began doing that, and while writing in my notebook, I started playing with words—images and rhythms connected to my parents, along with childhood memories.

This "playing around" felt inspiring—it wasn't about getting things off my chest. I was discovering a new world through language and the imagination. When I worked up the courage to show that same family friend what I'd written in my notebook, she said, "These are poems. You're writing poetry." Since that moment, poetry has been the mainstay of my life.

Heidi: Do you remember your first poem? What inspired that first poem or your first piece of creative writing?

Catherine: I don't remember my first poem. However, the experience of losing my parents became my subject matter once I began writing seriously. I naively thought that I'd write one poem about my mother and one about my father and that would be that. Decades later, I'm still writing about them. They, along with the water-filled limestone quarry I grew up beside, are the wellspring of my creativity. (Unfortunately, I had to sell the quarry-home after their deaths.) In some ways, I think writing about my parents is a way of keeping them alive, through the act of poesies.

Heidi: Was poetry your first creative outlet or was it another style of writing? Or another art form?

Catherine: I've always been creative, but I never thought poetry would become my outlet of choice. As a little girl I loved to draw. I also loved singing and putting on plays for my parents. Writing was never something I envisioned myself doing. Looking back, that saddens me. Unlike some poets, I never had that pivotal teacher who connected me to my writing self. Instead, tragedy served as connector.

Heidi: Do other forms of artistic expression or life experience influence your writing?

Catherine: The imagination works in mysterious ways. I pay attention to what activates my mind and heart—what provokes a visceral response within. I record these observations and experiences in my notebook. Nature, art, music, writing, dance—all influence my writing. Having a record of these triggers means I have something to go back to when I have time to write.

Developing Your Craft and Mentorship

Heidi: How did you (and how do you) continue to develop your craft?

Catherine: Studying poetry as an MA student in Northern Ireland helped develop my craft. Being fully immersed in poetry, away from my teaching job (at that time, I was an elementary school teacher) helped me become the poet I am today. I was exposed to numerous talented poets in workshops and readings: Carol Ann Duffy, Billy Collins, Jean Valentine, Michael Longley, Seamus Heaney, Allen Ginsberg, Czeslaw Milosz, Derek Mahon, Paula Meehan, Denise Levertov, Joan Newmann, Paul Muldoon.

I'm always thinking about poetry. And I spend much time reading poems and reading books on craft. Teaching poetry adds to my development—having to vocalize to students what poetry is and how it works (or doesn't work) deepens my engagement with the art.

Heidi: Influences—who influenced or encouraged your writing?

Catherine: The poetry community continues to influence me—poets near and far, dead and living. I'm blessed to have an editor I admire and connect with, Paul Vermeersch, who believes in my work. I'm also grateful to have numerous writing friends who support and inspire me, a few of whom I share work with on a regular basis: Ian Burgham, Merry Benezra and James Wyshynski.

Heidi: Looking back at the mentoring sessions with the contest winners, what advice would you like to share with other aspiring writers who are considering working privately with a mentor or an editor in the future?

Catherine: Be open to process; don't be tied to what really happened. The poem is smarter than you are.

UNPUBLISHED TO PUBLISHED

Heidi: What was your path to publication?

Catherine: My first poem, "Black Kettles," appeared in *The Fiddlehead*. My first publication, a chapbook titled *The Watch*, was published in Northern Ireland by Abbey Press. These poems grew out of my MA thesis—a daughter's attempts to come to terms with the deaths of her parents. The poet Mark Roper provided my first blurb: "Catherine Graham has done a remarkable thing: controlled and composed a deep personal grief. Her deft, lucid poems speak, with quiet authority, to and from the human heart." The poems from this chapbook were included in *The White Page/An Bhileog Bhan: Twentieth Century Irish Women Poets* and *The Field Day Anthology of Irish Writing, Vol. IV & V*. I was honoured, especially as a Canadian, to be in such esteemed company.

Heidi: What changes or new opportunities do you see in the publishing world in recent years that may benefit new writers?

Catherine: Poetry may not be a bestselling art, but it thrives and will continue to do so. The fact that it's one of the oldest art forms is proof of this. Small presses continue to publish poetry, as do journals and websites. Poetry tends to do well in the virtual world, as poems can be easily viewed and shared, especially during times of extreme emotion—joy or grief—when they speak to us most.

Heidi: What words of advice do you have for unpublished writers about the challenges they will face on their path to publication?

Catherine: The key isn't to seek publication. The key is passion for the art. That's what keeps you going. Challenges will always be there, but persistence is what counts, even more than talent. Finding time to write is essential to growth and development. Publication will happen eventually, if that matters to you. It's best not to rush the process. Quality is better than quantity when it comes to the written word.

INTERVIEW WITH JUDGE AND MENTOR, SHANNON BRAMER

Aspiring Canadian Poets Contest, 2013

Photo and biography courtesy of Shannon Bramer

Shannon Bramer is a poet and playwright. In June 2011, she enlisted the help of celebrated Toronto publisher BookThug to create *Think City: The Poems of Gracefield Public School*. She is the author of three books of poetry, most recently, *The Refrigerator Memory*, with Coach House Books.

Her first play, *Monarita*, was produced in St. John's, Newfoundland, in March 2010, and has since appeared in festivals across the country. Her new play, *The Collectors*, appeared at the Toronto Fringe Festival in July 2013.

Currently she is at work on a new poetry manuscript entitled *Precious Energy*. Visit Shannon's blog at poetintheplayground.blogspot.ca.

~~~

In the Beginning, an Aspiring Writer

Heidi: When did you start writing poetry?

Shannon: I started writing poems and stories as soon as I could write, like most kids! In Grade 4, I remember writing for fun and to "get my feelings out." I loved reading and wanted to be inside books a lot. *Anne of Green Gables* was a hugely influential book because before Anne, the idea of being a writer had never occurred to me. Anne loves poetry so much she acts out a (Tennyson) poem and nearly drowns. I remember finding that absolutely wonderful and hilarious. Anne is an orphan who uses her imagination to create space for herself in the world, to make a home. She faces disappointment and obstacles throughout the Avonlea books, but her creative spirit is resilient. I still aspire to be Anne-like in my adult life. Writing is as much a joy as a mode of growth and survival for me.

More specifically, when I was in Grade 6, we did a poetry unit in school that introduced me to the work of Canadian poet Irving Layton. It was a poem called *Song for Naomi,* and this poem made me feel wild inside. We learned about literary devices using that poem, and I vividly recall how I felt, trying to understand how it all worked, discovering how exciting language could be. But I was also really moved by the beauty of that poem. I wanted it to be my poem so badly that I copied it out in a notebook and changed the title to *Song for Shannon* and told my mother I had written it! It was after telling this big lie that I started to try and write my own poems.

Heidi: Do you remember your first poem? What inspired that first poem or your first piece of creative writing?

Shannon: All of my first poems were about love. They were about my feelings and dreams and fears. I'm not sure that much has changed over the years, but I've learned to let the mystery of language lead me more often. When I was sixteen, I was attacked on the street by a stranger, who tore my skirt off and ran away after I started screaming. I got away from him without being physically harmed, but it was terrifying and traumatic. I remember writing a lot to try and understand why it happened, to try and move on and somehow forgive this person. Several years later, I fell in love with a man and instead of a poem about him, there was a poem about his mother's hands. I never met her—somehow I knew I never would—but I knew her name. And writing about her hands was important—a poem about her hands would say everything I needed about the relationship with this man I loved. It would not be about him or me at all.

Heidi: Do other forms of artistic expression or life experience influence your writing?

Shannon: Other forms of art always inform and inspire work; the books I love to read, visual art, music and theatre are all interconnected sources of material and influence. My children are a source of inspiration; observing who they are and who they are becoming is endlessly fruitful and confusing and beautiful, as is trying to be a decent and present mother. Much of my poetry (and playwriting) explores tension and fluidity in relationships. My newest book of poetry is all about attachment and boundaries and identity; the painful fragmentation of real life can be unpacked and explored quite playfully with poetry.

DEVELOPING YOUR CRAFT AND MENTORSHIP

Heidi: How did you (and how do you) continue to develop your craft?

Shannon: My work has developed through a continuous process of experimenting and playing. It's also been important for me to devote time and energy to writing, in spite of all of life's other demands. This is has never been easy for me. Even before I had children, I found prioritizing writing difficult. But writing helps me understand everything better; I need to do it, and to do it I need to be alone. Like certain plants need shade alongside the sun. You must be devoted to the process and learn to embrace struggle, rejection and failure. You have to be able to accept criticism and sit on things, move on to new projects and let some work go. Artists crave love and appreciation like crazy, but I think it's important to know that sometimes we are writing for a room full of empty chairs. And you have to love those chairs more and more as time goes on. All artists grow because of their art, and what making their art forces them to see about themselves and the world. The way to keep growing is to keep practising, keep trying to see and feel freshly.

Heidi: Who influenced or encouraged your writing?

Shannon: This question might require a book-length answer, so I will have to give you the short version! My mother was the first person. She always supported my love of reading and writing. As a young adult, I loved books and was consumed by the work of Leonard Cohen, Gwendolyn MacEwen, Hans Christian Andersen, Yehuda Amichai, Eugene Ionesco, Janet Frame and the list goes on and on. Reading is generative. Whatever I have read and whatever I read next has an influence on my work.

Also, I have had many wonderful teachers over the years. I'll just mention two here. My drama teacher in high school (Oksana Cymbalisty) validated the creative, imaginative process for me in a way that helped me transcend my shyness and gave me the first taste of the joy of collaborative creative work. Her encouragement was a definite stepping stone for me on the path toward poetry and drama becoming fundamental to my life and identity. The next person who comes to mind is my university professor, (now deceased) Canadian poet Libby Scheier, who was the first person (after my mother!) to tell me that I could be a poet if I wanted to be one. She also offered the first genuine and thorough critique of my poems. She pushed me a lot and was as encouraging as she was critical. She taught me to be specific in my writing and to take risks.

Finally, the hugest source of encouragement has been my very own writer-husband, David Derry. He is an incredibly disciplined fiction writer, who gets up every morning at 4:30 to carve out writing time for himself before he heads out to the day job that supports us all. On the weekends, he relieves me as much as possible so that I get some time to write. It is often his belief in the value of my work, and probably more importantly the value of literature itself, that has kept me going even when I have often found the demands of motherhood too overwhelming to even scribble down a grocery list.

Heidi: What advice would you like to share from your writing mentors?

Shannon: I think the most important advice I've ever received was from a different sort of mentor, my paternal grandmother. The daughter of a Cape Breton coal miner and mother of seven children, my Nana Bramer always hoped that when I grew up I would *travel*. She meant this literally—that I should go to new places and see the world, go everywhere and go often. And I always think about that when I write. Is this work travelling? Does it have imaginative texture? Is it surprising and strange and vast, like a new place? I like to bring this question to my work, even when I don't always like the answer!

Heidi: Looking back at the mentoring sessions with the contest winners, what advice would you like to share with other aspiring writers who are considering working privately with a mentor or an editor in the future?

Shannon: Sometimes, a mentor and an editor are the same person; sometimes they are not. And you probably need both—we all do. I think it's a good idea to be upfront about what you need and want from a mentor. I'm not sure I've always provided exactly the right thing at the right time. Also, hiring a mentor or gaining a mentor through a contest is not the same thing as discovering one inadvertently, through some common project or interest. This is not to diminish the value of this experience; I think it means that the connection between the mentor and mentee may or may not always gel perfectly. When this happens, both people will learn and grow even more. So, I guess my advice would be to focus on the adventure of the process—try to notice the places in yourself and your work that are both open and closed to guidance, suggestion, commentary. Then be brave!

UNPUBLISHED TO PUBLISHED

Heidi: What was your path to publication?

Shannon: My first poems were published in small, independent journals and chapbooks while I was attending York University. To be honest, although I knew I wanted to write (and wanted the approval of my other writer friends), I was not very ambitious in terms of publishing. I loved the smaller, experimental, artful homemade publications that were prolific at that time (no Internet; no blogs!). I sent work out to Jay MillAr, and he was the first person to publish my poems (in small editions of beautiful, hand-sewn books that he made with his wife, Hazel). After university, my first book, *suitcases and other poems,* was published by Exile Editions, a small press run by Barry Callaghan and his son, Michael. That was entirely thanks to a beloved professor (of Canadian Poetry), Branko Gorjup, who recommended my work to Barry directly. I was lucky to be one of a circle of friends who were connected to Barry through Branko; I will be forever grateful to them both for opening that door for me.

Heidi: What changes or new opportunities do you see in the publishing world in recent years that may benefit new writers?

Shannon: When I first started publishing, there was no social media, and it's ubiquitous now because it's how so many of us informally communicate with each other. Publishers and writers can promote their work by engaging directly with readers and participate in conversations with other writers; there are real and beautiful communities online. However, authors continue to be desperate for passionate, curious readers. If you look around at most people on the subway in Toronto, they aren't reading books. They are sending text messages, playing games, watching shows or sleeping. Literary publishers are scrambling to survive while competing for the attention of the brains and hearts of human beings who would rather be doing other things—easier things. The act of writing and the process of engaging people to read is still a fight. When I visit middle schools to conduct poetry workshops, my first objective is always to show my students that a study of poetry is worthwhile even if the pursuit seems a bit hard or confusing at first. I must convince them of what I truly believe: that poetry is a style of being. That writing has the potential to sharpen our seeing and feeling and thinking. That when we read, we grow. And it is the distracted kid hiding the phone in her desk that I want to engage most of all.

Heidi: What words of advice do you have for unpublished writers about the challenges they will face on their path to publication?

Shannon: Only that you must write for a long time without worrying too much about publishing—the way a playwright tries to imagine a world without becoming consumed with all the details surrounding how her play will be staged. Devise a system for sending work out periodically, but don't let it sap your energy. You may have a lot of luck one year and then go for a few without being able to make anything happen. The important thing is to keep working on your poems, stories, plays, etc. Keep doing what you love and need to do. Write. And put your poems away in drawers and then pull them back out again. Go to readings and buy and read as many books as possible. Figure out what makes you happy when you are not writing and do that, too.

Interview with Judge and Mentor, Catherine Owen

Aspiring Canadian Poets Contest, 2014

Photo and biography courtesy of Catherine Owen

Catherine Owen lives in New Westminster, B.C. She is the author of 10 collections of poetry, among them *Designated Mourner* (ECW, 2014), *Trobairitz* (Anvil Press, 2012), *Seeing Lessons* (Wolsak & Wynn, 2010) and *Frenzy* (Anvil Press, 2009). Her poems are included in several recent anthologies, such as *Forcefield: 77 Women Poets of British Columbia* (Mothertongue Press, 2013) and *This Place a Stranger: Canadian Women Travelling Alone* (Caitlin Press, 2014). Stories have appeared in *Urban Graffiti, Memewar Magazine, Lit n Image* (US) and *TORONTO Quarterly*. Her collection of memoirs and essays is called *Catalysts: Confrontations with the muse* (Wolsak & Wynn, 2012).

Frenzy won the Alberta Book Prize, and other collections have been nominated for the BC Book Prize, the Re-lit, the CBC Award, and the George Ryga Award. Her photo series, *Skins (of grief)*, was given the Truth in Art Award from the New Westminster Record. In

2015, Wolsak & Wynn published her compendium on the practices of writing, called *The Other 23 and a Half Hours or Everything You Wanted to Know That Your MFA Didn't Teach You*. Her upcoming collection of short fiction is called *The Day of the Dead* (Caitlin Press, 2016). She works in TV, plays metal bass and blogs at Marrow Reviews at https://crowgirl11.wordpress.com/.

~~~

In the Beginning, an Aspiring Writer

Heidi: When did you start writing poetry?

Catherine: I began very early. Around four. I recall feeling the first impulse to write sitting beneath an oak tree near my kindergarten classroom.

Heidi: Do you remember your first poem? (Care to share a couple of lines?)

Catherine: I like trees / and things that are pretty. / I like me / and I like the city.

Heidi: Was poetry your first creative outlet or was it another style of writing? Or another art form?

Catherine: Poetry was first, and then much of my childhood I focused on fiction, returning to poetry through my teen interest in composing song lyrics.

Heidi: Do other forms of artistic expression or life experience influence your writing?

Catherine: All kinds of music, primarily. And as an appreciator, many forms of art. Watching nature, too. Just being there, in awe, for the moment.

Developing Your Craft and Mentorship

Heidi: How did you (and how do you) continue to develop your craft?

Catherine: Daily writing and editing. A definite discipline and structure and persistence. Lots of reading!

Heidi: Influences—who influenced or encouraged your writing?

Catherine: When I was a child, I met a few published authors, including Jean Little, who gave me the sense I could be a writer. Several teachers in high school made an impact by their acknowledgement of my talent. In my early twenties, it was Patrick Lane and my husband, the poet Chad Norman. And my parents, who have always been there.

Heidi: What advice would you like to share from your writing mentors?

Catherine: They just said, "Keep at it. Don't give up. You were meant to live this life."

Heidi: Looking back at the mentoring sessions with the contest winners, what advice would you like to share with other aspiring writers who are considering working privately with a mentor or an editor in the future?

Catherine: I think it is always helpful to have your work heard by another honed ear, or several, to get a sense of where you can't hear yourself failing to select the strongest word or most potent line break. You don't have to take all the suggestions, but regardless, the critiquing process will teach you avenues into your work you may not otherwise have accessed.

Unpublished to Published

Heidi: What was your path to publication?

Catherine: My first publication was in the Catholic school anthology when I was 11. Then, in literary magazines as a late teen, and finally, when I was 26, my book *Somatic: The Life and Work of Egon Schiele* emerged from Exile [Editions]. I just continued to submit and make connections with those who I found influential. And give poetry recitations!

Heidi: What changes or new opportunities do you see in the publishing world in recent years that may benefit new writers?

Catherine: A wider diversity of ways to publish one's work and a plethora of "writing advice"!

Heidi: What words of advice do you have for unpublished writers about the challenges they will face on their path to publication?

Catherine: Rejection isn't personal, but it is a moment for you to look again at the material. Always focus on the work itself and not merely the end results, whether publication, awards or any other external victory.

Interview with Judge and Mentor, Stuart Ross

Aspiring Canadian Poets Contest, 2015

Photo and biography courtesy of Stuart Ross

Stuart Ross published his first poetry pamphlet on the photocopier in his dad's office, one night in 1979. Through the 1980s, he stood on Toronto's Yonge Street wearing signs like "Writer Going to Hell," selling over 7,000 chapbooks. He is the author of more than 15 books of fiction, poetry and essays, most recently the poetry collections *A Hamburger in a Gallery* (DC Books, 2015) and *Our Days in Vaudeville* (Mansfield Press, 2013), collaborations with 29 poets from across Canada. The book *You Exist. Details Follow.* (Anvil Press, 2012) won the only prize given to an Anglophone writer in 2013 by l'Académie de la vie littéraire au tournant du 21ᵉ siècle. Three of his poetry books have been shortlisted for the ReLit Prize, and his short story collection, *Buying Cigarettes for the Dog* (Freehand Books, 2009), won the prize in 2010. His novel, *Snowball, Dragonfly, Jew* (ECW Press, 2011), won the 2012 Mona Elaine Adilman Award for Fiction on a Jewish Theme.

Stuart's many chapbooks include three released in 2014—*Nice Haircut, Fiddlehead* (Puddles of Sky Press), *A Pretty Good Year* (Nose in Book Publishing) and *In In My Dream* (BookThug)—and others from Room 3o2 Books, The Front Press, Apt. 9 Press, Silver Birch Press, Pink Dog Press and his own Proper Tales Press, which he launched 36 years ago. He is co-translator of *My Planet of Kites*, by Marie-Ève Comtois (Mansfield Press, 2015).

Stuart is a member of the improvisational noise trio Donkey Lopez, whose CDs include *Juan Lonely Night* and *Working Class Burro*. He is a founding member of the Meet the Presses collective, which administers the bpNichol Chapbook Award, and has his own imprint, "a stuart ross book," at Mansfield Press. Stuart has run poetry workshops in British Columbia, Alberta, Ontario, Quebec, Nova Scotia, and the Northwest Territories and coaches writers one-on-one through Skype. He lives in Cobourg, Ontario, and blogs at bloggamooga.blogspot.ca.

~~~

In the Beginning, an Aspiring Writer

Heidi: When did you start writing poetry?

Stuart: I began writing when I was about nine or 10 years old, inspired by reading poems by Tennyson, E. E. Cummings, Ogden Nash (!!!) and some others.

Heidi: Do you remember your first poem?

Stuart: I remember the first poem I sent to a publication. The publication was the *Toronto Star*, which of course didn't publish poetry, though they sent me a very kind rejection letter. Here's the poem:

If you double a bubble
You'll have two bubbles
But this information isn't worth
a pile of rubble.

A few months ago, I included that poem in a long sequence called *Grey Snotes*. I think there's room for terribleness in poetry, if done deliberately. (I mean, it wasn't deliberately terrible when I first wrote it, but now I am consciously including it as a terrible poem in that sequence.)

Heidi: Was poetry your first creative outlet or was it another style of writing? Or another art form?

Stuart: I probably drew before I wrote. I was very inspired by the *Beetle Bailey* comic strip as a kid, and I drew these guys called "the Slobs." They had long hair and big noses and wore baseball caps that covered their eyes. I was also inspired by Al Capp's shmoos, and I drew shmoos a lot. Plus, my childhood friend Mark Laba and I invented a creature called "the black bloop," which was basically a little scribbled ball with stick arms and legs.

But it wasn't long after that that I began writing poems and stories, including my "novel," *The Many Escapes of Specimen 939-399-X*, which I bound in an edition of one. Still have it.

Heidi: Do other forms of artistic expression or life experience influence your writing?

Stuart: I'm definitely inspired by film, occasionally by music, sometimes by sculpture, installation art and photography. Mostly, I'm inspired by my neuroses and by other writers whose works I admire.

Developing Your Craft and Mentorship

Heidi: How did you (and how do you) continue to develop your craft?

Stuart: I read a huge range of writers and I experiment continuously. I don't believe in "finding my voice." We all have lots of voices, and I explore and experiment and never get settled in one way of writing. My last poetry book, *A Hamburger in a Gallery* (DC Books, 2015), is mostly a collection of personal experiments, including scores of poems I wrote in my own workshops, where I encourage participants to try new ways of writing. I'm much more excited about an interesting, ambitious failure than some neat, pat, cookie-cutter poem.

Heidi: Influences—who influenced or encouraged your writing?

Stuart: I mentioned my first "influences" earlier. As I got into my teens, I discovered the works of Stephen Crane, David W. McFadden, Ron Padgett, Aram Saroyan, Victor Coleman … These were some of the writers who excited me as I was entering a more mature phase of my writing—my late juvenilia, I guess you could say.

I was also lucky enough to attend a pretty crazy alternative school in Toronto, and our creative writing class studied with Victor Coleman, Robert Fones, David Young and Joe Rosenblatt. How lucky can you be? There was also a lesser-known poet, but no less an influence, named Sam F. Johnson. As well, my friend Mark and I started attending a downtown poetry workshop when we were about 15, run by a brilliant poet named George Miller, a guy who has never really gotten his due. He was huge for us.

I did also get some great encouragement from my English teachers— in junior high school, and then in high school, where my teacher, Ann Smythe, wrote on one of my stories, "Why are all your characters such dolts?" I loved that! But she was very encouraging.

Heidi: What advice would you like to share from your writing mentors?

Stuart: My most recent mentor is a New York poet named Larry Fagin, a brilliant teacher and writing coach. I haven't seen him in a few years, but one of the most important things he told me was to stop trying to be so clever. Cleverness in poetry makes for bad poetry. I really see what he means: I see cleverness now as contrivance.

Heidi: Looking back at the mentoring sessions with the contest winners, what advice would you like to share with other aspiring writers who are considering working privately with a mentor or an editor in the future?

Stuart: First of all, they should work with *me*. Second, if they are spending the time or money to work with a mentor, they should give themselves over to the experience: don't stubbornly try to make your mentor fit your mould; experience what the mentor has to offer. And if you think it's all bullshit in the end, that's fine, too. The important thing is to have this very different experience from what you would normally do.

Unpublished to Published

Heidi: What was your path to publication?

Stuart: I already mentioned my first self-published "novel" in an edition of one. Next, came a small book called *The Thing in Exile*, with poems by me, Mark Laba and Steven Feldman (both of whom I'm still in contact with), when we were 15 or 16 years old. It was published by Books by Kids, which soon became Annick Press. After that, I published a lot in my high school magazine, *Akropolis*, and as soon as I was out of high school, I started up Proper Tales Press and began doing chapbooks of my poems and stories. I still do Proper Tales publications 36 years later. I also began publishing with lots of other tiny presses and magazines: 1cent, Coma Goats, This Tiny Donkey, The Front Press, Contra Mundo Books, Curvd H&z, and so on. In my mid-thirties, I began to publish with larger small-press publishers. I have about 15 full-length books out, from ECW Press, DC Books, Anvil Press, Freehand Books, Mansfield Press, The Mercury Press, and soon Wolsak & Wynn. I like to move around between publishers, especially geographically diverse publishers.

Heidi: What changes or new opportunities do you see in the publishing world in recent years that may benefit new writers?

Stuart: Well, online publishing has its huge downsides and huge upsides—way too much to discuss here. But the immediacy and economy and reach of online publishing—I'm talking here specifically about online journals—is a good thing. The problem is it is so much easier now to flood the world with horrible writing. I still advise anyone I work with to start up their own print magazine or press and self-publish and do little mags or anthologies of their friends' work, etc.

Heidi: What words of advice do you have for unpublished writers about the challenges they will face on their path to publication?

Stuart: Just publish yourself. Make little leaflets of your poems and leave them on bus or subway seats or tuck them into other people's books in bookstores. When you are looking to be published by others, make sure you submit only to journals or presses whose output you are familiar with—if you haven't read what they've published, why in the world would you send your own work to them? That said, never mould your work to fit a publisher. Write what you need to or want to write and then find a home for that writing.

Interview with Judge and Mentor, George Elliott Clarke

Aspiring Canadian Poets Contest, 2016

Photo and biography courtesy of George Elliott Clarke

George Elliott Clarke has issued 14 poetry texts, four verse-plays, three opera libretti, two novels, two scholarly essay collections and two edited anthologies. His plays and operas have all been staged, and his two screenplays have been televised. He has three titles in translation: one in Chinese, one in Romanian and one in Italian. He lives in Toronto but still owns property in his homeland, Nova Scotia. He is the E.J. Pratt professor of Canadian Literature at the University of Toronto.

Acclaimed for his poetry, opera libretti and novel, Clarke has also won laurels for his pioneering work as a scholar of African-Canadian literature. His honours include the Archibald Lampman Award for Poetry (1991), the Portia White Prize for Artistic Excellence (1998), a Bellagio Center (Italy) Fellowship (1998), the Governor General's Award for English-language Poetry (2001), the National Magazine

Gold Award for Poetry (2001), the Dr. Martin Luther King, Jr. Achievement Award (2004), the Pierre Elliott Trudeau Fellowship Prize (2005), the Frontieras Poesis Premiul (Romania, 2005), the Dartmouth Book Award for Fiction (2006), the Eric Hoffer Book Award for Poetry (2009), Appointment to the Order of Nova Scotia (2006) and Appointment to the Order of Canada (2008).

Clarke has also received eight honorary doctorates. He served as the 27th William Lyon Mackenzie King Professor of Canadian Studies at Harvard University, in the Department of English, 2013–2014. After completing his term as the fourth Poet Laureate of Toronto (2012–2015), Clarke was appointed the seventh Parliamentary [National] Poet Laureate (2016–2017). His newest book is *The Motorcyclist* (HarperCollins Canada [2016]), a novel, but also new are *Extra Illicit Sonnets* (Exile Editions), which is amatory poetry, and *Gold* (Gaspereau Press), a miscellaneous collection.

~~~

In the Beginning, an Aspiring Writer

Heidi: When did you start writing poetry?

George: Fifteen. I wanted to be a rock-star songwriter. To be popular in high school.

Heidi: Do you remember your first poem? What inspired that first poem or your first piece of creative writing?

George: "Major Pat Pending and the Spiders from Mars." (Apologies to Ziggy Stardust!) I wanted to be a songwriter. I wrote songs in different styles: soul, disco, country, gospel, etc. Can't remember the lines, but that half-plagiarized title is unforgettable!

Heidi: Was poetry your first creative outlet or was it another style of writing? Or another art form?

George: Studied trombone for two years: boring. Poetry was the ticket.

Heidi: Do other forms of artistic expression or life experience influence your writing?

George: Yes: jazz, giallo films, Africadian church music, Italian pop music of the 1960s, etc.

Developing Your Craft and Mentorship

Heidi: How did you (and how do you) continue to develop your craft?

George: Decided to study English at university. Took all three degrees (or "belts"), 1979–1993. I continue to develop by reading and reviewing other writers—my peers, Nobel laureates, classics.

Heidi: Influences—who influenced or encouraged your writing?

George: Miss Dee Aymooney, librarian, Halifax North End Memorial Library; Queen Elizabeth high school teachers, Carol Gibbons and Fred Holtz; mentor, Walter Borden; and—by long-distance osmosis—Ezra Pound, Pierre Elliott Trudeau, Malcolm X, Miles Davis, Bob Dylan.

Heidi: What advice would you like to share from your writing mentors?

George: Tell the truth—as you know it—and make it swing.

Heidi: What advice would you like to share with aspiring writers who are considering working privately with a mentor or an editor in the future?

George: Learn—and then forge your own style. (See William Blake.)

UNPUBLISHED TO PUBLISHED

Heidi: What was your path to publication?

George: First "real" poem published was "Watercolour for Negro Expatriates in France," written on New Year's Eve, 1978, into New Year's Day, 1979: a statement of a young Black Haligonian intellectual, envying Afro-Americans who went to France in the twenties and thirties to dodge U.S. racism. The first book—*Saltwater Spirituals and Deeper Blues*—came about because I won (still the youngest person to have done so) a provincial writing competition in Nova Scotia in 1981. I was 21 at the time. The book was published when I was 23.

Heidi: What changes or new opportunities do you see in the publishing world in recent years that may benefit new writers?

George: Internet networking, sharing, downloading.

Heidi: What words of advice do you have for unpublished writers about the challenges they will face on their path to publication?

George: Forge your own style and tell your own truth!

Aspiring Canadian Poets Contest Winners: Interviews/Poetry

Ana Rodriguez Machado

First-Place Winner, Aspiring Canadian Poets Contest, 2012

Photo courtesy of Ana Rodriguez Machado

Interview in 2012

Why did you enter this particular poem in the contest?

This poem is difficult and painful, so it wasn't an easy decision to put it out in the world. But when I presented it in a workshop, I received encouraging feedback from my peers and my professor. I'm so grateful that they were such hands-on editors and honest, constructive critics.

I decided to submit this poem because I thought it was one of my strongest pieces, but in all honesty, it never crossed my mind that it would win.

What's the backstory to the poem?

In February 2012, I travelled to Honduras to participate in a Habitat for Humanity build. The trip lasted just over a week, but the things I saw and the people I met are forever ingrained in my memory. It was an intense and gruelling experience, both physically and emotionally, and I came back to Canada with mixed feelings about everything I had seen and done. It took me a few weeks to be able to write about the trip, and even then, I had no idea how I would capture the experience. After many attempts and some inspiration from Carolyn Forché's *The Country Between Us*, I decided to keep things simple. That's how I came up with *An afternoon in Central America*. What I love most about poetry is its freedom of interpretation. I think a poem is most powerful when it stands on its own, without further explanation from the writer. Everything I wanted to say is in the poem. It can defend itself.

When did you start writing poetry?

I started using writing to express myself when I was really young. I kept journals, wrote unrequited love letters, kept little notes about my thoughts. When I was 10, I wrote an adventure series about a little boy that learns to live in an underwater world. It was probably 30 pages long. I printed copies for everyone I knew and felt like a pretty accomplished author. What started out as embarrassingly candid journals in my preteen years eventually became more well-crafted and conscientious writing. I've always loved poetry and I've been fascinated by the infinite effects words can have on us, whether it is to make us feel something new or to entirely change our perspective. I never really decided to be a writer. I just wrote.

Do you remember your first poem? Care to share a couple of lines? What inspired that first poem or your first piece of creative writing?

Oh, God, I'd rather not share that! It was probably a love poem about the boy I had a crush on in Grade 4. It probably even rhymed.

Was poetry your first creative outlet or was it another style of writing? Or another art form?

I'm trying to write more prose, especially non-fiction, but it still isn't as close to my heart as poetry. I think poems and music and painting were my first creative outlets. Poems have a certain freedom that's difficult to achieve in other writing styles, at least for me. I feel completely comfortable writing poetry because it feels open and free for both the reader and the writer.

Do other forms of artistic expression and/or life experience influence your writing?

I look for inspiration in all my experiences and the experiences of people I know, so my surroundings constantly influence my writing. I love travelling and getting to know different kinds of people, from the way they cook to the way they greet each other—everything about other cultures fascinates me. New places always bring about interesting images or narratives to explore. Wherever I am, my writing changes with me—everything from the language to the weather and even the sounds of the streets inspires something different.

Influences—who influenced or encouraged your writing?

My parents have always encouraged me in everything I do. They're the protagonists of so much of my writing and they're my biggest/ only fans. I owe a lot to my creative writing teacher in high school (shout-out to Mr. Bowering!) for helping me realize that I could write more than melodramatic journal entries. And of course, my mentor in all things writing: the infinitely patient Carolyn Smart. She believed in my writing before I did.

What do you do to develop your craft?

Reading helps. Workshops help. Finding a community of people to share work with helps. My biggest challenge has always been fear. I feel like I'm faking it most of the time, like I have to earn something to call myself a writer, like I don't deserve it. So sometimes the hard work is finding the courage to make stuff; to just be alone with the work; to say, "Screw it—I'm doing it my way."

Tell us about your mentoring experience with contest judge and mentor, Catherine Graham.

Working with Catherine was a challenging and unique experience. She was a candid and helpful critic, who took the time to get to know me as a writer and as a person. She was patient and understanding when I struggled, reassuring and inspiring when I thrived.

How will Catherine's guidance inform your future writing?

Catherine helped me realize that a poem is never truly finished—a new draft is always just around the corner. I hope to continue finding new poems in the old ones and to keep writing and writing and writing.

What advice do you have for new writers?

My only advice for anyone who loves to write is to keep going and to do it honestly and without fear. The best thing about writing is doing it for yourself—because it makes you feel something, because it makes you look at the world in a different way, because it allows you to say something that seems impossible to say. Forget about everything else. Enjoy it and the rest will come in time.

~~~

ANA'S POEMS

An afternoon in Central America (first-place poem)

The mountains danced in shades of cadmium and emerald.
The policemen came to thank us for coming from so far away.
We aimed their loaded M14s and posed for pictures.
Everyone laughed. Sand turned to stone.
Behind the girl with golden hair, a little boy ripped a worm in half.

In this place I delight in you

and as I delight in you, the breeze dreams
of melodies, your name along its blades of thread.
The oldest constellations go through me
with your conviction. The moon swings
its perfect delusion.

But darkness arrives with another
melody, my hatred battles the idle
dusk. I embrace what I cannot
keep. You are not here. Our flesh turns
weary, craving without promise. The shores
grieve when day anchors there.

I catch sight of myself omitted like
ancient weights holding ships in place. Now
and again I touch their serious
bodies, resist the ocean and arrive

at nothing. I choose you silently with these
distant fabrications. Here I feel you
and the line where sky meets Earth
buries you all for nothing.
Here I feel you.

This is a haven.
Secluded, the ocean responds to its own echoes.
There are times when I wake ahead of schedule and still my heart is
pouring.

Only
the weightless grief
of a sailboat. Now
and again fabric catching wind. Lofty,
soaring dust. A grey seabird
tumbles downward
from the sun.
Afternoons,
each one the same,
run after one another.
The moon blazes fireflies
in drops of rain. Amid vague
longings the breeze
removes its knots.

In this place I delight in you.

00:52:59

after Alfred Hitchcock's *Memory of the Camps* (1985)

(The reel winds. A voice hovers. No music, no colour.)

This is April 1945.

The stench of disease from barbed wire cages
drifts to nearby countryside, an inconvenience
to those who wish to enjoy the perfume
of orchard blossoms.

Cows graze amid fresh dew.

The barely breathing bones reside in a place beyond
humanity. Accustomed to excrement, they surrender
to piles of twisted joints and jagged eyes. Those who dare
resist their heavy eyelids pay the price—

heads are wedged on stakes to teach the rest a lesson.

The figures with straight postures and steamed uniforms
revel in well-fed bellies. They search for unusual
drawings in stacks of translucent skin and stretch
tattooed flesh to make lampshades.

Witnesses pick at dried blood beneath their fingernails.

The righteous arrive at the mass interment to find
e l e v e n   m i l l i o n silenced
11 000 000 nameless
eleven million skeletons rupturing through pallid skin.

Any number can be inconceivable if it is vast enough.

The witnesses and poised figures are forced

to greet the faces they had buried.
They weep in remorse
laugh in hysterics

insist they had not noticed the smell.

Dear Hitchcock,
you say it had to be seen to be believed and I have seen
the hollows filled with the limp and defenceless
I have seen the breathless bones dragged by their limbs across the dirt
beyond anything you could call humanity.

52 minutes and 59 seconds.
There is nothing common about a grave.

touch lightly

with each touch we recall
        a small start of forgetfulness
in every creation
        there must be a modest beginning of end
and *forever* is a word
        that must be temporary.

youth means once more
because we overlook everything:
the dim constant akin
        to a touch of lips.

in this moment–
        the less travelled darkness we rest on
        the path of rainwater flooding our souls
        the slender kindling sensing deprivation
we do not recall the colour of our optimism.

we touch lightly and the corridor of moon we held on to like a railway
    is beyond us.

then lay to rest a murmuring sound

—once more and forever—

each weightless touch
    a longing.

every petal feels the frost.

An empty bottle of Jameson

good morning, poison
in tinted glass
you twisted everything
again
hazy words
and lips and hands
I recognize them
from somewhere
my brain crawls
out of my throat
I look for a bucket
to put it in

good morning, poison
you twisted everything
in tinted glass
again
hazy words
I recognize them

and lips and hands
from somewhere
my brain crawls
I look for a bucket
out of my throat
to put it in

good morning, poison
in tinted glass
hazy words
and lips and hands
my brain crawls
out of my throat
you twisted everything
again
I recognize them

from somewhere
I look for a bucket
to put it in

to put it in
I look for a bucket
out of my throat
my brain crawls
from somewhere
I recognize them
and lips and hands
hazy words
again
you twisted everything
in tinted glass
good morning, poison

NORA GROVE

Second-Place Winner, Aspiring Canadian Poets Contest, 2012

INTERVIEW IN 2012

Why did you enter this particular poem in the contest, and what is the backstory to the poem?

I chose the Chirico poem as it was one of my most recent works. I had for a number of years been intrigued by Chirico's early surrealistic—or what he preferred to call his "metaphysical"—paintings. For me, they emanate a sense of mystery—a mystery with a foreboding edge that lies just below the surface of things. I sense a story in his works as if something dramatic has just happened or is about to happen. Through just a slightly skewed perspective and the juxtaposition of unrelated things, his paintings present a dreamlike psychic space. Many of the ancient piazzas I visited in Italy and Spain, like the Piazza Vecchio in Florence, surface in my mind's eye as I write my Chirico poems.

When did you start writing poetry? Do you remember your first poem?

As early adolescents, friends and I wrote and performed comic skits for our classmates at the Catholic high school we attended. During that period, I also remember writing silly rhymes and songs for fun. However, Dylan-like angst also surfaced at that time:

My life is lost
I feel the pain
Of winters washed
By freezing rain

This opening to one of my first "serious" poems is followed by many more heart-wrenching stanzas. No doubt, the seduction of teenage hormones coupled with Catholic guilt and fear of damnation fueled these dark musings.

Do other forms of artistic expression and/or life experience influence your writing?

I am inspired by the natural beauty of the Pacific Northwest, where I live. I am especially drawn to whatever emanates "soul" or what Lorca refers to as "duende." Music, literature, the visual arts, film and dance are all sources of inspiration for me. At my last poetry circle meeting, I was introduced to the term *ekphrastic poetry*. I discovered that some of my poems, the Chirico series and my poem inspired by Georgia O'Keeffe, for example, fall into that genre.

The news of the world often triggers feelings of outrage and compassion that fuel some of my poems. And certainly, whatever is happening in my own personal world re relationships, losses, grief, celebrations, travels all stimulate my writing.

Who influenced or encouraged your writing?

When I was growing up, reading was encouraged. My parents had a fine collection of books, and frequent trips to the public library were a ritual I continue to this day.

English courses at university introduced me to some of the English canon of literature. And although I enjoyed my English courses, I switched my major to psychology and sociology. As a result, poetry receded as an area of interest for me for some time. It was not until I attended an American Humanistic Psychology Conference, where the poet David Whyte was on the program, that my interest in poetry was reignited. Through his influence, I became inspired to read, memorize and write poetry again. I was fortunate to attend a 10-day workshop with David and John O'Donahue on the west coast of Ireland in the late nineties, where we had the opportunity to engage deeply in the culture and landscape of that special part of the world through the lens of the poetry, music and people of that place. A decade later, that experience still fuels my poetic soul.

At present, I am a member of the Roundhouse Poetry Circle, whose blog you can access at <u>roundhousepoetrycircle.wordpress.com/</u>. We meet once a month, and each participant takes a turn to present a poet of particular interest. Last month, I did a presentation on Margaret Atwood's *Journals of Susanna Moodie*. The process of researching that project was most rewarding for me. And although we haven't as yet presented our own writing, the reading and discussion about published and well-regarded poets does spark my imagination and inspire me to continue to write. I also subscribe to the Poetry Foundation blog, which supplies me with a wealth of poetry and articles discussing various poets and poetics.

Vancouver offers a number of poetry readings and a variety of courses on "creative writing." Just last evening, I went to a poetry reading by our poet laureate Evelyn Lau, whose work I appreciate.

I have also written a series of poems that are compilations of lines of poetry by well-known poets—G.M. Hopkins, T. Roethke, Machado, Lorca, Rilke, W. Stevens, Mirabai, E. Bishop, A. Akhmatova, Neruda— that are particularly meaningful for me.

What do you do to develop your craft?

I continue to take creative writing courses. When I lived in Victoria, I attended workshops and summer school courses sponsored by the Victoria School of Writing. I also attended a number of poetry readings sponsored by the University of Victoria and a local coffee shop. Victoria has a vibrant community of poets. I am particularly enamored with the poetry of Patrick Lane, who lives there.

Back in Vancouver, I have taken several workshops at the University of British Columbia and Simon Fraser University and attend a variety of readings around town. I also attend the Vancouver Writer's Fest and the Sunshine Coast Festival of the Written Arts, most years. These forums expose me to a variety of writers that influence and stimulate my own writing.

Tell us about your mentoring experience with contest judge and mentor, Catherine Graham.

I feel privileged to have had the opportunity to work with such a supportive, insightful mentor as Catherine Graham. Her feedback encouraged me to take a fresh look at my poems and to revise them with renewed vigor. Her comments were consistently helpful and positive. For example, she wrote, "the above are suggestions to help you see the poem through another reader's eyes . . . to see the poem in a new way and to make discoveries in the revision process . . . take what works for you. They are suggestions to help you along your own path." She was also encouraging, "nice edgy quality . . . this poem has bite . . . I like the lovely clean music and lines in this stanza."

She also referred me to other poets who were new to me. One of the main learnings I will take away from my mentorship is the reminder to make my writing accessible to the reader while still being challenged to "push the language to be more surprising." That and the discipline to carve out time, when I am not involved in a writing course—to write on a regular basis—are my ongoing challenges.

What advice do you have for new writers?

As a fledgling writer myself, I hardly feel it is appropriate for me to give advice to others. However, what I tell myself is, take deep breaths of life, engage all your senses in experiencing the world, explore outside your comfort zones, take the time to contemplate your experience. Also, attempt to listen, be aware, understand and empathize with your fellow beings. Do what you can to contribute to the world's well-being. Expand your world through exposing yourself to art, music, literature, dance, travel. Read . . . read . . . write . . . write . . . love . . . love . . . appreciate and enjoy your one precious life.

~~~

NORA'S POEMS

Chirico #1 (second-place poem)

a dog yaps somewhere around the corner
its sound bounces off stucco walls
like a batted racket ball

Chirico paints
blocks of sunlight and deep shadow
on the empty cobblestoned streets

is it siesta
or something sinister

why does it feel so familiar
I am a stranger here

Lorca knew
his poetry silenced
by black boots gun butts shovels

fear
leaks through window sills
under bolted doors

after dark things happen

people disappear
some cry out
while others cover
their ears and wait

no one knows
why or who is next or when

at dawn life resumes
in blocks of sunlight and shadow
in houses and on streets
where a dog's bark is heard

A Sacred Vow

No Angel Gabriel heralds your birth,
my son.
I am no Virgin Mary.
A teenager still
in ways a child myself
afraid of my swelling belly and breasts
and the world's harsh judgement.

I do not love your father.
I do not want to marry.
"I do", I say to the priest.
"I do not", I say to myself.
Your father knows.

A slap a cry a howl
you breathe.
Umbilical cord . . . circumcision
the first cuts.
As I cradle and suckle you

in my arms,
I whisper a prayer,
a promise . . . a sacred vow.

You will learn
the world is fierce and glorious.
You will be wounded
healed and love.
You will be challenged
and hurt and love
again and again
and wonder
at the mystery.

Now I am in the winter of my years
you are grown and strong,
I light a candle to give thanks.
Prepared as some ancient Inuit
to find an ice floe

I won't look back.
I know I kept my vow.

Still Time

another rush hour
the only still thing
a great blue heron stands
on one leg
on the shore of English Bay

a passing siren startles
heron's wings to flight
I watched
heron fly and just before

sunlight strikes the stained glass
windows of a West End church
heron's shadow glides like cloud
over broken pieces of coloured light
reflected across the stone floor
the colours scatter like amulets cast by a seer
to foretell the future

I don't know which is worse
the terror of knowing
or the terror of not knowing
I am growing old
all time is rush hour to me now
still
heron returns to the shore of the bay
distant horizons gleam
in its unblinking eyes

At This Time of Day the Church Bell Tower Casts a Long Shadow

1495

An excited mob,
inspired by priests,
taunt a woman
tied to a stake
in the square.

A masked executioner, torch in hand,
lights her hair and the faggots at her feet,
cowl headed monks chant Latin incantations
as she burns.

Microscopic traces of her remains

stain the cobblestones to this day.

2008

A long haired, teenage girl
in a short red skirt
rides her motor scooter
into the square.

Hasn't anyone warned her?

Berlusconi prefers virgins,
they say.
Well worth the price,
he says.
Her family says,
she is missing.

Is what ever happens
destined to repeat itself?

What ever happens,

the church bell tolls the hour

Jill Talbot

Third-Place Winner, Aspiring Canadian Poets Contest, 2012

Interview in 2012

Why did you enter this particular poem in the contest?

Stephen Dunn said, "Your poem effectively begins the first moment you've surprised or startled yourself," and that was exactly what I experienced. I was quite surprised with the places the poem took me. Sort of like it had all been hibernating in years of waiting. It was also the first time I edited a poem. I got rid of the "it's nothing, I just scribbled it on a napkin" defence. It was also actually the only poem I had written since high school, so there was that. I had nothing else to enter. Perhaps that is what drove me to submit—this poem was my last hold on life and I wanted to hold on. Finally, I knew this. I wanted to hold on.

What's the backstory to the poem?

I was in methadone withdrawal. All of my senses were on high alert. I felt like a bit of an animal myself and was disillusioned with the nature of academia. After having been partially dead on methadone for so long, and having been living in the city, the turkey vultures seemed to provide a new sense of meaning. Writing the poem also helped me fight my incredible sense of aloneness. I was there, alone, with no sense of where to go for a future—indeed, unsure if I even had a future. Nature gave me both a mirror into that and an escape from that. There was an honesty and aliveness on the beach that I had hidden from and yet longed for.

When did you start writing poetry?

I wrote a few poems in high school for assignments. However, I largely avoided poetry until this poem, *Vulture*, which I submitted to the contest. Poetry frightened me. It took me a long time to write because it took me a long time to face myself. I only took the required English courses in university. I wanted there to be a right and wrong answer. I didn't have a voice in life, and allowing myself to have a voice on the page would have made my life crumble. Thus, it wasn't until my life already was crumbling that I could write. It wasn't until I could hold on to the fractured moments that I could express it. Writing helped me become myself, but I could not write until I was willing to be a person. Anything I wrote prior to *Vulture*, and much that I wrote after it, was merely a copy of the image I had been given of who I was. I studied psychology because it was easy. I don't think I knew what an existential meltdown was until I sat through a lecture on rat laughter and rat maintenance in university, or when I read in my APA manual (the bible of the social sciences), to "avoid poetic language."

As addiction took over, and my existential angst about academia grew, the image I had been given began to show cracks. I was given too many images, and I had too many small instances of having a voice. Having a voice was addictive in itself; I was not willing to give it up. Sometimes, I loathe the cliché of being saved by writing or of the image of the suffering artist. Nevertheless, I had a teacher in high school who said that clichés become clichés for a reason. While I find this a hideous thing for an English teacher to say, in this one instance, she may have had a point. Make no mistake about it—only in this one instance.

People often ask me why I did not start writing sooner. I am tempted to say that it was addiction or mental illness, but this is false. I didn't start sooner because I was lost. Even the most fictional stories require some sense of self. This is even more true of poetry. The sense of having a voice had come and gone throughout my life, gaining more and more strength—the ability to live outside of mirrors and scripts.

I felt like most of my life was a script, and writing became a way of living out the script when no one was there and became a way of breaking free from it. This poem was one of the first breaking-free moments. I am still in shock that it came to be at all, for I was not reading poetry, and my life was crumbling. The places where writing was a way of living out the script, obviously, were not worth holding on to. This was something to hold on to.

Do you remember your first poem? Care to share a couple of lines? What inspired that first poem or your first piece of creative writing?

Actually, this question is quite terrifying, as I'm sure most writers would insist. It's hard to look back on my first work, as I'm quite disgusted at the clichés. One of the first poems I can remember and don't feel completely embarrassed about was about a clarinet. It was an assignment with the topic of secrets. I used to play clarinet and loved the smell of cedar and the look of the instrument.

Made in France it says / beneath the silver keys / waiting for someone to reveal / its secret

Was poetry your first creative outlet or was it another style of writing? Or another art form?

Photography was my main medium of expression as a teenager. Because I was acting more as an observer than an active participant, it was an easier mode of expression for me (at the time). Before that, my mom saved a short story I wrote in Grade 4. It was about a girl who pretended to be a boy so that she could go hunting. I think, when we are children, our work is quite creative because we haven't yet learned to use clichés, but when we are teenagers, all of our desires to fit in tend to play a huge role in our writing; at least for me that was the case. I needed to open myself up for my poetry to work, and that took time. Once that was in place, the words just came. As for other artistic mediums, sometimes I can use one to inspire the other or mix mediums together. Between the teenage years and this poem, there was a long, creative dry spell, largely due to addiction. Often people think that drugs assist creativity. I would have to disagree. Writing requires a self. Writing requires a voice. Heroin was my way of killing these things.

Do other forms of artistic expression and/or life experience influence your writing?

I'm a twin, and my sister was always the artistic one. Because of that, I sort of lost out in terms of art. As for experiences, all of my life experiences influence my writing. Fortunately and unfortunately, there's no way around that. Most of the experiences fall into some universal category or other, which is how poetry can connect with wide audiences. Falling in love, heartbreak, grief, teen angst, growing old and celebrations relate to everyone. In terms of specific experiences, my writing is influenced by my struggles with addiction, poverty, adoption, mental illness, prostitution and my social sciences background. It took me a long time to write about some of these things without doing it as a caricature. By making them a caricature, I could convince myself that they weren't really real, while getting approval for playing out what I thought others wanted. I am still getting there.

Influences—who influenced or encouraged your writing?

At the time I submitted *Vulture*, I wasn't reading any poetry. I was incredibly lucky when I started writing to get attention for it; I certainly hadn't done the work to deserve it. Eventually, I learned to put in the work. Since *Vulture*, I have become an avid reader of poetry and short stories. I have had various mentors, who have all added their own unique input. I am most inspired by women. The most influential poem was *Anger*, by April Bernard. It was so honest, so raw, so powerful. I think that anger is more difficult than sorrow and equally powerful when it works. And I don't mean the political poems; I mean the gut poems. The most influential short story was *Prizes*, by Janet Frame. Both can be heard online. This contest itself helped. I don't really remember how I came to think to enter a poetry contest. Most people start reading and writing first and then enter contests. My life rarely follows the regular track.

What do you do to develop your craft?

Unfortunately, when I was in university, I shied away from the humanities. After university, I took Sarah Selecky's online course, *Story is a State of Mind*, which was hugely beneficial. It was for short stories but also aided with poetry. I also took some poetry workshops that were a few hours long and a scriptwriting workshop, and I had a poetry mentor through the WoMentoring project online. I have a critique group online where we provide feedback for each other. *Bird by Bird*, by Anne Lamott, was a very useful guide for me. Otherwise, it is mostly just about continuing to read and write. When I started, I thought there was some secret that was being kept from me. It really is this simple: keep reading; keep writing.

Tell us about your mentoring experience with contest judge and mentor, Catherine Graham.

This was important for me to learn about editing. I was amazed at how many times we reworked certain lines. This process was new to me and very helpful. Having someone neutral is also important. Friends don't want to tell you where your poem doesn't work.

How will Catherine's guidance inform your future writing?

I will hopefully give my writing all of the attention and time that it needs, letting go of that which doesn't work. Writers can form unhealthy attachments to their work, which is something to be aware of. We've heard from several authors, from Sir Arthur Quiller-Couch to Ernest Hemingway to William Faulkner, to "kill your darlings."

And in fact, that's what I have to do. Daily. It takes discipline. And, like anything, sometimes we need someone else to keep us disciplined.

What advice do you have for new writers?

Don't listen to advice. No—seriously. The only useful advice I ever received was to just keep at it. Otherwise, I knew many people who wanted me to succeed so much that they took it upon themselves to try to take over. Don't let anyone take over. Since the advice often came from people who were not writers, it is not surprising that it was not helpful. Even as I begged writers for some secret that would solve my worries, they would not offer it. Keep writing, was all they would give me and yet, in giving me that, they gave me all I needed. They were also giving me permission to let go of all those voices who demanded that I start a blog, or win the Pulitzer Prize next week, or write about what they thought I ought to be writing about. There is no secret. There are only the words. Treasure them.

~~~

JILL'S POEMS

Vulture (third-place poem)

I want to be a part of it—
outside my Georgia Strait window, the turkey vulture circles and circles,
she goes to fetch her young and they take turns gnawing at a captured baby seal.

The lesson of the day is ruthlessness, selfish survival, a good eye.
I know it is a she because
when every battle is 'til death do us part and every piece of carcass—
continental breakfast—true bonds require the right hormones.

I know it is a she because the default is 'he'
Animals are all male don't ask me why. Stuffed animals, especially.
Whether I should refer to it as a she, as lesbian, gay or transgender,
half sea or half lion? (never half white) is something they'd never ask,
in the wild.

Locusts will travel thousands of miles, one by one, in great crowds.
Follow the leader, they frantically keep up with the pack, the locust in
front being the guide, and possibly breakfast, if he dares
stop.

We sit in classrooms discussing 19th century literature,
and I long for the mad waves on days
they tell me to bring an umbrella, I long for the grand entrance of
wind,
fighting the trees. I long for the Queen Ocean, powerful, unaffected
by the politics of land. Uninterested but angry.

You study DNA, forgetting about it when you go to the bar,
chromosome shopping. Terrified that you may have your own mate
call, terrified that you'd also fight to get your belly full.
Not knowing—somewhere there's a seal looking for its pup.
Somewhere there is a youthful vulture showing off.

You clutch your copy of the APA manual (4th ed) as if it might save
you.
You are half man, half suit, and a bit iPad3,
the vulture of the modern world
. . . or the baby seal?

Young Fools

There are kids
making out
on the couch
          Was I always so forward?
As if the rest of us
don't exist

I suppose to them, we don't

Oh, youth,

you'll look back on this and think yourself a fool

you'll look back and wish
you were still there

They whisper as if
anyone wants to listen

I don't
The same way I hide this page

from view

They have no idea how lucky they are
not being capable of knowing this
makes adolescence
so dreadful

Dear youth,
you will never look at that couch
the same way
Do remember

    it doesn't look as it is
from light-years away

And when you realize that others could see
know—their disgust—just

reminiscent heartache

Street kid syndrome

It's not their fault, really. Born into
a one bedroom or bachelor
suite. These kids walk like little armies along
the railway
to the shelter or the methadone
clinic, hoping there were white kid
rap, hoodie up.

The street kids run from popo with stolen bikes and
jib pipes and cycle the psych wards
fighting with the nurses.

I see them march.
Once I hear
"Hey I seen you, girl"
I don't
turn back.

Natalia Darie

First-Place Winner, Aspiring Canadian Poets Contest, 2013

Photo credit: refined photography, danielanaka.com

Interview in 2013

Why did you enter this particular poem, *Maroon*, in the contest?

I must confess that learning how to write, or at least how to give a coherent voice to my thoughts, has been a very slow process for me. In the past, I struggled through many drafts and revisions of poems and remained very critical of them. Over time, I learned that it is more important and satisfying to relinquish some control and allow thoughts, emotions and words to flow before revising and rethinking. This, I believe, has slowly added more authenticity to my work and allowed me to express myself more accurately. The reason I entered *Maroon* is that it is one of the few poems I feel most complete about. Many times, there exists a discrepancy between what I wish to express and the reality of the work. I feel that *Maroon* comes very close to depicting my feelings and thoughts at the time it was written.

What's the backstory to this poem?

Like most things in life, the backstory is a love story. The poem is based largely on the unique cocktail of feelings that appeared in me when I reconnected with an old lover whom I had not seen or spoken to in a couple of years. As we learned each other all over again, I was overwhelmed by the exquisite way in which old memories blended with the reality of the present to create an experience that was at once familiar and slightly alienating. It was like a perceptional paradox, and I knew I had to put it down on paper.

When did you start writing poetry?

When I was an overly dramatic teenager, I used to scribble words instead of doodling as a way to vent my angst. Slowly, as the hunger to articulate my emotions became more and more acute, I began to write. At first, the writing was very clumsy and free-flowing, mostly just an outlet for frustration. Over time, I began to love the writing itself over the purpose it originally served. What I love about poetry is the way in which it can seem aloof and yet be incredibly precise, the beauty of its conciseness and the powerful impact of the arrangement of words on a page.

Was poetry your first creative outlet or was it another style of writing? Or another art form?

My first mode of expression was short story composition. Over time, I became more and more fascinated with the ability to say more using less. I almost unconsciously started cutting sentences down into phrases and, eventually, into verses. It was much later that I started to incorporate rhyme and rhythm into my writing.

Do other forms of artistic expression and/or life experience influence your writing?

I am fascinated by the parallels between dance and poetry. Both art forms are highly fluid yet require discipline and, at times, restraint. Because poetry is rhythmic in nature, it resembles the graceful nature of dance; it is like a moving thought. Dance is also highly personal;

when I watch a dancer, I know that if another dancer were to perform the exact same choreographic scheme, they would probably do it differently, adding to it their unique essence. Poetry is also very subjective because it has the potential to capture even the most obscure and complicated of emotions.

Influences—who influenced or encouraged your writing?

The first poet I ever read was Sylvia Plath. Her work was truly transformational; I could sense the anguish in many of her poems, and her use of imagery astounded me. The work of Reinaldo Arenas possesses an almost dream-like quality, and his fearlessness is palpable in almost every poem. David Rakoff has been an inspiration in terms of his astute social commentaries and scorching humour.

I am exceptionally lucky to have an avid reader for an older sister. She has a BA in English from York University, and she exposed me to important writers such as Douglas Copeland, Michael Ondaatje, Chuck Palahniuk, and Gabriel García Márquez. I think it is important to have a strong guiding influence when one is young and to be presented with an endless variety of authors. My father, too, has been an inspiration in terms of my spiritual perspective; he has been immersed in Buddhist teachings for approximately four years and has propelled my curiosity in that area. This has heavily influenced my world view and, as a consequence, my poetry. Last but not least, my mother has been my pillar during many complex and often difficult conversations on topics ranging from death to happiness, and she has taught me that one can expand enormously on an idea simply by having an honest dialogue.

What do you do to develop your craft?

I feel like I read constantly. Reading, for me, is like experiencing different lives simultaneously. I believe that I will never cease to learn from and be influenced by other authors. I also immediately capture any words, phrases or ideas that come to me unexpectedly. (I have a notepad that follows me everywhere.) While I was in school, I completed a creative writing course at Ryerson University and I plan on participating in University of Toronto's creative writing summer workshop. I attribute a large part of my development as a writer to trial and error. I learn best when I experiment.

Tell us about your mentoring experience with contest judge and mentor, Shannon Bramer.

Shannon has been very effective at helping me to see my work from a new perspective, one in which well-placed words are more important than the number of words used. When writing, I think a popular inclination is to overthink ideas and, consequently, use too many words. Shannon taught me the importance of having a silence or pause after a meaningful word or line. This, in turn, causes the writer to be much more exact and to think harder before deciding to give a particular word the responsibility of conveying an idea or feeling.

How will Shannon's guidance inform your future writing?

Shannon has taught me that it is of paramount importance to stay connected to other writers and to seek advice from them. I think many fellow writers struggle with some of the same creative dilemmas and, because of this, they have many answers to these problems. Many times, a writing problem is like an equation that would take a very long time to solve solo. Coming in contact with other writers allows for a glimpse into their solutions and often reveals a new perspective within oneself.

What advice do you have for new writers?

I can only provide advice plucked from my own limited life experiences. I think the most important thing is to have a plan for dealing with the fear that will inevitably appear during the creative process. This fear is good, because it means we are questioning ourselves, but it should be informative rather than debilitating.

~~~

Natalia's Poems

Is She?

If everyone dies at the hands of another
Then lead me gently away,
For I will be frightened but willing.
The blood will rest on my shoulders,
Then rush to discover
The soles of my feet,
And I will
Feel that, perhaps, I have sunk under oceans.
Guide my head as it loses its balance;
Fold my neck neatly, and lie me down
In the moss of the cellar.

The Remnant

Body calibrated, severe hips
Pleated into patterns of inertia;
I don't own a thing.

A patch of skin thaws inside
An impatient mouth,
Under the dim light of momentum.
My flesh aches with love in April
When death bends, bones crouching
Quietly
Outside the window.

HEIDI STOCK

Blood fills a ribcage, swills
Around in a tall carcass;
A lone lung teeters
Above a great fall, frothy pink spit jiggling
With horror; swiveling heads
Revolve around the situation, crunching popcorn.
At high altitudes a stem begins to
Buckle imperceptibly; the crowd surges with scandal
Thrusting intentions; a fever soars.

Puddle in a paper bag, let a
Live wire pass through; my fingers twitch
As they soften like fruit; a switch
At the nape of the neck
Has been left on.

This Time

This seam of time
We're unfurling upon is a moon
Of changing proportions, revolving dim bulb,
Dumb, deaf;
Incoherent in the night
Holding on tight to a tattered sky,
By the light of a violent firefly.

Our hands read the body of a rock, eyes wide
Blind as milk; there is a path or a language
Under the knot.

This corner of time
We're huddled against is a famine
Grinding its teeth
Bare, black;
Massacre mind

Coursing through a savannah
Thirsting to strangle a supple jawline.

Our feet patter downhill, mud keeps us adrift,
Racing towards the old windmill.
Laughter fills the lungs
Of the bodies
We're hiding inside a book with
Pages recoiled, yellow curled
Boneyard of stories uncoiled.

This palm of time we're
Crawling along is a galaxy of sand
Churning the days
Molten and mute;
Animal old man hunched over his
Mound of dirt
Kneading a parody out of earth,
Polishing us till we dilute.

Growing Up Savage

Sky flings clouds, smudges
Flocks in an arrow.
Wind and sorrow tease each other; revolve
Hands held, faster and faster, until
Sweat slips, grime pulls, sticky
Fingers claw the air; tricky
Business, this staying midair.

Leaves on a tree die knowingly, sighing
Downward; the rot continues to
Trot for a time, on a surface, full gallop
Breaks underneath the lilies.
Again the ripe blush teaches a swollen

121

Moment how to gush.
A membrane reaches a high colour,
Anatomy spills its hot pallor.

We run naked in the sun
Deranged and lucky, in the meadow
Where everything that does not matter
Weighs so much; the ground hungry, waiting
For a weak moment, waiting
To swallow
The days, they scatter and there is
Chatter in the woods, beyond
The anesthetic of youth.

A Pang of Need Shrieks in the Night

Black elastic cat abbreviated
And a little unrelated
How for you I've neatly waited
To become uncomplicated.

The whole way through the fatal lives
You knew,
Fools in orbit would compare
You to love prepared bloody rare.
Blackout bastard
In the alley, flying pots like kites
Sucking dry the bloated nights.
All those people you've chewed bare
And still you refuse to share.

Eating, bleeding
Pleading all the while with a
Wide effective smile.

Whitney Sweet

Second-Place Winner, Aspiring Canadian Poets Contest, 2013

Photo courtesy of Whitney Sweet

Interview in 2013

Why did you enter this particular poem, *Brass Plaque and a Bottle of Beer*, in the contest?

I heard about the contest on the Internet when I Googled "poetry contests." I wanted to try and get a poem published, as being a writer was something new to me. It was something I always wanted to be, but I was afraid to admit it to myself; I felt like if I really tried, it might evaporate and that would make me so sad. But my husband encouraged me to try and I submitted my poem to the website and came in second place! I was very happy and proud and it has made all the difference in my confidence and my faith in my own abilities as a writer. Placing in the contest has helped push me to really work at being a successful writer.

I was taking an Intro to Creative Writing course at York University, with the amazing Priscila Uppal, and she stated at the beginning of the course that she rarely gives out A's on any work by second-year students. I wrote the poem for an assignment and submitted it. When I got it back she'd written something like, "You're making me give you an A, good work." So, I figured if she said it was good, I must really be on to something and that it was worth trying to get it published.

What's the backstory to this poem?

The backstory stems from when I was first dating my husband, and his uncle suddenly suffered a stroke. We rushed to Montreal to be with him before he passed away and the whole situation was very difficult for me as I had met most of his family only once or twice before this. I felt like an outsider, not only from the family, but also from the grief of the situation and from the language, because his uncle was in a hospital where everything was in French. I was sad because my husband was broken-hearted, but also because I didn't have a place yet in the family. I got my grief initiation into the family that weekend.

When did you start writing poetry?

I think I've always written poetry. I feel like I think in poems—that it is something I can't help doing. It's just a part of my being, I suppose. When I was a kid, I was very quiet and just observed everything and everyone around me. I think I stored all that information away in my brain, and somehow my mind churned it into poetry that flowed through my body. When I got older, probably in my teen years, I put those words down on paper.

Do you remember your first poem? Care to share a couple of lines? What inspired that first poem or your first piece of creative writing?

The first piece of creative writing I remember that really affected someone else and made me secretly desire to be a writer was a short story I wrote for my Grade 9 history class. The story was called *The*

Rose, and it was set in World War I, where a nurse and a soldier fall in love. Now that I think back on it, I'm pretty sure it was a rip-off of the movie made from Hemingway's *A Farewell to Arms*. But in any case, my teacher, Mr. Rothberg, said he cried when he read it, so I guess it was good.

In high school, I also took a Writer's Craft class and here is a poem I wrote. I think I was about 16 when I made this creation!

Pants

Flared, flood, sweat, plaid, dress.
Capri, khaki, taper-leg,
Tearaways and more.

Men's, women's, girl's, boy's
Pocket, pleat, flat front, zipper
hiding bottom halves.

With boots, or sneakers
Wear a belt or suspenders
Pants are never wrong.

Pants, pants, pants, pants, pants
No shirt, no shoes, no service.
Pants, pants, pants, pants, pants.

I remember performing this poem at the end of the year in front of the other students. I had them chant "pants" and snap their fingers to the rhythm of the poem. It was a lot of fun. As you can see, my work has become somewhat more serious as I've gotten older.

Was poetry your first creative outlet or was it another style of writing? Or another art form?

Growing up, I've always done creative activities, in particular, music. I took piano lessons, played the clarinet in high school, as well as sang in the vocal jazz band, and I taught myself to play guitar. I started out writing bad songs full of teenage angst. Then I went to culinary school and became a chef, which is certainly a creative job. I decided I would go back to school after a few years of working and get my English degree and ended up in creative writing, where I fell back in love with poetry. I've always read poetry for fun but didn't really understand how to craft it until I went back to school and learned about it. It has become my primary outlet for creativity, but I also like to paint, knit, cook and refinish furniture.

Do other forms of artistic expression and/or life experience influence your writing?

I think everything influences my writing. Walking outside and being in nature is important to me so that I can hear my own thoughts on life and my surroundings. That's where the poems come from, from everything I see, do, feel and know. Trying to answer questions inside my head is a good place for me to start when I write.

Influences—who influenced or encouraged your writing?

This list might be long! For starters, I must give my husband Paul a lot of credit for his support. Going back to school in my late twenties, when we were just starting out on our life together, hasn't been easy and he has sacrificed a lot to support me. He has also encouraged me to let my inner creativity flourish and be exposed to the world. I don't know if I would be answering these questions if it wasn't for him. Of course my mom and dad are also a great support. They encouraged me to go back to school and lent me the money to do so. My mom reads all my work and I know she is proud. Unfortunately, by father passed away before he could read the work I'm doing now but I know he would be happy I'm doing something I love.

Another person who has encouraged me is my high school English teacher, Steve Taylor. When I was in OAC, he said to me, "Never stop writing." I took that to heart, and I think it was part of the reason I decided to go back and get my degree in English. He made me feel that I had the talent inside me, only I wasn't ready to let it out. He and I are in touch on a frequent basis and I send him all of my new work, which he reads willing and enthusiastically (I hope!). He always has encouraging words to say. I've also had the privilege of reading his poetry as well, and I must say he is a talent.

I also find great inspiration from the work of bpNichol, as well as from Gord Downie's book of poetry, *Coke Machine Glow*, and the work of Robert Creeley, Williams Carlos Williams and Edna St. Vincent Millay. Because I've been attending university and taking several poetry classes, I've been very fortunate to read many, many poems and work by different poets. There are probably too many influences to name in this category.

What do you do to develop your craft?

The creative writing courses at York University are excellent. Other than that, I keep a lot of ideas in my head and a lot of random poem fragments in my phone.

Tell us about your mentoring experience with contest judge and mentor, Shannon Bramer.

My experience with Shannon was fantastic. We hit it off right away and seem to write in a similar manner. We also come from some of the same life experiences, so I believe we connected in that way as well. She encouraged me to write more words in my poems, as I tend to be sparse and to the point. This was an important lesson for me and a good exercise to try. Even if I didn't end up keeping the "more words" I'd written, it was good for me to explore where the poem could grow. Shannon's feedback was never pushy; it was always helpful and useful for each poem. She also left the final decisions for any edits up to me, because she understood that sometimes the poem decides what it will be. I believe we have begun a great poetic friendship and I look forward to keeping in touch with her for many years to come.

How will Shannon's guidance inform your future writing?

Shannon asked me to think about my audience. This is not something I considered much, but I will from now on. Knowing who I want to read my work is important, because if I'm trying to say something to the people out there and no one is interested or no one understands then I have failed.

What advice do you have for new writers?

Don't be afraid to write and put it out there into the universe. Chances are, someone, somewhere, will connect with what you are saying. There are beautiful words inside everyone, so take the chance and put them together. Who knows what changes a small act such as that will make to your life?

~~~

WHITNEY'S POEMS

Brass Plaque and a Bottle of Beer (second-place poem)

7:00am flight to Montreal
Hôtel - Dieu
I don't speak French
We sat watching you die

MENTOR ME

In English
I told you to

Wait
Until after lunch
Your sisters will be back

I held the baby
That wasn't permitted inside
"Votre bébé est beau"
The nuns said smiling
He cried fat, hot and hungry tears
I could not feed him

The funeral was at a Catholic church
Performed by a French priest
In broken English
It felt strange I'd only met you twice before

Your family is immeasurable
Me
An outsider
Grief initiation

They buried your ashes under a tree
Facing Covey Hill
Through a blue veined sugar bush
Over ankle breaker field stones
Past cedar scrub
By the elderberry field

They buried you with
A brass plaque
And a bottle of beer.

HEIDI STOCK

Between

                     Between

is   and   was   is

                gone

Going to Kansas

Darling grab your slippers
the emerald sky is changing
the clouds are rearranging
in the most peculiar way

Darling grab the dog dear
his little ears are twitching
we will stow him in our basket
so he doesn't fly away

Darling there are monkeys
flying past the door dear
I wonder what's in store
an evil spell's been cast

Darling build a fortress
a fortress in the basement
a fortress made of pillows
use the blankets for our roof

Darling there are lions
lions at the door now
I can hear them roar now
they are breathing down my back

The sky has all turned black.

Darling are you here now?
I no longer feel your fingers
those beloved fingers
I long to feel them linger

Darling are you gone now?
there is a hole in the ceiling
I seem to have the feeling
I am all alone.

On Grief

1.

Suddenly,
like a crow.
Large and silent
sleek and brave
black and iridescent.
Cawing.

Taking flight to ride the wind
waiting in treetops.
Ripping flesh from the carcass
sinew roiling in an empty gullet.

Fester and grind against shards of regret
oozing marrow from imagined moments.

2.

a child playing hide
and
seek

waiting

behind the curtain.

tiny toes visible
asking to be found.

3.

Grown like marigolds
to be measured
Inch   upon   Inch.

little bright green worms
hup across stems and orange flowers.

Stop and see how beautiful they are

4.

A dog with
blades rolling
tongue lolling
lungs panting
teeth gnashing
gnawing chains
Straining to freedom.   Dragging reluctance down sidewalks.

5.

Descending quietly like snow
drifting up windows
to smother us all.

6.

Soaring above
a kite on a wire.
Mylar tail flutters in
the quick breeze.

eyes turned upward to the perfectly
impossible eclipse
tugging us away from the picnic,
demanding attention.

7.

Gone.
Really gone.
Impossibly gone.
Everyday gone.
Forever gone.

8.

A rock.
Immovable   yet

                         crumbling.

Grains of grief
collect like sand
on a beach inside a heart
along the shoreline of a soul.

ISABELLA DE ALMEIDA AIDAR

Second-Place Winner, Aspiring Canadian Poets Contest, 2014

Photo courtesy of Isabella de Almeida Aidar

INTERVIEW IN 2014

Why did you decide to enter this particular poem in the contest?

I chose to submit this piece because of how wildly spontaneously and intuitively it came to me. Writing this piece was an interesting journey. I began writing it late at night while riding a bus, in the messiest chicken-scratch writing that has ever come through me. I'm surprised I could even read it afterwards. I'd had a very introspective and isolated week prior to writing this poem. After learning about the glosa form in one of my poetry classes, I was keen to try it out myself. I like the idea of interconnection between poems and poets. The glosa form in a way is like creating a web between writers and readers. Rather than just writing isolated pieces of work, we are able to bloom and expand on just a few short lines from another's poem.

It got me philosophizing about how, if multiple glosas continuously stem from the same poem, the essence of the poem itself becomes a timeless, consistently evolving and interrelated entity. I like that idea. It was a contrast to my introspective week and just the kind of writing style I needed to experience at the time.

What's the backstory to this poem?

My poem, *Ghosts, Animals & Tattoos*, is a glosa inspired by a ghazal by another poet named Chen Chen. Aside from Chen Chen's brilliant lines, the rest of my inspiration came from past shared, transient dazes with friends and lovers, and the juxtaposing states of both pleasure and shadow, fulfillment and abandonment, that we often find ourselves in—at least that I find myself in, I should say.

When did you start writing poetry?

I have been writing poetry since I was eight years old, before I even really knew what to call it. I started writing poems to make sense of the world I witnessed with my doe-eyed child eyes and also to add my own twists to it so it could look and feel exactly how I wanted it to.

Do you remember your first poem? Care to share a couple of lines? What inspired that first poem or your first piece of creative writing?

Aw, man. What a great question. I really wish I could dig that up. All I remember was that it had a cat and some lemons in it, haha.

Was poetry your first creative outlet or was it another style of writing? Or another art form?

I'd say my first love in writing was short stories with surreal, fantasy elements. When I was younger, I wanted to be a singer, but I think that ship sailed.

135

Do other forms of artistic expression and/or life experience influence your writing?

I'm a fire dancer and newly aspiring aerialist. I have a passion for the circus arts and creating rhythmic, sensual dance expression through the body.

Influences—who influenced or encouraged your writing?

Luckily, today, I have a plethora of contemporary and Canadian influences, but if I were to dig deep to my early writing days, I can't deny that it was the old classics that roped me in: Oscar Wilde, Emily Brontë, Albert Camus, Dostoevsky.

What do you do to develop your craft?

I'd say the main thing is a daily perceptive eye and consistent notetaking. Whether it's going inwards into the body, or outwards into the world, I try to observantly experience life as much as I can so I can write about it.

Tell us about your mentoring experience with contest judge and mentor, Catherine Owen.

Catherine and I connected via email, and I found her edits to be clear, easy to comprehend and full of "ah-ha" realizations about certain lines that I'd been feeling iffy about or secretly obsessing over. I've always loved her writing, and to be honest, one of the main reasons I decided to submit to this contest was because she was the judge. I wanted my work to reach out and connect to her somehow, even if I didn't win (though obviously winning is a huge bonus!).

How will Catherine's guidance inform your future writing?

Aside from encouraging me to play around with structure, compelling vocabulary and images, I have to say most of her guidance comes from simply reading her work. Catherine's book *Trobairitz* has always been a fave of mine. I like the way she parallels and shows the misogyny faced by women in the music world in two very different centuries— the 12th and 13th–century female troubadours who composed music with the modern-day metal rocker chick. I like the idea of digging into past and present eras and finding the same patterns, especially when they are cycles that need to be broken.

~~~

ISABELLA'S POEMS

How he approaches sex shop employees

He walks in, lips as donuts glazed
with spit, belt undone.

She stands behind the counter,
gliding her claws against glass displays.
Nude-faced, peach purée warm skin,
nails as beetles dipped in gold.

He says,
I'm looking for bondage ropes.

The air screams of latex
and plastic berry.
She reaches for scissors,
long, acrylic hoods towering
over stubby fingers.

137

HEIDI STOCK

She walks him past gaping mouths,
salivating tongues on cardboard packages.
Ice-blue silicone, fuchsia plugs,
white dicks, black dicks,
inflatable everything,
flashlights that aren't really lights—

past the corner where everything is
suddenly black, pleather, chains, restraints.

He wonders about the
cool of metal against goose bumps;
the friction of cuffs on thin wrists.

She unwinds the rope.
He pictures her voice as
a broken gag in his grasp.

Her nails tap the wall.
She asks: *how many feet do you want?*

He: *I want you.*

She shoves him with her
needle tips, scissors in the other hand,
she hollers—
get out.

Blind date with a marine biologist

I ask him if he knows anything about anglerfish—
(No)
I dive in.
This is how they mate:

The male bites the female
Bodies rush in and out
as grey-clothed flocks;
schools of sardines.

fuses with her flesh
Baristas extend arms;
squid tentacles that collect
crumb-ridden plates.

Male digests himself
My neon polka-dot shirt
feels too venomous frog for the occasion,
but this is how I dress.

eventually ending up as nothing
My tongue stretches, sea slug
that licks crumbs and drips from the edge of lips.

but a pair of balls attached to the female,
releasing sperm when needed.
He fingers the tea bag string of his
Earl Grey with a crab claw pinch,
stares at an ordinary photo of a lily on the café walls;
anything to avoid eye contact.

Bites his pretzel
as if it's rotten mussels; face sours
while he sips his tea like bitumen.

Submerged in an awkward silence,
much like under the ocean:
every sound is sharp.
sniffle sigh cough

HEIDI STOCK

Banana bread and black coffee
swish in cheeks as I chew –
is it *too* loud?

Bone Altar/Ego

In the alley, a dead crow.

Its rib cage protrudes
from severed feathers.

The naked brass chain
on my neck fancies its skull.
I give it to my lover's ex;
a red-haired taxidermist.

Our bonding moment –
We toast wine; blood-crimson
as the animals she strips.
She resents him, not me. She says
her beetles will gnaw the last of flesh,
she'll clean and coat the bones in resin.
I start to unfold bills, but she doesn't want money,
only the heart and wings in exchange.

So she cleans the bones and
makes death beautiful.
The heart didn't resist;
powdered and succumbed to rot
before her fingers could graze it.

Now the wings sit on her altar;
the skull around my neck.

The skull around my neck,
wings on her altar.
Fingers can graze them,

before they powder and succumb to rot.
The heart didn't resist.
It's a beautiful death when
bones finally clean her.

The heart and wings exchange -
she doesn't want money. I unfold bills
coated in resin. Clean bones
eat the last of flesh. Beetles
say she resents me, not him.

The animals strip her and
we toast blood; wine-crimson.
Our bonding moment.

I give my lover

a red-haired taxidermist;
naked, chained in brass.

My neck longs for the skull.
From severed feathers,
her rib cage protrudes.

In the crow, a dead alley.

Two filters

What else changes when you
open a book, peel a fruit?

HEIDI STOCK

You pierce your teeth into
an orange, suck all the juice
before eating the arid pulp.
You curse sticky citrus hands
and the girl across the street for
wearing a short skirt.

The wood shavings
in your voice melt to syrup
when you read poetry;
cold coffee in hand,
you still give the barista
an extra toonie.

Sometimes you're velvet,
other times straw.

James Hinds

Third-Place Winner, Aspiring Canadian Poets Contest, 2014

Photo courtesy of James Hinds

Interview in 2014

Why did you decide to enter this particular poem in the contest?

This poem was the most recent piece I had written and I felt it expresses my attempt to be real and original—although my literary and historical influences can easily be found in the words.

What's the backstory to this poem?

Poetry is a way I try to access the me that is authentic, and it expresses my experience in a sort of exaggerated and yet soulful way. I feel a deep connection to old culture—our ancestors—and their suffering. And so my reference to slavery and the Holocaust is a shout-out to and a shot at connecting with human suffering from different cultures, times and contexts. I like to think that if I honour them in my poetry, somehow they will protect and guide me.

The melancholy of a black slave in white rags singing soulful music as she picks cotton in the field, and the resilience of the Jewish spirit exposed to the horror of a gas chamber is inspiration for me to value life, and I love speaking to their experience. It's edgy and potentially controversial but respectful of our collective past.

Although I feel connected to that sort of suffering, my experience as a white, middle-class male is vastly different, and I am blessed to be privileged. So I am drawn to more difficult and darker life narratives because I want to learn how to be connected to a wide spectrum of human experience.

When did you start writing poetry?

I started writing poetry when I was 13 or 14, cooped up in my room in the basement, grounded for causing trouble to my parents, listening to Nas, Erykah Badu, Pink Floyd and Sublime, trying to find and understand myself. It was a time of introversion in my life, and also angst and rebellion, like any jilted teenager.

Do you remember your first poem? Care to share a couple of lines? What inspired that first poem or your first piece of creative writing?

I just looked through my first book of poetry for the first time in a while. The first poem I wrote is called "Lifting Latches."

Walking towards a deep horizon,
Coming to a point of happiness.
Feeling the earth move as the emotion swiftly
engages the body.
The desire slowly awaits the vast period of pleasure.

I'm not really sure what inspired me to write this, actually. I had this book with a bunch of sketches and drawings, and this was the first piece of poetry that came out.

Was poetry your first creative outlet or was it another style of writing? Or another art form?

I think poetry was my second creative outlet, after listening to music. With poetry I finally found a way to get my thoughts out of my head, to somehow see if they were logical or sane.

Do other forms of artistic expression and/or life experience influence your writing?

Spoken word poetry engages me and lights my fire in a way that other forms of art don't. Somehow, the silence behind the stage during a spoken word performance has a lot of potential, which the poet invites and uses. Most forms of art, like visual art, movies and music, influence and inspire me also.

Influences—who influenced or encouraged your writing?

I had two English teachers, one in Grade 11 and one in Grade 12, who influenced me. Once a month, one of them would have his students select something unique that represented who they were and present it to the class. He encouraged me in that way; I presented some poetry with Miles Davis playing in the background and a Rastafarian hat on. The other teacher got me to look at poetry in a fresh way by telling me to completely start over on a big project I had finished.

U2's music also influenced me to write. Also, Sage Francis and Buddy Wakefield's work has had an impact on my writing.

I had some friends in high school who were really into writing poetry, and we would always critique each other's poems. We were the kinds of kids who loved finding blue pens in the hallways—we would always have three or four on us and trade them.

What do you do to develop your craft?

I took a poetry class at university in 2006, where I was able to refine my skills. The class had eight students and was pretty intimate.

Going to spoken-word shows keeps me inspired and motivates me to connect with poetry—my own and others'.

Tell us about your mentoring experience with contest judge and mentor, Catherine Owen.

Having Catherine read and critique my poem was fun—it was great to get gentle yet critical feedback of my work and a second perspective on the style and format of the poem. I appreciated how her opinions helped to improve my work.

How will Catherine's guidance inform your future writing?

I think she helped me refine my style and taste.

~~~

James' Poem

Does Your Poetry Suffer (third-place poem)

Does your poetry suffer?
Do your rhymes bleed?
Do your words ask your syllables to love?

I tell you! this poetry really does suffer
to love -
that's why it writes.

I easily,

without pride,
prostrate to broken, raw, suffering poetry: a real and edgy life-tide.

These beautifully fractured words speak my truth!
and it's real - even though I'm deluded.

Does your poetry suffer?

Can your Inner Massa express 400 years of slavery with that willful
tongue - a - whipping?
Please do -
all your ancestors watch, wait, and weep -
celebrating your cotton-picking tune.

Hearts split open when your words are heard; eyes stream! with our
shared vision.
So if I'm stuck,
if I'm paralyzed by my own self-pity-like emo-rhymes,

this poetry will joyfully suffer,
for us.

Does your poetry suffer?

Can your inner Fuhrer capture the suffering of concentration camps
with your chambered words?
Zyklon B - a - foamin' from your lips,
Zundercommando's lies through your stained, unbrushed, chattering
teeth.

From the Promised Land they watch and ask us to remember,
they ask us to change -
they ask us to
let go.

HEIDI STOCK

My poetry suffers, because it is so.
My words lie,
my stanzas cheat,
my presence steals -
and my onomatopoeia just ain't buzzin' no more.

All pretense thinned,
no censorship to buffer;
my heart cracks open as this poetry suffers.

Does your poetry suffer?

These words pulse, beat and shake with the pain of its truth.

This poetry anguishes with a purpose
to break free of its iambic chains;
to escape the prison of its own expressions.

If your poetry is
raw
stripped bare
naked
pulsing
like this wildly beating heart,
then it suffers for joy;

your poetry suffers to be whole.

Does your poetry suffer?
Do your rhymes bleed?
Do your words ask those syllables for love?

Make your poetry suffer.

Chloë Catán

First-Place Winner, Aspiring Canadian Poets Contest, 2015

Photo courtesy of Chloë Catán

Interview in 2015

Why did you decide to submit this particular poem to the contest?

I wrote this poem for a class and wasn't sure how it was going to be received. Would it be too cryptic? Too disjointed? Too surreal? I knew these would be probable critiques, and yet every time I tried to change it before the reading, inserting perhaps a more obvious narrative or somehow explaining the images, I decided I didn't want to change one word. This usually works to my detriment, but this time, when I finally read it out in class, most of my colleagues reacted favourably. It was a huge boost, knowing that, for once, trusting my instincts had worked. Never has one of my poems been so little tinkered with after the first draft. I decided to submit it to the contest on the strength of those reactions.

149

HEIDI STOCK

What's the backstory to this poem?

It started as an exercise given by instructor, Ken Babstock. He told us to write six lines or so and somewhere in the middle make it obvious where the narrator is situated. So I wrote the first stanza (without the first line referring to Pessoa), thinking of a particular place where I grew up, the chalk cliffs in the South of England. It stayed like that until I decided to expand on it. At the time, I was reading Fernando Pessoa's *Book of Disquiet*, and the idea came to me to list other images that were lodged in my own "book of disquiet." Because they were disjointed, I linked each stanza by referring to the poem's first line. Of course, what I was writing, in a very organic way, was an anaphora. I won't explain the genesis of all the images, because I think part of the effect has to do with their strangeness. But I will say that each one is rooted in experience: a memory, or a dream, or something between the two. Each one, for its own reasons, stuck over the years and haunted me—perhaps because, in one way or another, they all deal with loss.

When did you start writing poetry?

I began taking creative writing classes about four years ago, enrolling in poetry, fiction, and creative non-fiction. I liked them all, but I keep gravitating back to poetry. It's not that I find it "easier" (they're all horribly difficult), but perhaps I tend to see things in moments. There's nothing like nailing a particular feeling or image or scene in a few lines, because when you nail it, you understand it.

I started taking classes a year after my father died, very suddenly and very young. His death prompted me to explore all sorts of difficult questions, and writing was part of this. It's not that I thought I'd "try out something different" or even that I wanted to write specifically about his death. It was a case of not being able to see a way forward after such devastation. Put it this way: being faced with one of my worst fears made the fear of succumbing to my creativity shrink in

150

comparison. I wish it had been something less terrible that made me put pen to paper, but something positive has come out of it.

Do you remember your first poem? Care to share a couple of lines? What inspired that first poem or your first piece of creative writing?

I'm not sure it's worth sharing my first poem from those classes, but funnily enough, there's a line from it in *Uprush*: "a slap and its sting." I do this quite often. Go back to my boneyard of "failed" poems and salvage one line or a couple of words. It's rewarding to know that all that work wasn't wasted and that saving discarded poems can sometimes come in handy when writing new ones.

Was poetry your first creative outlet, or was it another style of writing? Or another art form?

As a girl, I was always making things: drawings, paintings, jewellery, clothes, furniture. At the same time, I was always reading. I'll never forget the sense of relief and excitement when my mother would replenish the stack of books on my shelf. I felt that life was somehow safe if I had that alternative world to escape to. When the pile dwindled, I would feel anxious. I have the same feeling even now. I wasn't a huge writer, but I had notebooks as a teenager where I'd doodle or draw or paint or stick things in, and I'd also scribble down words or phrases. I don't think I distinguished much between words and images.

Do other forms of artistic expression and/or life experience influence your writing?

I'm an art historian, so I am always going to exhibitions and reading about art. I'm a big fan of modern dance and theatre. Film is also part of my weekly staple. I don't think any of these find their way directly into my poems. I wish they did. But they make me think and feel and experience the world in ways that are inspiring, and this probably rubs off in the writing, if only to get me in a particular mood.

As a child and young adult, I moved around a lot and lived in numerous cities and countries. I'm also bicultural (half British, half Mexican). For better or for worse, this instilled in me the vision of an outsider, which sometimes comes in handy when observing and writing. Perhaps not so much for living, although it does make one adaptive!

Who has influenced or encouraged your writing—which writers/authors, other artists, teachers or mentors, loved ones?

My teachers at the University of Toronto creative writing program have been amazing: Michael Winter, Ken Babstock, Catherine Graham, Paul Vermeersch, Christine Pountney, Pasha Malla, Shyam Selvadurai, David Layton, Allyson Latta, Alexandra Leggat. They are all inspiring and supportive, always inviting students to readings and literary events. Being included in these things is a big part of the encouragement. A class I took with Ken Babstock was co-taught with Jeff Latosik. He was the first one to say the words, "Send these out." If he hadn't said it, I probably wouldn't have done it. I'm grateful he believed in my work. Also, I have a great writing group. They are always encouraging and very fun.

There are too many influences to list. Poetry-wise, here's what's currently on my bedside table: Jorie Graham, Paul Ceylan, Anne Carson, Shane Book, Cassidy McFadzean, Matt Rader, Tracy K. Smith, Robert Haas, August Kleinzahler, Sina Queyras, Erin Mouré, Karen Solie, Ken Babstock … Yes, my poor little table is creaking under the weight. I'm not even going to get into fiction! But it's important to note that there's a mixture of established poets and newer poets.

What do you do to develop your craft?

Read, read, read, write. Read, read, read, write. That seems to be the pattern. Perhaps I'd be more prolific if it were the other way round, but I just can't stop reading! It's inspiring to see so many different voices out there, and I learn from all of them.

Classes keep me writing. Sharing work with colleagues makes all the difference. If the dynamic is good, it can make a solitary and often difficult process really fun. There are deadlines, of course, but also stimulating discussions that push me to look in places I haven't seen, or haven't seen in a particular light. The teachers—all incredible writers and editors themselves—always have insightful thoughts on the writing process, from inspiration to revision. They also make invaluable reading recommendations. This has expanded and enriched my knowledge, particularly of poetry, despite its unfortunate lack of visibility in bookstores.

Tell us about your mentoring experience with Stuart Ross.

One-on-one sessions with Stuart have been an incredible opportunity to get feedback on my work. It's a luxury, having the time to ask questions about the details: does this word work? This comma? This image or line break? And also to talk about broader questions such as submitting, feeling blocked, or expanding my style. It's a pleasure to talk about reading as well, and he always comes up with great recommendations based on my interests and leanings. What I like most about my sessions with Stuart is that he's open, encouraging and respectful, and this creates an excellent creative environment. I will always be grateful for him telling me that I could send him anything, meaning pieces that aren't finished or polished, or even just experiments. It takes the pressure off. I always feel I have to hand in something perfect, which of course is nonsense.

How will Stuart's guidance inform your future writing?

Stuart told me that he prefers the word "experiment" to "exercise." This is a wonderful way of looking at it, because it means that nothing is just a preliminary warm-up to writing a poem. Instead, the whole process of writing a poem is about experimentation. It's a liberating thought, not distinguishing between learning and actual composition, and the more poets I talk to, the more I hear them say that they are continuously learning through the process. It also softens the barrier between poems that are working and those that aren't. It means you're not racking your brain for a good one from the start. That tends to shut me down completely!

Reprint, originally published on Allyson Latta's website, www.allysonlatta.ca

~~~

Chloë's Poem

Uprush (first-place poem)

I've always been attracted to what's in the distance, and the hazy aqueducts. Fernando Pessoa

In my book of disquiet
there's a chalk glare,
the tail end of a country
I can't catch across the gap,
then again a rush of flint shingle
breaks against the parapet.

There's a sea lion I didn't see
swim to the surface, through
the ashes we'd strewn
with butterflies we thought would float,
but were now sinking with him.

There's a lion with a monkey's face
and a lady, slim as a question mark
holding a mirror in her hand,
and I cannot eat for looking
at the strange beauty of it.
There's walking the tight,

the rope, the stalag.
There's a slap and its sting
and I rain from the ground up.
There are suitcases, many of them
and rubble, furniture, toys
heaped in pyres on a ship—
a box, or is it a saw-in-half.
There are whales from the porthole.

Basia Gilas

Second-Place Winner, Aspiring Canadian Poets Contest, 2015

Basia's Poems

NEGATIVE CURVATURE (second-place poem)

Dr. Taimina was the first to crochet a model
of a hyperbolic plane. With what women do
when they have nothing else to do she taught
her students to handle an impossible.

Cosmologists once speculated the
universe might be shaped like a
potato chip, the geometric opposite of a
sphere. In hyperbolic geometry, things

aren't as expected. For example,
The sum of a triangle's angles can equal zero.
The Wilkinson Microwave Anisotropic Probe,
in showing off the universe's baby pictures,

proved the universe flat within a .4% margin
of error. It took 2,000 years to find a flaw in
Euclid's parallel postulate. Bolyai's father,
Farkas, said to him: For god's sakes please

give it up. Fear it no less than sensual passion,
because it too may take up all your time
and deprive you of your health, peace of mind
and happiness in life. My mother's plea with

equal urgency: Don't get pregnant. And

in teaching me how to crochet hoop-skirt
ruffles for Barbie atop the toilet tank,
unknown to me, there hid a hyperbolic plane.

Crenulated brain matter inside the skull
increases surface area for neurons like
sea slugs' anatomical frills provide
more surface area for them to filter feed.

OCCASIONAL BIRD

She was saying it might be in our
mouths, that you can't buy
what it tastes like to unlearn.
That we could play school and
make stuff up together
or continue to trace our hands
and all draw the same turkey.
She was saying
to touch you might take a thousand
strangers or more. That it might
not be in our eyes
where we buy what it looks like
we paid for. That we could eat light
and continue to feel hungry
or we could all eat the same turkey.
She was saying
to get our mouths around it
we might build a model of the moon.

for Stephanie Springgay

HEIDI STOCK

THE LOST

after Peter Gizzi's "The Quest"

It's fact: the skyline evacuates into
a whale, a tremolo fleeing its domain
in the shape of a pipeline

fortissimo, I require everyone
intensified in the universal white

embark anew huge astonishment
manufacturing symphonies to hammer the earth,
everything is exploding, eternal, presto

everything proclaims to everyone all things
10,000 worlds, also, could not bring into being.

ETOBICOKE TO EOR EWUASO

A warm swarm of hands met me from
across the field, touching the tops
of my feet, the writing bump on my finger,
the littlest one plucked at my hangnails,
amid laughter. With chin jutted, one girl asked,
if the dogs in my country really wore shoes.

A goat was brought as a gift for our hosts
and I missed its slaughter. I paid too
much attention to these children who did not
need tending to. I didn't know I could leave
the classroom, and the students would stay
to chew chalk, the corners of notebooks.

At break, I sat in the grass with the girls,
who taught me Swahili. A boy approached,
borrowed our notepad, wrote in it, gave it back,
and walked away. At first the girls refused
to translate it, said it read my hair looked like hay.
I looked it up myself: The chicken has no eggs.

As we nested around books I brought, some with
pictures of children who looked like them, we read
aloud, our bodies leaned on one another. And in
a pause Silvia looked up at me and said, "We are ugly."
And of the photo of the moose I shared she said,
"It has hands coming out of its head."

Marina Black

Third-Place Winner, Aspiring Canadian Poets Contest, 2015

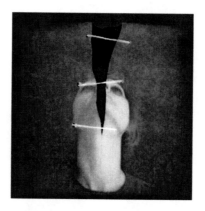

Self-portrait: Marina Black

Interview in 2015

Why did you decide to submit this particular poem in the contest?

I read this poem at my friend's party to a few writers and poets and received very positive feedback. The same night, I accidently stumbled upon the contest announcement, and I decided to submit. I have never participated in any contests before. This is my first submission.

What's the backstory to this poem?

Once I got an email from a friend of mine, who mentioned something about the winter light. The way he phrased it triggered in me this brewing mental activity of getting inside a poem almost instantaneously. I think I wrote it within a few hours, although kept going back with editing. A plain word—light—has been made new by bringing up memories related to my childhood: the train trip, the fever I had while travelling from a small writers' village, where a poet, Anna Akhmatova, used to live. I think that's what's interesting about memory—when you listen to its voices, sometimes they click into place and there would be things you find there. And this memory creates a shape around which something lives—and how it gives hints about what that thing is but does not reveal it entirely. The strangest thing—you suddenly end up noticing things post-factum that you never had noticed before.

When did you start writing poetry?

To be honest, I've never had an easy relationship with being a poet. I like to write, but I haven't written much, and although I persist, I never assumed it as a profession. I loved poetry from my early adolescence; however, it wasn't something I thought was in me to actually do. In the Soviet Union, where I grew up, there was this tradition of *samizdat*, where people reproduced censored publications by hand and passed them from one person to another. Because I couldn't buy books of poets I liked (Tsvetaeva, Akhmatova or Brodsky), I would exchange poems with friends, and we would retype the copy for the next reader. It was kind of a secret that had an element of danger and thrill in it and also gave a sense of being accomplices to a strange crime.

Do you remember your first poem? Care to share a couple of lines? What inspired that first poem or your first piece of creative writing?

I think it was a poem I wrote when I was a teenager about tea and honey, and what happened and didn't happen between people. (I don't recall the exact lines.) It seems I was already on the verge of this "looking back" moment when I was interested in why things did or didn't happen and their effects on people—why we say "yes" or "no," for instance, why we speak or remain silent, why we know anything at all if nothing lasts or remains the same.

Was poetry your first creative outlet or was it another style of writing? Or another art form?

When I immigrated to Canada, the question whether to be an artist or a writer was solved on its own because English isn't my mother tongue. And for some time, I couldn't write even in Russian. It was a rather painful experience that I can compare perhaps to a phantom limb effect. So I became busy with becoming an artist—a photographer, specifically. However, I realize how much these two mediums feed into one another, at times intentionally and at times not. There's a way to think of it as a continuance. It's all one poem, essentially. If I am lucky there's some sense at the end that both are an example of a life lived and reimagined in a search for music through contemplative experience.

Do other forms of artistic expression and/or life experience influence your writing?

Photography and music, mostly. Because photography, the one I am interested in, behaves the way poems behave—they make a sound. The experience becomes direct—images and poetry, like music, are a direct transmission. When photographs or poems are true, they do that. I often see images first and then pile sounds on top of them to make a poem.

Another thing, after having lived in Canada for more than 16 years, I can consider myself bilingual. And bilingualism makes one aware of the gaps in how different languages model the way we think and the world around us. It also makes you worry yourself with a lot of "maybes," with misinterpretations, misreadings, mispronunciations, as well as with strange things that occur with foreign language acquisition, when expressions appear strange, even arbitrary, and the sentences' structures clash in all kinds of unusual ways.

Influences—who influenced or encouraged your writing—which writers/authors, other artists, teachers or mentors, loved ones?

Where do I begin? In no specific order: Paul Celan, Marina Tsvetaeva, Louise Gluck, Osip Mandelstam, Anne Carson, Sylvia Plath, Robert Haas, Dylan Thomas, Wallace Stevens, Carl Philips. A couple of years ago, I took a poetry course at the University of Toronto with an extraordinary Canadian poet, Ken Babstock. His mentorship has been important to me. And of course, my friends. Some are poets and writers themselves; some are not—just thoughtful people.

What do you do to develop your craft?

Reading, for sure, but mostly, I walk. As I walk, I occasionally jot down ideas, words or sentences. I took this habit after Erik Satie. He used to walk long distances to write his music.

Tell us about your mentoring experience with contest judge and mentor, Stuart Ross.

Stuart has this amazing ability to recognize, feel, when there's something hovering beneath the verbal, that mysterious emotional place in a poem that makes it work. To see enough unknown in it to be brought out. Besides, I absolutely adore his quick sense of humour when he would say things that are constructive but funny and encouraging at the same time.

How will Stuart's guidance inform your future writing?

Looking closely and rerouting the patterns, looking in the unexpected places, or, as he put it himself, "Write what you don't know."

~~~

HEIDI STOCK

Marina's Poems

The winter light (third-place poem)

Forget the ink of spruce greening alongside the tracks.
The train Vyborg – Leningrad rushes past villages with bullet's velocity. Past
the twilight of twitching eyelids - the cataracted eyes in whiteness, not in history. Past
Finland Bay. Ten times the trees. Endlessly. Finally. The city. Everything.
Ceaseless air. Idle in low temperatures. And the childish snow falls sidelong
onto mansard roofs. Past
spell silver-laced windows that are partly faces. And suddenly
the colonnades of Nevsky prospect are overturned by Akhmatova's funeral. Drone dull buzzing folding into the traffic of legs
stiffened in numbness trotting their way.
One step.
        Two steps.
                And steps.
You were holding the coffin over the wound ached on the lovelorn paper. Clucking
jaws. There is, it seems, no heresy like the heresy
of saying good-buy. All I do now
is listen to your music. For nobody,
for no living ears: as I am
your syllable. I am
an animal
and I – am poem
in the midst of matrons in furry hats, crows, cobblestones,
wide open mouth of bridges and clumsy jackets.
As if a traveller seized
by the dark thirst. The North is driving herd
into the Baltic, heads down whining in sorrow.

The Savior on the Blood is ink-bleeding its tower-knots of fire, licking
your shivering body with tongues whose blood is not your own. How
fathomless
it is to be embedded in glacial light. How fragile
the winter light is after all, perched precariously. How always
on the verge of disappearing. And then
you are no more either. And I
remember things that have been said lead-onto-white, pain-onto-
wire, sinews, tautology – the knacks for catching dying life's moth or
violated pale virgin flakes with their busted gills –
bitter wad of silence.

Just letters left, preserved
by wonder. If yes –
in what language?

Postcard

Imagine her riding a horse through the cemetery. Clatter
of hoofs, blending in the clouded silence
that is infinite space: a painting. Twilight
descends but never falls
on flattened sage-green field. The harness of the horse shining.
Eyes hyper-vigilant. Nutmeg-stained between water and desert.
She learns to fall silent. She thinks of
a painting. Of how the words made her.
How she once talked to cover herself
in broken places. Such as: our relationship
isn't working. Such as: I like
your tie.
                                    Thirty years ago
she felt that a painting was always 'the first time'. Today
it's the last time she ever sees anything, which is: like 'the first time'.
Which is: like desire full of endless
distances. And then the lift of the brows cropped by chemo

165

but still alive. A long shadow of her former shadow: I am fine.
Or was it a question: Am I?
She thinks: her birthday is coming soon.

The Alchemist

My doubt grows and blossoms every day
mouth-marked in the shape of desire.
I surrender. Type the word
on the white sheet:
some dim idea of a poem.
What do the sightless see when they dream?
Every morning I wake to the handful of vowel notes. Sail saying-slips.
Silence awaitings. Fatherless lies and motherless sorrows - fellows of
the dark
waters of your bellows. Maybe you are not
a smile but a childless cry. Maybe
smiles assume we hold the same belief, yet
lose the substance. When your body is broken
you turn to what you know best:
the twig-whispers from the ghosting
bramble nest turning into a distant rumble. I tuck them
under my eyelids. They
ooze or laugh at me. What to do
with this knowledge?
                    We watched
boats rocking farewell to the poor stone buildings of men. The night
added breeze to the multitude of renewals. I threw the pebbles into
the sea's factory
so they'd be ground as weeds.
Now, outside of the dream, I remember thinking
the truth of things might come easier on a quiet night
like this. When the world is in delay.
I stand in a wasteland sending signals
into the throttled universe. They are, perhaps, only small coins

crowned with coats of arms. To just be grief
             Where have you been? In the house,
whose walls are songs, convictions crumble
like abandoned witnesses.

Poetry: Essays

Erase, Expand, Escape:
How to Travel on the Page

by Shannon Bramer

ERASE

Erasing or blacking out words within an existing text allows a writer to move inside a work, to touch it, to interact with its patterns and spaces and silences. Taking words away or hiding them under a physical mark impacts the reader visually and causes the poem to refract, to split open somehow. Erasing words means you will leave other words behind. These words now have more work to do. They become louder or quieter or funnier or possibly sad and pensive. If the words have been sleepy, the disappearance of their friends wakes them up. What is removed from the text is still part of it; a poem created using this technique is full of tiny ghosts in open doorways. I don't always work this way, but when I do, I find the whole process pleasurable and mysterious. This technique has helped me understand how to love the bones of language as much as the skin.

Experimenting with this technique requires nothing more than text and a sense of adventure. You can create a rule or rules for yourself when approaching a text, like, no words with the letters "s" or "t" inside them; cut every fourth word or any word you don't like. You can also erase words and whole chunks of text like chipping away at sandstone—randomly or mindfully—to see what emerges. Below is a poem created using only the text in the first paragraph above:

within a move to touch
patterns hiding under

Erasing words means
you will leave

words behind.
sleepy disappearance
of friends

What is still part of it; a poem
of tiny ghosts in open ways

find bones
        skin.

Erasure can also be likened to a process of unravelling. For me, so many of my own little poems resemble a unique strand of yarn tugged loose from a heavy sweater.

EXPAND

The flipside of erasure is expansion. Instead of working with a text that you are uncovering by stripping it down, expansion requires the writer to add layers of thought and meaning to the work being created. To thicken or fatten up the piece of writing, rather than thin it out.

I think this technique is important because it forces discovery in the opposite direction, especially if you are a writer like me, whose impulse is toward minimalism, restraint and caution. This technique is not a formal one—*expand* is just the word I use. It is not only about adding words, but thought, energy, pauses, breath. Expansion requires the writer to relinquish some control over the work by using free association and a stream of conscious process to keep going with an idea or an image in a place where she or he would rather stop.

This idea came to me through prolific Canadian poet, Patrick Friesen, who mentored me during the creation of my third book, *The Refrigerator Memory*. He pushed me to "write longer lines" because I was always writing short ones. It was a simple yet profound suggestion. Trying to write longer lines forced my thoughts to roll out differently on the page, and the result was a manuscript with more surprises, more texture and less lyric predictability and inhibition. Although my inclination is still toward brevity and short, halting rhythms, his advice stays with me and makes me push outside my comfort zone.

Like with the erasure technique, applying an expansion approach to your work has many possibilities, such as, I am going to get back inside this poem and add three more lines; I'm going to rewrite this piece as a block of prose; I'm going to choose six places to add six words. This process is meant not as a means of perfecting work but rather to cultivate a sense of play, detachment and patience in creating and developing new work and seeing where a stuck piece might be able to go with the right amount of pressure applied. Below is a new version of my poem, with three lines added. In this case, I decided to return to the original paragraph to see if I could source three long lines and experiment with where to put them in. Along the way, I altered some of the other lines and found myself adding the little word "her" to the piece:

within a move to touch her
patterns hiding under her

her skin poem the ghost of text sleeping

Erasing words means
you will leave

words behind her

sleepy disappearance
of friends

her refracted split open poem now whole

*

What is still part of it; a poem
of tiny ghosts in open ways

her essay patterns this space of mystery inside

 bones
           skin

ESCAPE

Both the erase and expand techniques are meant to help writers of all ages and experience escape or disappear within the piece of writing and revel in a process of play and mystery. When I allow myself to work with pieces using these methods, whether it be my own or a piece that I am editing, I find I am able to focus on how the poem is working outside of my own hopes for it. It makes me feel free because the shape of my thoughts blossom out of the language itself. It might feel mechanical and dull for some writers to work in this way, or to impose any prescribed process onto a piece of writing; I recommend these techniques as a possible means of discovery and adventure, as a way to travel to new places with your writing. But ultimately, the journey is your own and these are just two of many possible paths to explore. For fun, here is a third version of the poem, finally with a title:

Sadie Writes Poems in Sunlight

within a move to touch her
patterns hiding under her

her skin poem the ghost of text
of sun sleeping

Erasing words means
you will leave

words behind her

cold hands on the page
this sleepy disappearance
of friends, words

her refracted split open poem now whole
like my daughter writing

*

What is still part of it; a poem
of tiny ghosts in open ways

she writes in sun here
her essay patterns this space of mystery inside

bones
            skin

MENTOR ME: AN INSIDE VIEW OF SESSIONS WITH POET, SHANNON BRAMER

by Heidi Stock

This is the first inside view of mentoring sessions in this book. It is literally "mentor *me*," as I am the student. These sections are included in the anthology to give the reader a sense of the experience and benefits of one-on-one mentoring with a poet, songwriter, screenwriter or producer. It is only meant to give a sense of what private mentoring sessions may be like for you. Every mentor and every student is as unique as the relationship between them.

GETTING STARTED

I wanted to start my first session with poet Shannon Bramer with a review of a handful of my poems. If you read my essay in the first section of this book, you'll see that I wrote about having just a handful of poems with potential for development. So it's with those poems that we started. I emailed the poems to Shannon and asked a few questions about areas of concern, strength and weakness.

Here's what I learned:

Heidi: Upon first read, do you connect emotionally with these poems?

Shannon: I found myself drawn to the themes of these poems, and I felt the longing and questioning of the woman inside them. These are poems about seeing and being seen. I like the questions they ask. There is an interesting combination of directness, confidence and assurance presented alongside a heartbreaking kind of hesitation and immobility.

174

Heidi: Do you find the voice to be authentic?

Shannon: Yes. The speaker of the poems is being herself. More unfolding and opening of the self *and* the language is necessary, however, for the poems to really engage the reader deeply.

Heidi: Is the heavy use of rhythm or rhyme manipulative?

Shannon: I don't find the use of rhythm or rhyme manipulative, but the poems do lean a bit too heavily on them at times. This can create a feeling of flatness in the poem—causing the reader to get stuck on the surface of the poem—when I think there is a depth here that needs to be explored.

Heidi: Are these poems outdated? Does the heavy use of rhythm or rhyme pull these poems away from modern poetry? Are they poems, but spoken-word poems? Because of the rhyme, are they songs or pieces of song lyrics and not poems?

Shannon: These are questions we will answer as we look at the poems individually; I will say that *Mirror Mirror* and *Outdoor Art Show* feel like very modern poems to me and not songs or spoken-word pieces.

And so the mentoring begins. I chose to work on my poem *Outdoor Art Show*. It is my reflection on a painting, Spring Thaw, that I bought at the Toronto Outdoor Art Exhibition years earlier.

This may have been the right choice, as my poem *Mirror Mirror* does in fact become a song during my poem-to-lyrics mentoring sessions written about in the Songwriting section of this book *(see p.258 for the essay,* Mentor Me: An Inside View of Mentoring Sessions with Singer–Songwriter Luther Mallory)*.

Below is my original version of *Outdoor Art Show* that Shannon read:

HEIDI STOCK

Outdoor Art Show

There's beauty in the skeletal fountain grass, dead

yet living. Four anorexic trees, three headstone grey,

one red-brown like the earth, exposed, thawing

from the distant sun gnawing and casting a ghostly shadow.

Look at the pool of blue at the centre. I loved it. I paid for it.

Content, I keep the mystery of its greatest feature: ground level perspective.

Sunken too, I'm drawn into the scene, imagining I am

a 20-year-old running from her captor or an 80-year-old driving into the ditch.

If this were the last place I'd be alive yet dying, it would be okay.

And here is the poem in its first revision by Shannon, using the *erase* technique. The title has also been changed to that of the painting.

Spring Thaw

Skeletal fountain   grass,
    anorexic trees, three headstone

Grey, or red-brown earth,
    exposed, thawing

Distant sun gnawing my
        Shadow—

pool of blue at the centre? driving ache
I love I pay

I keep sunken too, I'm drawn into
   my running from her

the last of me alive, dying, alive

Erase and *expand* are common techniques in poetry to deconstruct or add to the original poem, which allows the poet to see his or her poem in a new light. Shannon provides an overview of and instruction on this technique in her essay, *Erase, Expand, Escape: How to Travel on the Page* (p.169).

Now I'm seeing my original poem in a new light! **I respond to Shannon with my impression of this first revision of my poem under the erasure exercise:**

The emotion is richer or strengthened with the changes to "driving ache," "the last of me," "I love I pay" (double meaning of I pay with money and I pay with my life).

The voice of the subject, the "I," is quieted. I feel that the removal of the narrative of the 20-year-old kidnapping victim, the 80-year-old driver and the subject diminishes the voice and the perspective of the "I," the subject of the poem. She is one of three dead women who are like the three dead (headstone grey) trees and yet she sees beauty in dying: "There's beauty in the skeletal fountain grass, dead/yet living" and accepts her potential death in this environment: "If this were the last place I'd be alive yet dying, it would be okay" (original version). In the highly narrative original version, the subject's voice dominates. In the erasure version, there is distance from this voice, which creates mystery in the poem and allows the reader to use his/her own imagination.

177

The concept of the soul/spirit is introduced with the new phrase, "my running from her" as "my running (physical body) from her (soul emerging at time of death) and "pool of blue at the centre" (at the centre of the self is the soul). This phrase is unchanged from the original version but now it moves beyond the literal meaning of pool of blue (puddle of blue water) in the centre of the painting.

Two new words and new formatting added. The words ache and last were added to the poem and there are changes in formatting (spacing, stanzas, italics, punctuation). "Ache" and "last" are powerful additions to the poem because in the original version the pain of the dying process wasn't clearly expressed, as it now is with "ache." As well, "last" clearly expresses the finality of the physical form in death, while "alive yet dying" and "dead yet living" create ambiguity.

And now, it's time to expand. Here's the poem in its first revision by Shannon using the expand technique.

Spring Thaw

There's beauty in the skeletal fountain grass, dead

yet living. Too much beauty? Four anorexic trees, three

headstone grey, splitting one red-brown like the earth, exposed,

thawing this open—a greedy leaning in, an ache from the distant sun

gnawing and casting a ghostly shadow. Is it me

in the painting? *Look at the pool of blue at the centre.*

I loved it in Northern California.

I paid for it, didn't I? My body is still content.

Look at the pool of blue at the centre of you, lady.

I keep at the mystery of its greatest feature like a small black dog

Digging: this is my sunken ground level perspective.

I'm drawn back into the scene, the dead grass, trees as skinny

as I am when I am 20 years old. When I am 80. This painting

of me running. Or is it me driving myself backwards into you?

Into the spilt of the earth, the ditch, the blue

at the centre – look at it.

Again, I'm seeing my original poem in a new light! **I respond to Shannon with my impression of this first revision of my poem under the *expand* exercise:**

The more narrative, the more wordy the poem becomes under the expand exercise, the more reflective and "interactive" the poem becomes with the reader. The subject asks, "Too much beauty?"; "Is it me in the painting?"; "I paid for it, didn't I?" "Or is it me driving myself backwards into you?"

Twice, *you* is mentioned. This version of the poem is demanding the attention of the reader: "Look at the pool of blue at the centre of you, lady" (this could be the blue in the reader's heart or in the reader's soul) and, "Or is it me driving myself backwards into you?" (creating a relationship with the reader) and making demands to look again "at the centre—look at it." The reader may either love or hate this kind of manipulation by the subject of the poem. The questioning nature of the subject (the "I" of the poem) asks the reader to ponder death and dying along with her and possibly the depression and despair stage of dying, with the reference to "blue" twice and the addition of "my sunken" in front of "ground level perspective," while the "I" in the original version of the poem lays out her view of death and dying as the later stages of acceptance and surrender.

The more words, the more descriptive and more specific the poem becomes in its setting and imagery and the more the poem controls the imagination of the reader may be a pro or con. Like the poet and the painter of the oil painting, the reader may imagine a familiar, rural scene, but with the addition of Northern California, the reader's imagination is controlled as it would be for the reader of prose, who is immersed in a setting determined by the writer. With the increased narrative, there is also the addition of a new "character"—the dog—which is an interesting new addition because the dog brings life to the still scene with his activity (digging).

The increased narrative builds on the imagery and the meaning of the poem. The new phrase, "My body is still content," has a double meaning: the literal meaning that my body remains in its physical form and also that my body continues to be content, as in peaceful. The double meaning of "I paid for it," from the original version (literally paying for the oil painting and when life mimics art, the subject and the poem's characters pay for it with their lives) is emphasized in this expanded version by bringing it to the attention of the reader in the form of a question: "I paid for it, didn't I?"

This expanded version puts the subject, the "I," at the centre of the poem. Other "characters" (the young kidnapping victim and elderly driver) are gone and the 20-year-old becoming an 80-year-old is now the subject: "trees as skinny as I am when I am 20 years old. When I am 80." What's new and interesting with this change is the enhancement of the image of "skinniness." The skinniness of her 20-year-old self (perceived either as a healthy slenderness or unhealthy weight like the anorexic trees) and the skinniness (the unhealthy frailty and/or dying) of the 80-year-old self.

With the literal driver removed and replaced with, "Or is it me driving myself backwards into you?" in this expanded version, there's an opportunity to interpret the "you" and the "I" at different times in her life. At age 80, she goes backwards to age 20, backwards before her physical life began, if the "you" she addresses is her soul—"the blue at the centre"—rather than the "you" being the reader of the poem.

Based on my learnings from the *erase* and *expand* exercises, it's time for me to create a new draft. Here's that poem:

Spring Thaw

Beautiful skeletal fountain grass,

dead – yet living. Four anorexic trees,

three headstone grey, one red-brown like the earth

exposed *thawing,*

aching from the distant Son casting a ghostly *shadow.*

Pool of blue at the centre.

Body still content, but sunken too,

A 20-year-old hidden from her captor,

an 80-year-old driven in the ditch.

The last place we were alive – yet dying,

Alive! Look at it.

I explain to my mentor, Shannon, my choices:

I changed the opening line from the original version—"There's beauty" to "Beautiful skeletal fountain grass"—so there's no declaration of its beauty; it becomes fact, an assertion. Also, the rhythm of those four words, the three-quarter time, waltz-like nature shows the beauty of its movement in the breeze.

The pauses created with "– yet living" and "– yet dying" and the spacing between the words "exposed" and "thawing" and the words "Body," "still," and "content" were used to make the reader pause and pay attention to them.

Putting the words "thawing," "aching" and "shadow" in italics was done to mimic the physical positioning, the leaning of ice or snow as it thaws, the leaning of the physical body when it is in pain, and the leaning nature of a shadow.

A new and unexpected change that did not come out of the erase or expand versions is the change of the word "sun" to "Son". This brings in a new image of life, death and afterlife in religion (Christian in this case), the Son of God, with the words "exposed," "aching" and "Alive!" supporting this. Putting the words "hidden" and "driven" in a smaller font size was done to mimic the physical nature of being hidden or driven into the ground.

I kept the "characters" of the victims of violence (20-year-old) and the car accident (80-year-old), in addition to the subject, the "I," so that it is "we" ("the last place we were alive"). The experience of "body still content," of "dead yet living" and "alive yet dying" is a shared experience, just as finding beauty in the rural roadside scene was the shared experience of the artist (the oil painter) and the buyer of the art (the poet whose reflection on the painting called *Spring Thaw* created this poem).

From the expand exercise, learning from the insistence of the subject, the "I," for the reader to be reflective and observant, is the new phrase to close the poem, "Look at it," which is simple and effective in its direction and authoritative in its single syllable sound: "Look at it."

And here's Shannon's response to me regarding my draft poem:

Heidi—I had a chance to look carefully at this poem (following our conversation and discussion) and also went back to your original. What struck me most was how, through our process, you have really moved away from a more prose-like piece and found a lovely balance in terms of the narrative and the minimalism in this current version. I especially like the building of the first three lines, growing longer until there is a sense of running out of breath, of brokenness by the fourth line—when things begin to thaw.

I love italics in poems sometimes, though sometimes they can be distracting and unnecessary. In this piece, I like them on "thawing" and "aching" but wouldn't keep them on the word "shadow". Also, I wonder about improving the phrase "ghostly shadow"—this is unfortunately a bit hackneyed and needs to be fresher for more impact and clarity as an image.

I think we already spoke about keeping the words "hidden" and "driven" in the same font as all other words in the poem, correct? I don't think it's helpful to readers to have too much imposed upon them visually in the case of a poem like this, where the small words are already doing their work. I think you should change "Son" to "Sun"—the ambiguity will come through in a close reading of the work, and I think it's important that a poem retain its mystery—that too much isn't directly pointed out or explained away.

A few more comments/observations:

Perhaps too much punctuation in the bottom half of the poem? Consider dropping some; see how it feels/looks/sounds.

"Body still content, but sunken too": This needs something—not sure what, but there is a vagueness here that distracts me. I'm not sure what the "body" refers to in this line—body of water, human body, her body—perhaps all three at once? I think you should play around a little more with this line, especially as it follows "pool of blue at the centre." Add and take away from it. Push it a little further.

Anyway, I hope these comments are helpful and not too overwhelming. As you know, this process is both challenging and exciting! These little poems are as hard as diamonds but somehow so fragile at the same time.

Based on Shannon's feedback above, I created my final draft:

Spring Thaw

Beautiful skeletal fountain grass,

dead – yet living. Four anorexic trees,

three headstone grey, one red-brown like the earth

exposed *thawing,*

aching from the distant sun casting a shivering shadow.

Pool of blue at the centre.

Body still content, but sunken too,

this 20-year-old hidden from her captor,

this 80-year-old driven in the ditch.

The last place we were alive – yet dying...

Look at it.

These are my comments to Shannon on the changes I made to create my final draft, above:

I agreed with changing "ghostly shadow" and removing the italics on "shadow" and substituting it with "shivering shadow." The anorexic, aching tree, the kidnapping victim in fear or due to the cold, and the accident victim in shock would all shiver.

I changed "a" and "an" before the 20- and 80-year-olds to "this", because they are specific to the poem, not just any. The sound of the end of the word—*this*—suited the sounds of the poem and the hissing sound of fountain grass swaying.

The challenge to re-examine the punctuation was exactly that to me—challenging! One change I made was the ellipsis (...) following the second-to-last line: "yet dying..." This punctuation gave it a "to be continued" feeling (dying but reborn/alive). The "to be continued" leads to the demand to the reader to "Look at it," with the first letter in "Look" capitalized for emphasis. The ellipses also represents the three "characters": the young kidnapping victim, the elderly car accident victim and the subject/voice/"I."

I removed the word, "Alive!" in the last line, which seemed less important and impactful since the removal of the "Son" (i.e., the Son of God). The simple, three-word ending, "Look at it," was more powerful without it.

I hope that sharing these exercises, drafts and comments from my poetry mentoring sessions with Shannon Bramer has been helpful and informative. In our last mentoring session, Shannon shared this about the mentor and student relationship:

"Please know my comments are meant to encourage and uncover more than they are meant to correct. Also remember that a different reader might have a completely different take on your work, and my ideas are simply the ideas of one person."

Well said!

185

SONGWRITING

Interviews with Songwriting Mentors and Contest Judges

Interview with Contest Mentor, Luba

Singer–Songwriter Mentor Experience, 2014

Photo courtesy of Luba

Luba first burst onto the Canadian music scene with the smash hit, "Everytime I See Your Picture." The single shot to the Top 10 on singles charts across the country, prompting the release of her first major album for Capitol Records, *Secrets and Sins*. Released in 1984 and produced by Daniel Lanois (U2, Peter Gabriel), the album produced Luba's first gold single, "Let It Go." The song, written by Luba, stayed at the top of the charts for over 40 weeks, eventually reaching the #1 position across the country.

In 1986, Luba released her second album, *Between the Earth and Sky*, which produced the Top-10 hits, "How Many" and "Innocent," and became her first platinum-selling album. "How Many" was chosen to represent Canada in the Tokyo International Song Festival, where Luba made it into the finals category. Her 1987 hit, *Over 60 Minutes with Luba*, featured her heart-wrenching rendition of the classic "When a Man Loves a Woman," also a Top-10 hit. *All or Nothing*, released in 1990, was Luba's second album to be certified platinum, achieving sales of over 100,000 units in Canada.

Throughout the years, Luba has won many awards: three Félix awards, numerous Casby awards and five Juno Awards, including the Best Female Vocalist title three years in a row. She has collaborated with such talents as Bryan Adams, Pierre Marchand (Sarah McLachlan) and Narada Michael Walden (Whitney Houston, Aretha Franklin), who chose Luba to sing "The Best Is Yet To Come" for the soundtrack to *9 ½ Weeks*, which also included the hit, "Let It Go."

In the spring of 2000, Luba made her comeback with a new album on her own, newly formed label, Azure Music. *From the Bitter to the Sweet* marks the strong return of the singer–songwriter. Luba, pulling from her life experiences during the past years, wrote all 11 songs. She considers this to be her most honest and revealing album to date, with a collection of songs reflecting maturity of sound and direction. The album features Luba's trademark heartfelt vocals, intertwined with a modern rhythmic approach and acoustic instrumentation, resulting in a truly transporting atmosphere.

The first single, "Is She A Lot Like Me," a Top-20 radio hit, firmly planted Luba back into the Canadian music scene. The single was a mainstay on Canadian radio throughout the year 2000, ending the year in the #19 position of the year-end BDS Canadian AC chart. The song is a take on love, loss and curiosity after the fact. Everyone can relate—and this thread of human experience weaves its way throughout the new album.

"Being at the helm of my own label has afforded me artistic control and greater involvement in the day-to-day workings of the company," says Luba. "*From the Bitter to the Sweet* marks a rite of passage for me. From conception through to the release, I have been involved in every stage."

Although Luba had been out of the public eye for some time, she was very busy devoting herself to her writing and singing. "Some people believe that if you aren't continuously releasing albums or touring, then you cease to exist as a musician," she says. "That's simply not so. I decided I needed to take time after the release of my last album to re-evaluate my life and career and to set a new course for the future." During this period, Luba encountered many challenging experiences, including the break-up of her marriage and the loss of her mother to ovarian cancer in the mid-90s. This led to a period of reflection from which Luba drew her inspiration for the words and music that would become her next album.

Canadian media embraced Luba's return with appearances and performances on Canada AM, CBC Morning News and features in many magazines and newspapers, including *Maclean's* and *Billboard*. Luba was also the focus of a one-hour performance on the MusiMax video channel. In November 2001, Luba's spectacular performance at the Montreal Spectrum was the subject of a television concert special— aired nationally on the Global network. She continued to impress audiences throughout the year 2002, with concert appearances across Canada.

Luba continues to record new music; in 2007 she premiered the new songs "Time" and "Heaven" and is currently working on a new album. She remains one of the more successful female artists in Canadian music history, despite never charting in the U.S. Her three consecutive Juno Awards for Female Vocalist of the Year put her in select company—only Anne Murray (nine) and Céline Dion (six) have more. Luba's journey has indeed been *From the Bitter to the Sweet*. It has all led her back to sharing these experiences with her audiences through her music. And they have welcomed her with open arms.

Bio courtesy of Luba from her official website, www.philfogel.com/luba/luba2013/biography.html

~~~

Heidi: What are some of your earliest memories of artistic expression?

Luba: Singing, at approximately age three, on the grounds of a Ukrainian camp, using a picnic table as my stage and performing for my parents and their friends. I knew from then on that music was in my DNA!

Heidi: Which artists have inspired and influenced your songwriting?

Luba: Elton John, Carole King, writers from the great Motown era, Heart, Annie Lennox, Van Morrison, David Bowie, Sting and last but not least, Joni Mitchell.

Heidi: What other art forms do you enjoy, and have they inspired your songwriting?

Luba: Singing (live shows and studio recording), photography, fine arts (multi-media—pencil, pastels, charcoal).

Heidi: How did you (and how do you) continue to develop your craft?

Luba: Practise, practise, practise! And listening to as much music as possible in every genre, from classical to R&B, from world music to rock and pop!

Heidi: How were you discovered and signed to a major record label?

Luba: Playing for anyone who would have me—performing covers but also including my own songs, which wasn't such an easy sell back in the late 70s and early 80s. Sending demos out to every record label imaginable and being persistent! Finally, two major labels began to show interest, and Capitol/EMI won out in the end.

Heidi: Do you define success differently now from the way you did at the beginning of your career?

Luba: Success for me has always been about learning and growing as a singer–songwriter and musician—to be the best I can be!

Heidi: What is your creative/songwriting process, and has that evolved or changed over time?

Luba: It has pretty much stayed the same. Sometimes the melody comes first; sometimes the words. Then I begin putting the pieces together, much like a puzzle. Every note, every syllable, must fit perfectly.

Heidi: What role has collaboration played in your career?

Luba: I tend to be a loner when it comes to songwriting, although I like to fine-tune a song with musicians with whom I have a good rapport and are fun to work with. Making music should be fun!

Heidi: Thank you for mentoring our contest's top three grand-prize winners. What do you hope they learned from their mentoring sessions with you?

Luba: That criticism isn't always a negative thing, compliments should boost your confidence and to learn to follow your gut instinct—believe in yourself, first and foremost!

Heidi: What direction or advice from your collaborators or mentors do you still follow today?

Luba: Trusting my gut—the voice inside me does not lie.

Heidi: Your advice to aspiring songwriters?

Luba: Songwriting is not an easy path to pursue. Make sure you hone your craft, work harder than those around you and keep the creative process positive and fun.

Heidi: The music industry has changed, with fewer album sales and less revenue to artists. Unsigned artists must also be proactive and be "DIY musicians" or "artist entrepreneurs," managing their own careers. What do you think of these changes and the challenges new artists face today?

Luba: It's a whole new world out there and, as always, people have to find a way to adapt and use these new technological tools, as well as social media, to get their music out to as many people as possible. The sky's the limit.

Heidi: You released a greatest hits compilation, *ICON*, in 2014. What are your upcoming plans?

Luba: Right now, I am juggling a few projects. A mini-tour is in the planning stages, songwriting is a daily exercise, not unlike meditation, and I am slowly writing a book (very slowly!). I would also like to somehow combine my photography with my words and music—and the circle shall be complete.

INTERVIEW WITH FINALISTS JUDGE, LESLEY PIKE

Singer–Songwriter Mentor Experience, 2014

Photo courtesy of Lesley Pike

NOW Magazine said, "Pike's got the goods," and Canadian indie darling Lesley Pike is back to showcase those goods on her new album, *Tug of War*, where she blends pop sensibility with her signature vocals and heart-on-sleeve lyrics, creating her own emotive sound.

Pike has been touring extensively through North America and Europe for the past four years and is known for her engaging and oftentimes hilarious live shows. In 2013, she was Gibson's featured artist at Robert Redford's Sundance Film Festival at the famed O2 Arena. Lesley has also shared the stage with Jason Mraz, Darius Rucker, Joan Osborne, Matisyahu, Tristan Prettyman, Ari Hest, Justin Nozuka and countless others.

www.lesleypike.com.

Bio courtesy of Lesley Pike and her management

~~~

Heidi: What are some of your earliest memories of artistic expression?

Lesley: Apparently, belting out tunes in the sandbox at approximately three years old! I basically got involved in everything I possibly could as a kid: school musicals, summer camp band, choirs, music lessons, you name it.

Heidi: Which artists have inspired and influenced your songwriting?

Lesley: There are so many, but off the top of my head: Peter Gabriel, Annie Lennox, Tori Amos, Ani DiFranco, Tracy Chapman.

Heidi: What other art forms do you enjoy, and have they inspired your songwriting?

Lesley: I do pottery as a hobby when I have the time—very inspiring to work with the hands in a different way and see such tangible results. Being at the wheel is almost a form of meditation—it gives me lots of time to think, reflect, and occasionally even come up with song ideas.

Heidi: How did you (and how do you) continue to develop your craft, and when did you discover that you wanted to pursue music as a career?

Lesley: I try to surround myself with people who are also doing something they are passionate about and that they work hard at; that inspires me to keep challenging myself. I think I've known since I was very young that music would be a big part of my life in one way or another, and I decided when I was in my late teens to commit to it and simply see where it takes me.

Heidi: Have there been any defining moments or turning points in your career when you felt you were on the right track and achieving success as you define it?

Lesley: There have been many serendipitous moments when things just seemed to click and I have felt that I am exactly where I was meant to be. I have learned, however, that those tend to come on the heels of, or in the midst of, great struggles and when putting in a whole lot of hard work!

Heidi: What role has collaboration played in your career?

Lesley: For the first several years of my career, I was a solitary writer and thought I had to be on my own to be creative and to express myself the way I wanted to. Over the past two or three years, I opened up to the idea of collaborating, and it has been one of the best decisions of my professional life. Co-writing and collaborating with friends and colleagues on both writing and performing has resulted in some of the sweetest, proudest and most enjoyable/inspiring moments in my professional life. Being able to share and capture an experience or moment with someone else (or several others) is magic. It has made me a better writer, performer and human being.

Heidi: What direction or advice from collaborators or mentors do you still follow today?

Lesley: There have been a few times—at shows, especially—when I've started to second-guess myself, compare myself to others, etc., and my producer/guitarist, James, always says, "Lesley, you just do *you*." Regardless of the setting, the situation, the scenario—just be yourself. That's good advice in all walks of life!

Heidi: Your advice to aspiring songwriters?

Lesley: Make a commitment to simply "show up" and do the work, without being too attached to the outcome. Sometimes it will flow;

sometimes it will feel impossible. Just keep showing up and making yourself available. Inspiration has a way of finding the people who consistently show up.

Interview with Semi-Finalists Judge, Luther Mallory

Singer–Songwriter Mentor Experience, 2014

Photo courtesy of Luther Mallory

Luther Mallory is a musician and a band coach living in Toronto. Raised in the Ottawa Valley, in the small town of Arnprior, Ontario, he moved at the age of 19 to London, Ontario to go to college—and find a band. After 40 seconds of college, Luther gathered bandmates, started Crush Luther, and moved to Toronto, where the Canadian music scene was.

In Crush Luther, Luther was the songwriter and singer, and the band was together from 2002 till 2010. They released two albums internationally, toured Canada five times, and performed on the east coast of the United States with a Warped Tour festival. They produced five music videos, including two #1 hits on Canada's music TV station, Much More Music.

Somewhere in the middle of all of that, Luther managed stints as a music journalist, A&R [artist and repertoire] director for an independent label, producer/co-writer, label owner, artist manager and musical director/bass player.

In 2011, Luther started an independent record label out of Toronto called Daycare Records (slogan for "babysitting your stupid band") with *Rolling Stone/Billboard* journalist, Karen Bliss. On the Daycare roster were battle rapper Kid Twist and indie/pop band The Danger Bees, both of which Luther produced and managed.

The following year, former INXS frontman, J.D. Fortune, asked Luther if he would be interested in producing his solo record, which led Luther to a brief but intense nine months as the producer/co-writer/ bass player for J.D.'s new band, Fortune (which Luther says "folded due to blah blah blah").

In 2013, Luther began coaching bands on how to beat their fears of criticism, connect with their music and their bandmates on stage, and build their fan bases (www.luthermalloryproductions.com). Recently, he started a new rock band out of Toronto called The Bow and the Blade with his brother, Devon, and lifelong drummer P.J. Herrick. By the time of this printing, hopefully The Bow and the Blade will have won all of the Grammys and Junos for "Best Everything."

After trying so many things for so long, says Luther, "This industry is like a mosquito lamp for me. It will probably kill me and I don't care. I can't stop myself. It's too intriguing."

Biography courtesy of Luther Mallory

~~~

Heidi: What are some of your earliest memories of artistic expression?

Luther: My music obsession was gradual. I had no "moment" where I fell in love or anything. I can remember vividly when I discovered that artistic expression was an actual thing, and that set me off to find more of it.

I wrote a poem in Grade 8 and I showed it to my friend. I tried pretty hard at writing, but I did the classic downplay when I let her read it, saying it was just something stupid I wrote in 15 seconds or something—you know, to save my self-image. She was floored by this poem. She was totally buzzing, and I was part confused and delighted. She told me she wanted to get it tattooed on her, and I said, "Definitely don't do that." I remember having this weird sense for the first time that creativity, when shared, can really affect someone on a different level. I went chasing that.

All I remember about the poem was it had the line, "I took a bath in flowers" in it. No, I'm afraid I'm serious.

Heidi: Which artists have inspired and influenced your songwriting?

Luther: I made a funny discovery about a year ago: When my brother and I were kids, my dad used to have a huge red van we called "the Super Van," and the only two cassette tapes in the van were compilation records of the hits of the year.

We'd be bumping those tapes front to back all day, every day. I now realize that my love for pop came from exactly that experience. Nothing but hits and no filler, my whole childhood. I love great singers, and I love simple songwriting. If my dad had been listening to Patti Smith in the Super Van, I'd be an indie guy, but pop was filling up that van, so that's what I love.

Savage Garden and Billy Joel were the biggest teen-year influences. I eventually moved into lyrically driven stuff like Lyle Lovett and Rickie Lee Jones, which influenced my vocal delivery heavily, as well as my lyric writing. Darren Hayes from Savage Garden is my hero, though.

Heidi: What other art forms do you enjoy, and have they inspired your songwriting?

Luther: Creative presentation of any sort is my preferred art. I enjoy a speech as much as a song, and a great presenter is as good as a great singer—watching confident people share ideas with passion and belief and watching the real-time effect it has on an audience. The connection to the audience is the art form I intensely love.

Heidi: How did you (and how do you) continue to develop your craft, and when did you discover that you wanted to pursue music as a career?

Luther: There has to be a separation between the analytical and the emotional. I was born to collect data and analyze everything until it's a mud puddle in my brain. That's important for improving as a writer or player. You have to do more than listen to improve.

But my kind of music is about emotion first and precision second. Analysis of everything gets me thinking, and that thinking buries my ability to feel. Feeling is where the heart of it all is and what the audience is after. I had to learn how to take the thinking cap off at times and let it be about emotion alone.

A few songs did that for me:

"By The Sea," by Bobby McFerrin (YouTube it. I've only ever seen or heard it live as a solo performance.)
"This is a Rebel Song," by Sinead O'Connor
"Mercy Street," by Peter Gabriel
"Skeletons," by Rickie Lee Jones

Heidi: Have there been any defining moments or turning points in your career when you felt you were on the right track and achieving success as you define it?

Luther: In Crush Luther, our first video for *City Girl* went #1 on Much More Music. I stared at the TV and thought, "This is happening." It was cool. I had girls' pants on at the time. It wasn't cool.

Heidi: What role has collaboration played in your career?

Luther: I learned a hard, critical lesson about collaboration on my first-ever co-writing session with a guy who worked at EMI Publishing. We basically sat across from each other holding guitars, and stared at each other until I went home. I was too precious about my ideas. He would suggest something for something I had started, and I'd politely pass, thinking it wasn't a good addition to my idea. Very self-righteous. I learned that nothing gets done without other people and I learned to embrace help. Especially in music, no artist is an island.

Heidi: What direction or advice from collaborators or mentors do you still follow today?

Luther: A very important business mentor of mine told me, "It's easier to do what is impossible than what is simple." He meant that if a goal is looked at as impossible, then you'll have to push with everything you have to achieve it. That kind of pushing forces you to be creative, ingenious and innovative, and to use all of your internal and external resources. Collecting that momentum from that kind of intensity makes you actually achieve what seemed impossible.

Some simple goal like calling a radio station to find out how to service your song to them—you won't do it; it's too easy. It gets put off like laundry or finally dumping your boyfriend. I like big goals, and then I like to exhaust myself working toward them. I fail and I succeed but it always takes intensity.

If you're serious about your music career, set a goal like "Get a song into a Disney film." If you're truly serious, and you're not just a talker, start attacking that goal and you'll pass all of your other "simple" goals on day one because of the sheer size of the big goal.

It reminds me of a quote by Jim Rohn: "Don't become a millionaire so you can have a million dollars. Become a millionaire because of the person you'll have to become to get there." Amen.

Heidi: Your advice to aspiring songwriters?

Luther: This isn't your final project. You'll fail another five times before you know enough to succeed. I know you're giving everything you have to this band or this album or this tour and that's exactly what you should be doing. When this one falls short of your vision for success despite how hard you've worked, you *can't* let it permanently defeat you and run you out of town. The next one will be better and easier. And eventually, if you stay in it, you'll see rewards. The only people that last are the risk-takers and the soldiers. If you break a leg in battle, rip it off and throw it at somebody! That's a leader. Be that.

Interview with Preliminary Judge, Katie Rox

Singer–Songwriter Mentor Experience, 2014

Photo courtesy of Katie Rox

As the former lead singer of the industrial-rock band Jakalope, Katie Rox found the success she had always dreamed of. From a Top-3 track on the Japanese pop charts to her profile on *MTV Cribs*, from international tours to multiple Much Music Video Award nominations, Katie has had her taste of life in the fast lane.

But the days of being a major-label rocker are gone as Katie has chosen a much softer and more personal path with her music. Her three self-released solo albums, *High Standard, Searchlight* and the 2011 release *Pony Up* have taken Katie on multiple cross-Canada tours, performances at the 2010 Winter Olympics, the legendary Calgary Stampede, a 2011 Japanese tour, and a collaboration with Simple Plan's Sébastien Lefebvre that resulted in the 2010 EP release *Christmas Etc.* She has also completed songs for an independent feature film and TV pilot to go alongside her previous placements in *Degrassi: The Next Generation, Lost Girl* and *Bon Cop, Bad Cop.*

Katie was raised as a farm girl on the Canadian prairies of Alberta, so her music has evolved naturally into a warm, acoustic and roots-based embrace. While some have referred to her as one of the talented new voices of Americana, she prefers to just call herself a singer-songwriter. Yet it was on a recent pilgrimage to Nashville when Katie's eyes were opened to an important new distinction in how she thinks of herself—as a storyteller.

"Being in Nashville and watching these incredible songwriters perform, it really dawned on me how the story itself is much more important than just a catchy hook. If someone can write a song about an old yellow car that makes you want to cry at the end, then they've created something truly memorable and clearly done their job."

Katie's recent efforts, inspired by her trip to Nashville, paired her with producer Jamie Candiloro (REM, Willie Nelson, Ryan Adams). The two just finished recording her fourth studio album in Candiloro's Los Angeles studio, released in late 2013.

"We just clicked, musically and personally. He pushed me to the point that sometimes I wanted to say 'I can't give any more!', but yet I always could. He made me dig deep, and I think it will show in the album we created."

Inspired by the power of a good story and breathtaking melody, Katie Rox is clearly leading by example, travelling her own DIY musical journey.

Biography courtesy of Katie Rox. Visit www.nicehorsemusic.com.

~~~

Heidi: What are some of your earliest memories of artistic expression?

Katie: I remember at first I didn't want to sing in front of anyone! I was just a kid, taking lessons because my sister did, but I didn't want to compete or sing in recitals. When I did my first recital, I started to sing and burst into tears and ran to my mom! But at the end of the recital, I did it again and completed it. When I was about 12, I finally entered my first singing competition. It was in musical theatre, and I won! I was hooked after that.

Heidi: Which artists have inspired and influenced your songwriting?

Katie: So many . . . it depends on what I'm listening to at the time. I love old country music; it doesn't always come out in my writing, but it's there! I also love John Mayer, Jason Mraz, The Civil Wars . . . and Michael Jackson.

Heidi: What other art forms do you enjoy, and have they inspired your songwriting?

Katie: I am absolutely no good at any other kind of art!

Heidi: How did you (and how do you) continue to develop your craft, and when did you discover that you wanted to pursue music as a career?

Katie: I write with a LOT of different people. No matter what style of music, I will write it. I have attended some songwriting camps as well. Sometimes just some dim lighting and a glass of wine will help, too!

Heidi: Have there been any defining moments or turning points in your career when you felt you were on the right track and achieving success as you define it?

Katie: Remember that TV show, *Pop Stars*? I auditioned for that when it came to Calgary. And I was a Calgary finalist! That was the moment when I thought maybe I might actually have a real shot at something. It gave me confidence beyond my friends and family telling me

I was good. It meant people in the industry thought I might have something, too.

Heidi: What role has collaboration played in your career?

Katie: Huge! Being in Jakalope was one big collaboration, from the artists involved in the writing to the ones who toured the project. As a solo artist, it's also still a collaboration, just more of a "behind the scenes" kind. It's important to surround yourself with people whose careers you admire, or whose musical stylings you feel connected to. Also your peers—those who can understand the triumphs and the struggles—the many, many struggles you face as an artist! You'll need a bouncing board, a think tank and a cheering section. Usually, you'll find that in the very people out there doing the same thing as you.

Heidi: What direction or advice from collaborators or mentors do you still follow today?

Katie: To always say yes to opportunities that come up, and to try everything at least once.

Heidi: Your advice to aspiring songwriters?

Katie: Never stop learning, developing, growing and trying new things. You never know what they might lead to. It's important to be yourself, but it's also important to keep reaching and going out of your comfort zone—you just might learn new things about yourself that you didn't know were there.

Interview with Preliminary Judge, Melanie Durrant

Singer–Songwriter Mentor Experience, 2014

Photo courtesy of Melanie Durrant

Melanie Durrant is a seasoned veteran who embodies real artistry through her unique, edgy and soulful music style. Born and raised in Toronto, Melanie attended the Earl Haig School of the Arts. She trained at the Royal Conservatory of Music and worked on an eclectic array of projects before she became an alternative hip hop/ soul artist. Citing influences that range from the soulful swoon of Minnie Ripperton to the hard-knock of Aerosmith to the "mercy me" melodies of Marvin Gaye, the radiant singer–songwriter has no problems crashing through the wall of sound.

She has received multiple accolades throughout her career, including a Much Music Video Award for her single, "Where I'm Going," and she is a Stylus Awards winner for Single of the Year for her song, "Bang Bang," by Kardinal Offishall. In 2013, Melanie's reggae-influenced lovers rock single, "Made For Love," was nominated for Reggae Single of the Year for the 2013 Juno Awards.

This multi-talented artist was also a featured performer in the Canadian production of *RENT*. Being a regular in the ensemble allowed her to work with her good friend and cast-mate, Jill Scott (Hidden Beach/Epic Records).

In addition to performing her own shows for audiences across Canada and the U.S., Melanie has shared the stage alongside Jay Z, 50 Cent, Jill Scott, Common, Sean Paul, Kardinal Offishall as well as many of Canada's top artists. She has graced such magazines as *Honey* and *Coco*. Melanie has performed and done interviews with MuchMusic Canada, MTV Canada, Star Daily and CTV Network, to name a few. She has had a variety of video production releases aired nationally on MuchMusic Canada. Her songs have been in high rotation on Toronto's Flow 93.5 FM, as well as other radio stations across Canada. Melanie's music has been featured on numerous compilation releases and DJ mix-tapes around the world.

Currently, she has been working diligently on new material for her sophomore album. Full of melodic surprises, heavenly harmonies and bold direction, Melanie embodies the voice, attitude and sound that have blessed Canada and that the whole world has been waiting for.

www.melaniedurrant.com

Management: Maurice Laurin

Biography courtesy of Melanie Durrant and her management

~~~

Heidi: What are some of your earliest memories of artistic expression?

Melanie: My earliest memories of artistic expression would be singing and dancing with my mother at home. We did that a lot. My mother is a professional singer/performer and has been her entire life.

Heidi: Which artists have inspired and influenced your songwriting?

Melanie: I would say my mother is my biggest inspiration. She is an amazing artist and as a young child, she introduced me to Motown and soul music and artists such as Aretha Franklin, James Brown, Gladys Knight, Diana Ross and The Supremes, Smokey Robinson, Michael Jackson and Stevie Wonder, to name a few.

Heidi: What other art forms do you enjoy, and have they inspired your songwriting?

Melanie: I enjoy photography but I can't say that it affects my songwriting in any way.

Heidi: How did you (and how do you) continue to develop your craft, and when did you discover that you wanted to pursue music as a career?

Melanie: After attending one of my mother's live shows and putting on my own show for my kindergarten class, I was convinced that music was the path for me.

Heidi: Have there been any defining moments or turning points in your career when you felt you were on the right track and achieving success as you define it?

Melanie: Attracting the attention of the president of Motown records, through one of my singles, "Where I'm Going," and then him signing me to the company, were very gratifying and definitely made me feel I was on the career path, considering some of the greatest artists in history were signed to Motown.

Heidi: What role has collaboration played in your career?

Melanie: Collaborating with other artists, writers and producers has been very educational. From word play to melodic styles, working with talented musicians can bring something different to what you regularly do on your own. In my experiences, it has helped teach me different approaches to creating a great song.

Heidi: What direction or advice from collaborators or mentors do you still follow today?

Melanie: Working with a wide range of musicians and taking in all the information by listening and learning has been one of the keys to my growth as a songwriter. You also have to be true to your vision and be on point when it's your turn to share that input. And make sure to always bring a pen and something to write on!

Heidi: Your advice to aspiring songwriters?

Melanie: My advice to aspiring songwriters would be to listen, research and write as much as possible. The saying, "Practice makes perfect" definitely holds weight in the world of songwriting. The more you work at it, the stronger your skills will develop. Stay at it!

Interview with Preliminary Judge, Theo Tams

Singer–Songwriter Mentor Experience, 2014

Photo courtesy of Theo Tams

Fun should be the chief component in anyone's life—smiles, laughter, jokes—a general bounce in every step you take.

But until recently for Theo Tams—pop singer, songwriter, international performer and Gemini Award–nominated final *Canadian Idol* champion (class of 2008)—it was the one element missing from his life.

"I tend to be quite serious and intense," Tams admits on the eve of his upcoming six-song EP, the follow-up to his 2009 debut album, *Give It All Away*. "But I feel my new music sounds younger and is more fun than anything I've done before."

You can hear it in his ebullient and electrifying self-penned pop songs—whether it's the piano-driven romance of the energetic "Stay," the entertaining "Steal Your Love Away," or the pining "When You're Not Around"—it's a live-wire sound that seems to boast an extra spark or two.

213

"I've learned to have fun, enjoy the ride, the journey and not take things so seriously," confesses Tams, who is signed to EMI Music Publishing and has a development deal with Slaight Music.

"And I think that's really reflected in my new music. There are still those really intense ballads—that's a huge part of the music that I make—but I've also thrown myself into a different sound and just kind of let go."

Prior to *Canadian Idol*, Tams, who plays trumpet and piano, lived in the Lethbridge suburb of Coaldale, population 7,493, in a strict, religious household, where he taught himself to write songs. "I think that writing just became my voice," he admits. "I tended to write about everything, the majority of my songs from personal experience."

Influenced by Sarah McLachlan, Jann Arden and the team of Bryan Adams and Jim Vallance, Tams—who scored a No. 1 AC hit here with Ali Slaight for their charity duet, "Do You Hear What I Hear?"—is ready to introduce Theo 2.0.

"I'm much more aware of who I am, not only as an artist, but as a person, and I feel that this music is the best I've ever created. I'm eager to share it with the rest of the world."

Biography courtesy of Theo Tams

~~~

Heidi: What are some of your earliest memories of artistic expression?

Theo: Music has always been a part of my life. I remember watching and listening to my sisters play the piano, and that was the first thing that really sparked my interest. Around the age of 12, I started taking the poetry I wrote and setting it to music—so that was my first introduction into the realm of songwriting.

Heidi: Which artists have inspired and influenced your songwriting?

Theo: Mostly all Canadian artists. I love the stories that Canadian artists tell: Jann Arden, Sarah McLachlan, Bryan Adams. All were really big influences on my music and the way I continue to write songs.

Heidi: What other art forms do you enjoy, and have they inspired your songwriting?

Theo: I've always enjoyed visual art: drawing, painting, sketching, photography. I'm not sure I'm that great at it, but every now and then I'll bust out the art supplies and create something. I'm also a huge fan of cooking, which I believe is an art form in and of itself. Some of the best meals are created the way songs are, by adding or taking away certain parts to create a masterpiece.

Heidi: How did you (and how do you) continue to develop your craft, and when did you discover that you wanted to pursue music as a career?

Theo: I just wrote. I wrote and wrote and wrote. About everything. And to be honest, a lot of the songs I first wrote were crap. I still think a bunch of the songs I write are crap. But then there are the gems—the diamonds that come from the piles of coal. That is what I think beginner songwriters need to learn, and it was a hard lesson for me as well, that not every song you write is going to be great, or a hit, or useable. And there is nothing wrong with that; it is the process of writing songs—many of them—that brings you to your greatness.

There was always a part of me that knew I wanted to pursue music as a career. I guess it just came down to a time when I really believed it was feasible. Probably my early 20s, I thought maybe I can do this.

Heidi: Have there been any defining moments or turning points in your career when you felt you were on the right track and achieving success as you define it?

Theo: Obviously winning *Canadian Idol* was a pivotal moment for me. It not only allowed for the move from small-town Alberta to Toronto, but it also put me in touch with a great number of people in the business. The first couple of years after *Idol* were like Music Industry 101—I learned a lot and made a lot of mistakes, but I have no regrets. The lessons I learned prepared me for longevity in this business and the bumps and hurdles along the way. The last year is probably the most secure I've felt in this industry, simply because I have taken things into my hands, collaborated with some brilliant artists, and surrounded myself with a really strong team of business people to take my career to the next level.

However, I think any artist will tell you that the definition of success constantly changes. Is it selling millions of singles, or is it paying your bills for the year? Success is on a spectrum, and that spectrum is constantly wavering.

Heidi: What role has collaboration played in your career?

Theo: Collaboration is key, in every respect, to succeding in this business. Collaboration, also referred to as *networking*, is not just creative—it is business as well. Co-writing was really hard for me at first, but now I thrive on it. It is the recognition that, as a songwriter, you have strengths to contribute, but you may also (and probably do!) have weaknesses in the songwriting process. Collaborating with other songwriters allowed me to realize what my strengths and weaknesses are, and knowing your weaknesses can only help your entire craft become more well-rounded.

Heidi: What direction or advice from collaborators or mentors do you still follow today?

Theo: Debra Byrd, the vocal coach on *Canadian Idol*, told me to get a small pocket recorder, or use the voice memo app on my phone, and start recording everything, everywhere. No matter where you are, if a lyric comes into your head, record it. If a melody or little lick comes into your head, record it. If a guitar riff comes into your head, record it. Then and there. Don't wait for a structure to form or a complete song to be written. Get your ideas. It is these little sound bites that become the very basis of some great songs. Record, record, record.

Heidi: Your advice to aspiring songwriters?

Theo: Write often, and write about everything. Put the names of cool song titles into a jar, and when you are at a loss for what to write about, pick a name from the jar and write that song. If you're not a performer yourself, put another jar full of names of artists that you really enjoy listening to, or would love to write for. Pull a song title and an artist, and all of a sudden you are left with the challenge of writing a song called "Every Little Window" for Rihanna, or a song called "Lily" for Chris Brown. It's a way of pushing yourself creatively and making it interesting and fun when your "inspiration well" is just a little empty (it happens!).

Interviews with the Songwriting Contest Winners

Interview with Amir Brandon

by Allyson Latta

First-Place Contest Winner,
Singer–Songwriter Mentor Experience, 2014

Photo credit: Alyssa Balistreri

Amir Brandon was the first-prize winner in the 2014 Singer–Songwriter Mentor Experience. He has now completed his mentoring with multiple Juno Award–winning, Canadian singer–songwriter Luba and industry mentoring from contest judges Luther Mallory and Theo Tams. I interviewed him about his creative process, career aspirations and advice for other aspiring songwriters.

Up-and-coming singer–songwriter Amir Brandon is making a statement. He was born and raised in Ottawa, Ontario, and the first glimpse of his potential was seen at the age of two, when singing along with recordings of greats like Michael Jackson. Amir began songwriting and performing at community events at a young age, eventually moving to Toronto, Ontario, to expand his musical network and artistry. His music has been positively received by blogs, magazines and fans and is promoted through live performances and social media. Most recently, his song "Millions" won the prize for best original song in a national songwriting competition promoted by industry partner, Songwriters Association of Canada. Amir is known for his soulful, melismatic vocals, through both originals and cover videos posted on YouTube. He is grabbing the attention of the public for his true-to-self songwriting as he steadily builds his repertoire of original music. Currently, he is working on his second studio EP, set to be released later this year.

"I know that if I write something from my heart, no matter how personal it is, there are people out there who will connect with it; there are people out there who need to hear it."

Visit Amir's website at www.amirbrandon.com.

~~~

Why did you decide to enter this particular song, "Millions", in the 2014 Singer–Songwriter Mentor Experience contest?

"Millions" just puts you in a happy place. It's a fun song, and I've gotten a lot of positive response to it from fans. It's honest, it's catchy, and it's something that everyone can relate to. It sounds like something a bunch of friends would sing along with on a road trip, don't ya think?

What's the backstory to this song?

I bought a ukulele a couple years ago, learned a few chords, and started improvising until I came up with a chord progression. I'm able to gather certain feelings from chord progressions alone, and the one I came up with inspired me to write about celebrating life and living in the moment. It's a happy-go-lucky kind of song. We tend to focus so much on the future and accomplishing our goals that we forget about what we already have. Writing "Millions" inspired me to spend more time with family and appreciate the little things.

When did you start writing songs?

From a young age, I was really interested in pop music and what made hit songs so good. I listened to (and critiqued) the songs on my mom's favourite radio station in the car. I learned a lot about songwriting just by listening all these years. I've always loved the idea of writing music and being a performer, and I've been doing it since grade school.

Was songwriting your first creative outlet or did you experiment with other types of writing or art forms?

I started writing short stories in Grade 2. Just kiddie stuff. Then I was introduced to poetry and began creating my own poems. I was in love with creative writing since I could remember, and it eventually morphed into a love for songwriting. The lyrics of my music are usually conceived last, though; the melody, the vocals, and the arrangement of a song play a huge role in my creative process.

How much of your songwriting is based on your own memories and experiences?

All of it! It's funny because I usually don't have a specific theme or life experience in mind when I'm writing a song. My songwriting process usually starts with a melody. A melody alone can make me feel a certain way, and with that I create the lyrics and chords. So really, the song speaks for itself and decides what I'm writing about, and from there I smear my personality all over it!

Do other forms of artistic expression and/or life experience influence your songwriting?

Visuals are a huge deal for me. I'm inspired by film, dance and photography. Music videos in particular can make such an impact on your perspective of a song. Some music videos surprise you when they define the song in a way you would've never thought of yourself. Some of my favourite music videos are *Remember the Time* by Michael Jackson and *Paparazzi* by Lady Gaga. Both tell an unpredictable story and create a setting that complements the music. It's something I'm keeping in mind as I work on my new EP, since I'm so eager to create more music videos of my own.

Have you written songs just for yourself, knowing you won't ever perform them?

I always write music with the intent of releasing or performing it. I might keep the song private if I feel like it's not ready for people to hear yet. I know that if I write something from my heart, no matter how personal it is, there are people out there who will connect with it; there are people out there who need to hear it.

Who has influenced or encouraged your writing—which songwriters, other artists, teachers or mentors, loved ones?

Some of my favourite songwriters are:

- Sade for her simplicity
- Michael Jackson for his versatility
- Mariah Carey for her vocal artistry
- Lady Gaga for her unapologetic confidence

Outside of music, my mom is my greatest inspiration. She's the bravest, most outgoing, and most loving person I know. She motivates me to step out of my comfort zone. As I work toward my dream, I always remember how much I want to make her proud; it keeps me going through thick and thin.

If you could meet a famous musician or songwriter, spend an evening jamming—or even just talking—with him or her, who would it be?

I wish I had had the chance to meet Michael Jackson. I love how sincere and real he was. He spoke his mind, he said what he meant, and he meant what he said. He really seemed like a wonderful person. I would've loved to get to know him better.

What do you do on an ongoing basis to develop your craft?

I work on my original material every day. Writing, rehearsing, recording—all that. Even when I'm out in public, I catch myself humming new melodies. I live and breathe my art. I challenge myself when I'm writing; I'm never satisfied. I tend to rewrite the same song a few times before I'm really happy with it. I want to make sure I'm 100% proud of what I plan on releasing.

As part of the contest prize, you received songwriting mentoring sessions with Luba as well as industry mentoring from contest judges, Luther Mallory and Theo Tams. What advice did you receive?

Some of the best advice that I received, as simple and obvious as it is, was from my mentoring session with Theo Tams. That is, "Be yourself, and don't be sorry about it." We all need to be reminded sometimes. As artists, we're somewhat obligated to be public people. We have to be genuine not only through our music, but through our personalities, the way we speak and present ourselves. I know first-hand that it's easy to feel self-conscious when we have interviews (ha!) or need to speak our minds. We need to stop caring about what people think, and honestly just be ourselves. Nobody else is like me; nobody else is like you.

What advice do you have for new songwriters?

Step out of your comfort zone. Make mistakes. Never stop writing. Listen to a lot of music. Did I mention to step out of your comfort zone?

Reprint, originally published by Allyson Latta at www.allysonlatta.ca/

Interview with Elias James

Second-Place Contest Winner,
Singer–Songwriter Mentor Experience, 2014

Photo courtesy of Elias James

How did you hear about the 2014 Singer–Songwriter Mentor Experience and why did you enter?

I believe I found out through the Songwriters Association of Canada. I guess I entered because I'm always looking for new opportunities for my music, and I had just finished a bunch of new songs for my upcoming record.

Why did you decide to enter this particular song, "My Biggest Mistake," in the contest?

It was something that I was particularly proud of at the time and also one of the songs from the new album that I was most comfortable with, considering I had been playing it live quite a bit. I knew the song was strong, and it lends quite well to how I was recording my submission: just guitar and vocals.

225

What's the backstory to this song?

I think my first idea ended up being in the first couple lines of the song, something about "what you looked like in this light" because I have this little bedside lamp in my room that casts some strange shadows late at night. The guitar part was a combination of a few things I picked up from a couple of my favourite artists. Then I'm always just trying to match up music with lyrics, putting puzzle pieces together slowly.

When did you start writing songs?

I got into the music game fairly late, when I turned 18. I took my first songwriting classes at probably 20 but was too shy and apprehensive about it to actually write anything. In my second year in music school, at Grant MacEwan University, I signed up for a songwriting class and I was forced to write a song a week for two semesters, so those deadlines really helped me get my first songs out.

Do you remember your first song? Care to share some of the lyrics? What inspired that first song or your first piece of creative writing?

The first song I wrote was called "From Afar." I kinda ripped off a bit of a Jack Johnson-y guitar part and wrote a song about being so into the idea of a girl you've never met before that you don't actually want to meet her because there's no way the reality could live up to the expectation you've built up in your head. The chorus was "If it's alright with you, I think I'll stay alone/Until this heartache has completely run its course/If it's OK I think I'll leave you with the stars/I'd rather love you from afar." Kinda silly.

Was songwriting your first creative outlet or was it another style of writing? Or another art form?

My first solidified creative outlet was songwriting, yes. I was never into visual art; actually, I was really bad at it. I was a good writer in school, but that was always academically. I didn't consider myself "creative" until I started playing guitar.

Do other forms of artistic expression and/or life experience influence your songwriting?

Artistic expression, not really (other than my album being named after a painting I saw at the Art Gallery of Ontario), but life experience, definitely. Most of my songs are exaggerations of real life events, based somewhat in truth on something that happened in my life. A lot of the time the emotion is real, but the facts are skewed. "Never let the truth get in the way of a good song," my mentors used to tell me.

Influences—who influenced or encouraged your writing— which songwriters, other artists, teachers or mentors, loved ones?

John Mayer was a big one at the beginning; Paul Simon. My biggest influences have been my songwriting teachers and mentors over the years, including Kim Fontaine, Jay Semko (The Northern Pikes), Dean McTaggart (Amanda Marshall), Robert Walsh. Ralph Murphy and Pat Pattison (both of whom I've met and taken online classes with).

What do you do to develop your craft?

I've taken a ton of songwriting classes, both online and in person (casually and at a university level), read pretty much every book there is to read on the subject and studied popular music on my own for hours and hours and hours. All of that, though, can only heighten your "taste level", as I call it. It doesn't really make you "better"; it just gives you a higher definition of what "better" is. Practice is the only way you get better, which means writing as much as possible.

Tell us about your mentoring experience with our contest mentor, Luba.

Luba was a positive affirmation that the path I'm on is the right one. She encouraged me to move to a bigger centre from my smaller city. She had a lot positive to say about my songs and my writing and plenty of wisdom to share with an emerging songwriter, which is always great to hear from an industry professional.

How will Luba's guidance inform your future songwriting?

Luba was another strong push forward in an industry created to set you back. As someone who hasn't seen a lot of success yet, at least from a financial standpoint, having someone acknowledge your direction is a great gift.

What advice do you have for new songwriters?

Write every day, and finish what you write. Get all of those crappy songs out of the way; you have to write them before you can get to any of the good stuff.

INTERVIEW WITH REBEKAH STEVENS

Third-Place Contest Winner,
Singer–Songwriter Mentor Experience, 2014

Photo courtesy of Rebekah Stevens

How did you hear about the 2014 Singer–Songwriter Mentor Experience, and why did you enter?

I heard about the 2014 Singer–Songwriter Mentor Experience while browsing the Internet one day for possible gig/musical opportunities and decided it would be fun to enter and see what happened.

Why did you decide to enter this particular song, "All In Good Time", in the contest?

Initially, I was going to enter a song from my first EP but realized in the contest rules that the song entered couldn't have any co-writers attached to it (which all of the songs from my EP did), so "All In Good Time" was the song that I felt most proud of that I had written on my own.

What's the backstory to this song?

I wrote the song a couple years back, when I decided to pursue music full time. A lot of people were telling me that I was crazy for trying to get into the industry and that there were hundreds of people just like me trying to do the same thing. I had doubted myself for years before and at the time of writing this song, where I finally felt like I was ready to pursue my dream, I wrote it as a way to kind of put those doubters in their place.

When did you start writing songs?

I remember sitting down at the piano and writing my first song (with sheet music paper and everything) when I was about eight or nine years old.

Do you remember your first song? Care to share some of the lyrics? What inspired that first song or your first piece of creative writing?

I do remember my first song, and the song is actually really pathetic. It was basically about having a "Happy Morning," (which is the song's title). I'm too embarrassed to share any of the lyrics, but my mom and I still sing the song all the time around the house as a joke!

Was songwriting your first creative outlet or was it another style of writing? Or another art form?

Songwriting was indeed my first creative outlet. I remember as a young preteen/teenager, I had a whole collection of notebooks and diaries absolutely filled with songs that I had written.

Do other forms of artistic expression and/or life experience influence your songwriting?

My songs are definitely influenced by life experience. Whatever I'm going through or experiencing at the time, instead of talking to somebody about it, since I'm not much of a "feeling-sharer," I'll write a song about it. It's my form of therapy.

Influences—who influenced or encouraged your writing—which songwriters, other artists, teachers or mentors, loved ones?

I grew up listening to a lot of James Taylor, Billy Joel and the Beatles, so they all became artists who I really admired and who influenced my songwriting a great deal. I love the stories that they tell through their music. As for current artists, Sara Bareilles, Ed Sheeran and John Mayer all have very poetic and metaphorical writing styles that I admire a lot and try to emulate.

What do you do to develop your craft?

I try to take note of how current songs are being written, how songs from the past were written and take the little bits and pieces that I like from both and incorporate them into my own writing, all while still remaining true to who I am as an artist. Co-writing, especially with people who have been writing songs professionally for a while, is also a really good way of improving your craft. You're really able to learn the ins and the outs of how a good song is put together that way.

Tell us about your mentoring experience with our contest mentor, Luba.

My mentoring experience with Luba was awesome! It was great to talk with someone who has been in the business for so long and hear her stories of when she was just starting out as an artist. She gave me a lot of really good advice, as well as many kind words about the song I had entered, and I left the mentoring session feeling really encouraged and motivated!

How will Luba's guidance inform your future songwriting?

Luba basically told me to keep doing what I'm doing, which was really encouraging to hear. I will definitely take her advice to heart and just keep writing and trying to improve my craft along the way.

What advice do you have for new songwriters?

Just write and write often! Write about anything and everything. Also, learning your strengths and weaknesses as a songwriter is really important so that you're able to highlight the strengths and work to improve upon those weaknesses.

Visit Rebekah's website at www.rebekahstevensmusic.com.

Advice from the Music Industry

Interview with Music Manager, Maurice Laurin

The Role of an Artist Manager

Maurice Laurin is a music manager and executive based out of Ottawa, with over 17 years of music business history. Throughout the years, he has been credited with management, development, consulting and shopping of a bevy of talent, including Melanie Durrant, Tone Mason, Arthur McArthur, Midi Mafia, Frank Dukes, Mims and Boi-1da, to name a few. He's been involved in projects for artists such as Drake, Jay Z, Kelly Rowland, Big Boi, Tyga, Nas, Rick Ross, Ludacris, 50 Cent, Fantasia and others. Many of those records have gone on to achieve gold and platinum status. Maurice has also negotiated and secured major publishing deals for several of his clients. He is also co-owner of Canada's most recognized online source for hip-hop culture, HipHopCanada.com.

~~~

You are involved with HipHopCanada.com and manage R&B/soul and hip-hop artists and producers. What's new and promising in this genre, particularly in Canada?

As a co-owner at HipHopCanada.com, I'm always coming across great untapped, homegrown talent throughout the country, from east to west. I've had some amazing success doing management for over a decade, and in the last few years, I've witnessed winning stories like

Drake, The Weeknd, Melanie Fiona, Classified, K'naan and a host of others. I can attest to the fact that more eyes are on Canada than ever before, and it certainly doesn't stop with artists alone. We have a new generation of young producers like Boi-1da, Noah "40" Shebib and T-Minus, who have helped expand the awareness of Canadian producers on an international scale. I speak with many high-level executives on a daily basis and one of the common questions I'm asked is, "Who's the next big superstar or producer from Canada?" People around the world are interested in what we have to offer. It's definitely a promising time for our young, up-and-coming talent.

What are the challenges and rewards of being an artist manager?

In my case, the challenges I face differ depending on the client. When it comes to an artist, the challenges can be a wide variety of things— from finding the right producers/co-writers for a Melanie Durrant project, to gaining proper radio support in the Canadian market, to getting booked on the right tours and other key events necessary to showcase your artist on the main stage, these challenges can all be complicated at times. The challenges are different for a music producer who creates the backdrop for your favourite songs. Sonically, things change from time to time, and one of the biggest challenges I face working with my producers is finding that balance between creative freedom and staying current with the trends. It's very important to find that balance in order to stay true to the producer's vision, but it's just as important to be able to sell their product to a potential artist.

As for the rewards, I would say one of the ultimate rewards that each of my clients share is the recognition—or, more importantly, the appreciation—received from the fans and the public. Even as a manager, I always get a rush when something I've been a part of is well received and people genuinely love the music. It makes you want to continue on.

What makes a good relationship between an artist and his/her manager?

I have amazing loyalty with my clients and the only way it works for us is by teamwork, communication, honesty and education. I refuse to be the type of manager who keeps my clients in the dark in order to be in control. I know too many stories of artists who were not savvy enough to know what they were walking into and ultimately regretted the scenario they became stuck in. Besides helping them be creative, it's so important to cultivate your clients and help them grow on the business level so they'll be better prepared to understand the basics of how the music industry works. It makes them better decision-makers with the choices and options that come across the table throughout their careers.

When is a new artist ready for management? How can he/she find a manager?

In my opinion, an artist needs to be patient and take the time to develop. They need to understand who they are and what their vision is. Hit the local circuit, try to meet people in the music industry and get some constructive criticism before you rush to find management. Once you've tested the waters, be honest with yourself, and you should be able to know if you're ready or not. It's also important to take your time when choosing a manager. Ask questions and do your research on any candidate that you're looking at. And be careful about filling that important role with a "friend" or "family member" who really doesn't have the necessary experience for the task at hand.

How do you find new talent?

Experienced managers search and find talent everywhere. From YouTube, to word of mouth, to competitions, to talent shows, to websites like HipHopCanada.com, I've found talent in many places. I met Canadian producer Arthur McArthur through an online beat contest when he was about 18 years old and have represented him since 2007. Another example: one of my business partners found a young singer named B Smyth on YouTube and went on to sign him through a worldwide deal with Motown/Universal in New York. In this age of technology and social media, if you create the awareness, people will find you.

Reprint, originally published in Ottawa Life Magazine, December 5, 2013, interview by Heidi Stock, www.ottawalife.com/2013/12/the-role-of-an-artist-manager-an-interview-with-maurice-laurin/

CONVERSATION WITH VOCAL TEACHER, RYAN LUCHUCK

Maximize Your Voice and Your Potential

Photo and biography courtesy of Ryan Luchuck

Ryan Luchuck is one of Canada's busiest voice instructors, balancing a roster of over 200 students. After fixing his own vocal limitations, he developed a passion for teaching others.

Ryan has studied intensively with some of the most highly regarded vocal instructors in the world. He has been mentored closely by highly respected Hollywood voice coach, Dave Stroud (www. davestroud.com) since 1997. Despite his success, Ryan has never stopped his quest for the most up-to-date, cutting edge knowledge of the voice. Most recently, he has studied vocal science and anatomy with Dr. Ingo Titze (www.ncvs.org) and breathing coordination with Robin De Haas (www.breathingcoordination.ch). He holds an outstanding background as an early Certified Speech Level Singing

(SLS) Instructor (2006–2011), having also held a post as a prestigious SLS Education Advisory Group (EAG) member.

Ryan's clients include Juno, SOCAN and Gemini award–winning artists and musical theatre stage leads. His ability to quickly diagnose singers of all styles and provide them with a clear, logical path to success has been the key to his phenomenal success.

In addition to his mastery of vocal technique, Ryan has travelled nationally as a performing songwriter, released two critically acclaimed CDs and logged over 2,000 performances as a musician and singer. An exceptional instrumentalist, he has worked professionally on piano, guitar, bass guitar, double bass, trumpet and drums, in addition to his work as a singer. He also serves as an orchestral arranger and studio producer for many of his clients.

Most recently, Ryan helped to create Vocology in Practice (ViP), an international organization of voice instructors committed to maintaining the highest standards in voice instruction (www. vocologyinpractice.com). He has also been working hard on the development of his own unique training system, MusoVox, which combines his expertise in technique with a more musical, fun approach.

www.ownyourvoice.com

~~~

Heidi: What was your path to teaching and mentoring?

Ryan: For me, it started because I had so many problems with my voice. So I had to work very, very hard to get my voice up to a point where I could go out and work professionally. I did that for a long time. I had studied so hard on my voice and watching my teacher as a mentor to me, it was always just in the back of my mind that maybe someday I would do this, too. Then, for about five, six years of doing music as my main living, I felt at a little bit of a standstill. I had invested so much money in trying to get my music career off the ground and I was a little frustrated about playing in bars all the time. I thought, well, maybe now is the time to try it. I started doing it and I *loved* it. In a lot of ways, I actually enjoy it more than performing. So that was kind of the path. It took a lot longer than that for it to gradually happen.

Heidi: That can be a kind of natural evolution, too, right— starting out as a singer–songwriter and performer and then mentoring?

Ryan: Yeah, I think a lot of us go in that direction. I know for me it was very obvious when I started doing it that if you believe in fate or direction of the universe or that sort of thing, as soon as I did it, things came so easily to me. Whereas everything in trying to build a career in music was a massive struggle. So it was just sort of inevitable that as soon as I opened my doors to accept students, it didn't take long. In about a year, I was almost full. Obviously, there was something about the set of skills I had that I could really help people, whereas I was struggling to compete out in the artist world with people who might have had a better voice than me, or were more charismatic on stage, or whatever. I was doing okay, obviously—I was making a living—but that was *so* much harder than going behind the scenes. I realized that my skill set is more valuable behind the scenes than as a front guy.

Heidi: On your website, you list singing myths, including the myth that only a chosen few are blessed with the ability to sing. Is it true that everyone can sing or learn to sing better?

Ryan: Well, certainly the second part of that question is true. A hundred percent. Everybody can get better. I've never worked with anybody who, if they properly applied their time, hasn't improved a lot. Definitely, some people are more gifted than others. There's no question. Not everybody necessarily has the ability to be a *great* singer, but I think that most people, if they apply themselves, can be decent. The thing that a lot of people don't realize is that we're using our instruments so far below their potential. Even for people who are great singers, they make a great sound, but they could be so much more if they took the time to learn how to maximize what they have. If you think about it that way, if the average person is using maybe 30 to 35% of their potential, well that's a lot. They can still get a lot of juice out of the instrument. So back to your question, yeah, I think that's true. I've yet to see somebody who really applied himself or herself who didn't become decent; let's put it that way.

Heidi: With those singers who we would call naturally talented, is it genetics, mechanics? Is it that their instrument is just constructed that way, or is it an ability to hear music and replicate it?

Ryan: It's all those things. You can look at artists and see how they can be gifted in different areas. Some people have incredibly flexible instruments but are somewhat disadvantaged when it comes to their ability to hear music, and that can be a different kind of dilemma. Then you have people who are incredibly musically gifted with very little genetic ability to sing. If you had to choose between the two, I'd probably choose #2 because I've seen people with very flexible instruments but their innate understanding and their ability to get music is something that they're going to have to work very, very hard on. I'd rather be someone that's naturally gifted musically than someone who isn't musically gifted but doesn't have to work hard on their voice. There are artists who seemingly have it all, you know, like a Michael Jackson or someone like that, who has this incredible musical sense with the gymnastic voice to go with it.

But there are a lot of really successful artists who we love who didn't have a lot of natural vocal co-ordination but used what they had to incredible effect—David Bowie, for example. You would never say that he was the most skilled singer in the world from a purely physiological point of view. He didn't have as much range as a lot of people. In terms of frequency, there was tension in his voice, but he was much more effective than a lot of singers because he was incredible at communicating emotion and he made a great sound.

Heidi: Why is voice training important for new songwriters like myself who may prefer to be behind the scenes and not sing or perform their own songs?

Ryan: Well, you could certainly make the argument that it isn't, but it's so competitive now that I think you have to give yourself every advantage, and for you, as an up-and-coming songwriter, it's about presenting your material. I mean, let's face it, right, the best tasting cake with ugly icing, people are not going to gravitate toward that. They're not going to try it. You could have the greatest song but if it's not performed well, very few people can hear through that kind of unsophisticated performance. So if you become a relatively good singer, and you're trying out your songs on people, they're automatically going to think they're better songs.

There are artists who do a lot of songwriting and are then able to launch careers. Carole King is a famous one. When they talk about Carole King's demos for her songs, artists used to say her demos were really intimidating because the vocal on them is so good, but at the same time, the fact that the vocal was so good put across the song. It's all about first impressions.

The other side of it—it's going to save you a lot of money and hassle. Instead of having to hire demo singers and find the right one, you become the demo singer. I also think we tend to write, for the most part, with the exception of someone like a Burt Bacharach, what we can sing. So you're going to probably write better and more interesting melodies if you can walk through a lot of different pitches.

I think it's just as simple as, the better the song sounds in every way, the better your chances. So if you're a sloppy guitar player and you're out there performing a song, people aren't going to think it's that good. Any musical ability you can bring to the table increases your odds, even if you have no intention whatsoever of being the performer.

Heidi: Moving on to performance, what are common hesitations or fears about performing?

Ryan: If you don't do a lot of performing, in general, it's extremely nerve-wracking. The voice is very sensitive to people, you know. People feel that their voice *is* themselves. When you get on stage to sing, it's very naked, you feel vulnerable and people really do, deep down, feel that if their voice is rejected, they're rejected. I think getting on stage and singing for people is much more difficult for the most part than getting on stage and playing guitar or any other instrument.

I think people also have unrealistic expectations in the beginning. They put a lot of pressure on themselves to be very advanced performers way too soon. Part of the issue is that we don't have a lot of outlets. We don't have a lot of opportunities to get on stage in a supportive environment where you feel you can fall flat on your face and there's no consequence to it. So for a lot of people, the first time performing is at an open mic, and that's nerve-wracking. There are a lot of people there you don't know, you might be waiting around for three hours to get on stage, and it plays right into your nerves. It's really common. The solution is to find as supportive an environment as you can and then do it *a lot.* That's the other thing—people never realize how many times professional performers have been on stage before they get to that level, and 99.9% of the time, it's hundreds and hundreds of times.

Heidi: I liked what you said about being a vocal performer. I can see now, with having played an instrument as a child and being on stage, I'm behind the instrument—I'm not the instrument. But as the vocalist, I *am* the instrument.

Ryan: You are the instrument, yeah, and it's very hard to separate psychologically.

Heidi: What's the difference between a good performance and a great performance?

Ryan: A great performance has an element of transcendence. It goes beyond a sort of perfunctory phoning in of something's that been rehearsed hundreds of times and it's very much in the moment. You can tell. Certain singers do it. Adam Duritz from Counting Crows is a good example of someone whose performance is a little different every night and you really feel that he's completely into it 100%. To me, that's a great performance. When I walk out of there feeling, "Wow, I was really touched by what that singer was communicating," that's different from, "Wow, they sang the song very well."

Frankly, and this might be controversial to some people, but I think a lot of times, especially when you're dealing with star performers—celebrity performers—there's a lot more good performances than great performances because they're on tour, they're doing it a thousand times. The element of celebrity gives them a pass on a lot of things because we go to the concert and we say "Wow, that sounds just like whoever," and we're pleased to be in the same room with them, so they get away with murder sometimes. But everyone's mileage varies. What I think is a decent performance versus a great performance could be totally different from someone else.

Interview with TV & Film Composer, Daniel Ingram

Photo and biography courtesy of Daniel Ingram

Daniel Ingram is a multi–award winning and four-time Emmy nominated composer/songwriter, whose unique and versatile approach to music has established him as one of the most identifiable voices in animation and family television. He has been featured in Rolling Stone and has had seven Top-10 Billboard-charting children's soundtracks released on iTunes, with over 1 million downloads to date.

Daniel's songs and underscore can be heard in 180 countries worldwide, on such popular family shows as *My Little Pony: Friendship is Magic, Equestria Girls, Littlest Pet Shop, Pound Puppies, Martha Speaks, Kate & Mim-Mim, Dr. Dimensionpants,* Universal's *Nina's World* and soon-to-be-released Netflix original, *Lalaloopsy.*

Daniel is one of the most active composers in the children's/family songwriting business. He has received over 250 song commissions including eight television theme songs in the past seven years, some of which have attracted over 100 million views on YouTube, as well as thousands of cover videos by fans of all ages. In addition to being a prolific songwriter, Daniel has scored over 300 episodes of animated television.

Daniel is currently writing songs and score for his first wide-release animated feature film, *My Little Pony: The Movie*, for Lionsgate/ Hasbro Studios, which is scheduled for release in October 2017. He and his team are based in Vancouver, B.C.

~~~

Heidi: What was your path to becoming a composer/songwriter for animation and children's television? What are some of the challenges and rewards of writing for this audience?

Daniel: Honestly, I didn't actually plan to work in animation, although coincidentally, if you asked me what I wanted to be as a kid, I would have said, "an animator" because I loved cartoons so much. I studied music as a teenager and followed through to university, where I completed my degree in music composition. I gravitated toward "interdisciplinary" projects and scored modern dance, theatre and film projects in my 20s.

It wasn't until 10 years later, in my early 30s, that a chance meeting with veteran Vancouver-based film composer Hal Beckett led me to an apprenticeship in music for TV and film. Among other things, Hal had scored hundreds of locally produced cartoon episodes. I was mesmerized by the process and liked the humour of the genre. He showed me the ropes and encouraged me, when opportunities came up, to score my own projects. Within a few years, I was scoring shows out of my home studio in Vancouver. Now things have really grown, and I have a professional studio space downtown, with a fantastic team working alongside me. Life can be so unpredictably serendipitous!

As you see with Disney, Pixar, Dreamworks or a host of other top-tier animation companies, family entertainment doesn't necessarily mean childish or simplistic. The challenge in writing songs and music in this genre is to keep it sophisticated enough to appeal to all ages, while not alienating young kids by going over their heads. On *My Little Pony*, this balance worked out very well, and I think the majority of feedback I get is actually from teens to adults, who appreciate the music despite its perceived audience being much younger.

Heidi: Which artists have inspired and influenced your songwriting?

Daniel: I've always found the idea of influences hard to quantify. I mean, in my teens I listened to the Beatles, Led Zeppelin and Jimi Hendrix. I studied 20th-century classical composition in my 20s and listened to just about everything under the sun in my 30s, including a lot of Broadway musical theatre. Each song commission I get is like an assignment, usually with pretty specific parameters around how it needs to sell a product or tell a story. I'll usually do research and then follow my gut instincts. In animation, you explore every genre of music under the sun, so you're constantly drawing upon a lifetime of listening to music. At the end of the day, though, I try to infuse a unique and personal voice into the DNA of everything I write, regardless of the genre.

Heidi: What role has collaboration with fellow musicians and artists played in your career? What advice from collaborators or mentors do you still follow today?

Daniel: I've always been a big fan of collaborating. In the case of songwriting, that might come in the form of co-writing the lyrics with a scriptwriter or working with a third party to orchestrate or produce a song that I wrote the chords and melody to. I think if I did everything single-handedly from start to finish I would have burned out years ago, and my music would have long since become repetitive. Instead, collaboration pushes you to grow and develop as an artist and also just gives your music a chance to live up to its full potential.

For example, I'm a mediocre guitarist at best, but I can hack out some chords. After writing a pop song, I might bring in a super creative, pro guitarist who'll hear what I did and add their spin on it, taking it to the next level. It makes the whole process so much more exciting and satisfying. As far as advice goes, I would say, don't be ashamed to leave some space in your art for pleasant surprises to happen, because a singer, or an arranger, or another musician might have an idea you didn't think of that really completes it.

Heidi: Increasingly, over the past decade, songwriters have been encouraged to seek placement of their music in film and television to gain exposure and another source of income. What advice do you have for songwriters pursuing this?

Daniel: This isn't an area I've had much experience in because all the work I've done has been on a commission basis, but I do have some opinions on it. If you're a singer/songwriter and you've got your own sound and write the music you want to write, and it gets placed in a movie, that's awesome! I mean, it's free money! But I know musicians who spend all their time writing songs in various genres solely in hopes of getting a placement. There are library companies that gather up this kind of music for pennies on the dollar. This feels like selling out to me. You're spending all of your time creating a one-off product in hopes that someone somewhere will want it one day, and it's usually for very little money. Like with stocks, it's hard to predict the next trend in music, so usually these libraries are behind the curve anyway. If you're writing music and don't have commissions, then find some— score student films, amateur theatre or dance productions, etc. If you're a band or a singer/songwriter, focus on your art and your audience. The rest will come naturally. If you're good, your management team can worry about the placements.

Heidi: What upcoming projects are you excited about?

Daniel: I'm excited to be writing songs and score on a new Netflix original series, *Lalaloopsy*, produced by MGA. I'm also very excited to be writing songs and score on the *My Little Pony* feature film, scheduled to release in October 2017, where I've had the opportunity to work with some fantastic Hollywood talent.

Songwriting: Articles and Essays

Aspiring Canadian Writers Contests Co-Partners with Songwriters Association of Canada to Launch the 2014 Singer–Songwriter Mentor Experience

by Juliette Jagger

Aspiring Canadian Writers Contests Inc., founders of the Aspiring Canadian Poets Contest, recently announced an opportunity for unsigned singer–songwriters across the country, through the creation of the 2014 Singer–Songwriter Mentor Experience.

With support from the Songwriters Association of Canada, the contest has been designed to provide the winning songwriters with mentoring sessions from acclaimed singer–songwriters, in hopes of building a foundation for and nurturing the abilities of our homegrown talent.

"Like our annual poetry contest, what I'm trying to do is offer aspiring artists, in this case, unsigned singer–songwriters, an experience and an opportunity to learn from industry professionals," says Heidi Stock, founder of Aspiring Canadian Writers Contests Inc.

Heidi has modelled the 2014 Singer–Songwriter Mentor Experience after the Aspiring Canadian Poets Contest, which just completed its second year. The songwriting contest will run for one year only.

249

"The top three winners of our poetry contest won online mentoring sessions from a published poet," says Heidi. "We got a great response from unpublished poets and the writing community in general. So, being that music has inspired a lot of my own poetry, I thought it would be rewarding to apply that same model to a singer–songwriter contest."

The contest, which opens October 8 and runs until December 22, 2013, or until 300 eligible entries are received, will be judged by a panel of singer–songwriters, including: Lesley Pike (Gibson's featured artist at the 2013 Sundance London film and music festival), Luther Mallory (former frontman of Crush Luther), Katie Rox (former lead singer of Jakalope), Melanie Durrant (2013 Juno Award–nominated artist), and Theo Tams (Gemini Award–nominated artist and 2008 *Canadian Idol* champion).

The top three grand prize–winners will receive private online songwriting mentoring sessions with multiple Juno Award–winning artist Luba, personalized social media promotion on behalf of the judges and mentor, and annual memberships to the Songwriters Association of Canada (which will be awarded to all top-25 finalists). The first-place winner will also receive a one-hour, one-on-one music industry mentoring session with semi-finalist judge Luther Mallory, who is a band coach and cofounder of the independent record label, Daycare Records.

When asked about the importance of mentoring new talent, specifically in the digital age, Luther had this to say: "Every artist that comes online as soon as they record their first demo has intensified the signal to noise ratio problem our industry has always dealt with. A lot of bad, a tiny bit of great. Endless, non-stop noise and just a little bit of signal. But that signal is the great, well-crafted, well-performed music out in the digital sea. Mentorship and instruction from someone knowledgeable about professional standards is a way for an artist to fast track their progress and hopefully improve to the point where they can break through the noise."

When asked about his hopes for both the contestants and the mentor experience alike, Luther expressed this sentiment: "Any initiative that works to help the creative community by encouraging artists to improve and progress belongs in the world. My hope for the contestants is that this contest brings them steps closer to understanding who they are as artists. Understanding that more fully will bring them closer to making important music. That's all we want to make and that's all we want to hear."

Reprint, originally published in A Journal of Musical Things on October 7, 2013. http://ajournalofmusicalthings.com/aspiring-canadian-writers-contests-co-partners-with-songwriters-association-of-canada-to-launch-the-2014-singer-songwriter-mentor-experience/

Juliette Jagger juliettejagger.com/

Collaboration, The Live Show, Your Music: Hobby or Business

by Luther Mallory

Photo courtesy of Luther Mallory

Collaboration—Don't Be Precious.

Collaboration is a tough skill to develop. Especially because artists think they need no help and because they feel that no one could possibly add value to their vision.

The first co-write I ever did was useless, and it was my fault. I couldn't part with my ideas. I couldn't relax my artistic ego enough to realize that collaboration works only when you don't judge ideas.

You can scrap ideas after they've been seen through, but you can't say no to someone else's idea before you've given some energy to developing it and finding out if it's worth something. It takes a bit of musical/life maturity to really practically realize that there are other creative people who know more than you about a particular skill you need to complete your project.

Often, you'll fall short of professional quality if you insist on doing everything yourself. Then you risk being that artist who proudly states, "I do everything myself," and everybody can tell because the mix and the drums sound terrible because you can't have all the skills! Look at creative collaboration as outsourcing for the skills you don't have or you need help with.

Resist the urge to feel like co-writing or sharing credit diminishes your involvement in your art. It doesn't make you less important to the art, and it doesn't make it less yours. Mostly, collaboration works like asking your friend for relationship advice. You can't see your terrible relationship for what it is because you've been living in a bubble, asking and answering your own questions and buying your own delusions about how it's going and what should happen next.

Then you ask your friend, who has no emotional obligation to your relationship, what he thinks and he tells you exactly what has been absolutely true all along. Your relationship is terrible but you were too close to see it. Your song might also be terrible; some outside input could easily make it great.

The many artists who resist collaboration for fear of losing the illusion of control over the art, or for fear of devaluing the art by sharing the credit, needs only to look at the most acclaimed artists in history to see that teamwork is exactly how they achieved that acclaim. Very few world-class artists are doing it alone.

Michael Jackson had Quincy Jones and co-wrote almost everything, sometimes even accepting songs with no writing credit. Nobody ever cared, because his artistic and expressive skills meant more to people than the fact that he didn't have skills as a mix engineer, or as a sole writer, or as a bass player.

253

Spend energy mastering the skills you're gifted at and that you love. Outsource the rest to people who understand it better than you and the project will be better and sound more professional. Don't be precious. It's a waste of time and a missed opportunity to learn from another artist.

Your Music—Hobby or Business?

Music and business: a critical formula. The dream for every musician is this—a career making music instead of a career working a "real" job. That's it. Not all musicians think it's possible, but that is the hope for all musicians.

That word *career* can be fairly solidly defined as something you spend time at that makes you money. That money is what musicians are after. Money is the thing that would make it possible for them to turn music into a career—the dream.

Fans. A fan of your band is a potential source of revenue for your band. In order to make a fan, one simple thing has to occur and if it doesn't, making a fan is impossible: you must share your music—your product.

People who have never heard your music won't buy it. A person must hear your music and like it enough to become a fan who's willing to spend money to support what you do—buy a shirt, come to a show, buy an album, pay into your crowdfunding and so on.

You did all the things—record, play live, print albums, print shirts, make a website—and now you're out there sharing. Are they buying? Are you making fans who are spending money? Probably not enough yet to reach the dream.

The problem: business. We get great at making music and neglect getting great at doing business. But we've determined that the formula relies on both music and business to reach the dream.

Making music is a hobby. Making money making music is a business. Business, as we've determined, is the only way to get a career. So that makes business at least as important as music in the equation.

Sharing isn't enough. How many times have you driven by a storefront and thought "Why is this a business? Who opened a store dedicated to handmade rubber ducks? How could it possibly be making money?"

It's not. This person simply had an idea, got it ready and shared it. This person rented the storefront, made all the ducks, built the website and put an 'open' sign on the door. Starting a business doesn't automatically make it a good business idea, or a smart one.

Sharing an idea doesn't automatically mean people will want to invest in it. If you play a show on a stage and 30 people are there, none of those people are obligated to become your fan, even though you've shared your product with them.

You have to do something more than share. You have to do what successful businesses do: sell. But sales is hard and feels a bit scummy.

Making music is fun, and it requires no courage. You write it on your bed; you practice it with your friends in your jam space. It's totally safe.

Selling your music requires a lot of courage. You have to talk to people, shoulder criticism, call industry people for advice and help, promote the show and adjust strategies when something isn't working. This is what entrepreneurs do. It's a life dedicated to learning and adjusting strategies, not just creating and sharing.

Musicians want to think it's only about music, but if we agree that the dream is a career making music, and we agree that it will require doing business to make that career happen, then we can no longer ignore what is fundamentally missing—business.

THE LIVE SHOW IS THE KEY TO SUCCESS

The live show is everything. You can prove your value on the stage, and it's real, in front of real people. Yet artists still talk about royalties, and record sales, and publishing as the things to chase after—as if getting a song in the background of one scene of *Big Bang Theory* will scale into success.

Nothing is certain because there are too many factors. Too much has changed, but not enough artists have adjusted. The industry has no money to develop artists so it doesn't. The solution for the industry is to wait for artists to prove themselves before it offers real help to them. Artists have to show the industry that they can interest a market.

The only control an artist has, and the way to interest that market, is to make the live show undeniable. If the live show is amazing and the music is great, the audience will respond and that will build a fan base.

What is superior about music fans is they have no investment in the artistic process or the industry—they only care about what tickles their ears and what moves them. They are purists. It's about a feeling for music fans; it's about statistics for the industry. But the statistic the industry is after is how many music fans are feeling the music. So the fans tell the industry who is good. The industry always believes the numbers.

And the fans won't become fans if your song is on *Big Bang Theory*, because it's buried behind the dialogue track and people are too lazy to look it up on Google anyway. But at the live show, you have a chance to focus an audience and capture them. They are waiting to be electrified—all you have to do is take the chance.

Taking the chance means building the skills until you're a master. Study songwriting, instrumentation and stage performance until you're a master. You know you're a master when the audience starts responding and then showing up at more than one show. Don't be fooled thinking that if the audience cheers or compliments you, you've made it. They have to come back. If they come back, then it means you've got enough for them to re-dedicate energy into sourcing you out again to having another experience with your music.

Skill building isn't the hard part, though. The hard part is facing the judging eyes of the audience and having the guts enough to pull off your vision in front of them, knowing they might not think you're cool. It's a risk.

If you're creative, you can dream up a great show, and you can improve it based on how your audience is responding. But getting the grit together enough to actually pull off what you've dreamed up is the hard part. The practical application of the vision is where artists fall short. It's easy to decide you're going to jump off the drum kit into the audience at the next show, but when the time comes, and it's time to do it, you don't. Not usually.

All music fans and audience members want at a show is to see somebody let go and show them something fearless. As artists, achieving that level of self-expression and fearlessness is near impossible—there is so much risk. But, we know that we could succeed if we could master the skills and present that to them fearlessly.

The work must be done and not underestimated, because the live show is the key to success. The live show is in our control. The live show can make us fans. And if the live show is great, the fan base will grow. If you can bring 300 people out to a show in your town, the industry will see value and become interested.

Then you get to decide if you need the industry's help at all. Forget about royalties and publishing for now; put your focus on mastering your skills and then making sure the live show is undeniable.

Visit Luther's website at www.luthermalloryproductions.com.

MENTOR ME: AN INSIDE VIEW OF SESSIONS WITH SINGER–SONGWRITER, LUTHER MALLORY

by Heidi Stock

This is the second inside view of mentoring sessions in this book. It is literally, "mentor *me*," as I am the student. These sections are included in the anthology to give the reader a sense of the experience and benefits of one-on-one mentoring with a poet, songwriter, screenwriter or producer. They are meant to give the reader a sense of what private mentoring sessions may be like for you. Every mentor and every student is as unique as the relationship between them.

GETTING STARTED: POEM TO LYRICS

My goal in my one-on-one singer–songwriter mentoring sessions was to turn one of my poems into lyrics and then a song. I had hope! Some songwriters begin their creative journey as poets before they start writing songs, and I routinely referred to one of my poems, "Your Eyes On Me (Boy)," as a song. That poem is in fact based on the structure of a song that happens to have verses and no chorus.

I wanted to start my first session with my mentor, Luther Mallory, by sharing two poems that I thought had a good chance of becoming song lyrics: "Your Eyes on Me (Boy)," mentioned above, and "Mirror Mirror." In determining which poem we would choose for my exercise in poem to lyrics, Luther had a look at both.

Here's what I learned from Luther: "There's better structure in "Your Eyes on Me (Boy)" in the lyrical repetition. Lots of lines repeating (the first, third and last line repeat in each stanza). Perhaps determine what could be a chorus in this lyric set, too. That will get us closer to an answer about which poem is the one. Obviously neither needs a chorus, but for the exercise, it will be helpful to see what might work."

Here's stanza 1 (or potentially verse 1) of "Your Eyes on Me (Boy)":

Your Eyes on Me (Boy)

Your eyes on me, boy

50-something boy

I can feel them.

New face on the train

Hair swept, unkept again

but you're gazing still.

The skinny jeans teen on my left turns,

now I can see that it's actually me.

You see me.

The other poem-to-lyrics option was my poem, "Mirror Mirror."

Mirror, Mirror

Inside out, this black cashmere sweater

and now the words I can't contain.

Fine lines surfaced and without permission

tattooed my face --

259

inking squints, smirks, and smiles.

Years of emotion engraved.

I am 40. Inside out, disoriented, exposed.

So I apply, morning and night, as directed,

filling cracks, trying to remove tracks

but the inner self, stubborn,

won't be masked anymore.

It refuses treatment,

locks the bathroom door, intervenes,

leaving me, face to face with myself.

But upon closer examination,

these are expression lines.

Powerful, potent, they won't shut up.

Confident, curvy, they are as sexy as

an Etta tune, a bare midnight sky,

a treasured truffle savoured slowly,

as sexy as the word itself.

I mentioned to Luther that the structure of "Your Eyes on Me (Boy)" was inspired by the untraditional song structure of the Alanis Morissette song, "Unsent," which I found incredibly interesting as a song (it has five verses and no chorus). It can easily be structured as a poem, which obviously never has a chorus.

Luther said to consider the following about lyric writing: "You have words, melody and rhythm, melody being the new guy here since you're used to poetry. Alanis and Peter Gabriel have a good knack for ignoring the rhythmic part and shoving words in wherever they want and it still connects. Bob Dylan, too. Consider the following methods."

Two Lyric-Writing Methods

Lyric writers often start with a melodic and rhythmic pattern. They determine the pitches and the pitch durations without using words, like in the "Na na na" part of "Hey Jude," and then imagine that as the rough draft of the melody before words are written to replace the Na na nas.

Another common way is to write the words (as you have with "Mirror Mirror") and then try to figure out how they fit into a melodic and rhythmic pattern.

A pop or country song will rarely take the second approach because so much about those styles of music rely on simple, repeating patterns to stick in the brain of the listener. So it's more important to have consistency in the melody and rhythm that someone will remember than it is to convey an important lyrical message that compromises the stiff structural idea.

Have a look at the song, "Mercy Street," as another example—along with "Unsent"—of a song that doesn't have to rhyme or follow a very structured pattern to work. The punishment becomes a more lyric-focused song that won't be such an instantly recognizable song to the listener. And that's okay!

On the other hand, have a listen to a very structured pop melody like "Roar," by Katy Perry, that does not leave the box for the function of staying completely easy to consume.

There are, of course, songs that live in between the structured and the unstructured. Have a listen and a think on these ideas. Then we'll get into where we want to go with these poems!

NEXT STEPS, NEXT SESSION

I have to say, listening to music as homework wasn't work at all! I listened to "Mercy Street" and "Roar," while weighing my options for which poem of mine to use, and I got back in touch with Luther for another discussion.

Here's how it went.

Heidi: There is a hint to the style that could be used for my poem, "Mirror Mirror," in my line about an Etta tune. That's for Etta James. I wonder if it's possible for "Mirror Mirror" to be in that genre—R&B/soul. When I thought of turning the poem into song lyrics, I thought that Etta line was very fortunate. Considering chord progression for blues compositions was as far as I got with that idea. Over the past few months, too, I see it as a piece within a play, being sung by an actress. I don't know if these thoughts help. Any thoughts on the ease of turning "Mirror Mirror's" lines into song lyrics and what genre the theme and the structure would fit?

"Your Eyes on Me (Boy)," as a poem or future song lyrics, needs cleaning up. If it was unstructured (no chorus added), like the Alanis song "Unsent" that inspired it, it could be really interesting but a big challenge. What do you think?

Luther: "Mirror, Mirror" may work as a soul song. These are your next steps. In the spirit of poetry, spot where potential rhymes, even soft rhymes, may exist within the stanzas of "Mirror Mirror." This may give us an anchor to some melodic structure, even if it's loose.

Also, determine what the point of the song is. We're searching for the "hook," here. Look at verses as the details of the story, and the chorus as the big point—the line that generalizes the story down to one fine point. These ideas can stay interpretive, as they do in "Mercy Street," or become completely obvious like in "Roar."

Let's break down "Roar":

The verses do the "I used to..." repetition thing—the details of a story about how she used to act. She's got a pre-chorus in this song that we won't likely have, but it's an option. The function of the pre-chorus is to transition us into the chorus. Her pre-chorus documents her becoming this stronger woman. It's no longer "I used to this or that"—now she's singing about recovering strength. It's her climb to the chorus, both musically and emotionally in the lyrics.

The chorus is the triumph. That's the point we're after in the song. It's a metaphor, obviously, and it works as the point and also as a great hook.

So, although it seems "Mirror Mirror" is already more interpretive, determine the possible structural anchors and the hook that might be the big point of the song.

FINDING THE HOOK

Below is my review of "Mirror Mirror," which includes my first attempt at a chorus, based on what I feel is—as Luther said—"the big point of the song." "Mirror Mirror" was in fact always the title of the poem, without the word mirror ever being mentioned in the poem.

HEIDI STOCK

Mirror, Mirror

Verse 1

Inside out, this black cashmere sweater

and now the words I can't contain.

Fine lines surfaced and without permission

tattooed my skin --

Years of emotion engraved.

I am 40, disoriented,

exposed.

Chorus:

Mirror mirror

Tell me the truth

Am I beautiful now

or in my youth?

Mirror mirror

I confess

I'm searching for

my happiness.

Verse 2

So I apply, morning and night, as directed,

filling cracks, trying to remove tracks

but the inner self, stubborn,

won't be masked anymore.

It refuses treatment,

locks the bathroom door, intervenes,

leaving me, face to face with myself.

Chorus:

Mirror mirror

Tell me the truth

Am I beautiful now

or in my youth?

Mirror mirror

I confess

I'm searching for

my happiness.

Verse 3

But upon closer examination,

these are expression lines.

Powerful, potent, they won't shut up.

Confident, curvy, they are as sexy as

an Etta tune, a bare midnight sky,

a treasured truffle savoured slowly,

as sexy as the word itself.

In creating the chorus, I thought I needed to be concise—use few words but at the same time, reveal the theme, or as Luther said, "the big point of the song."

I think the chorus hits the big point of the verses, and in the end, the verses answer the questions of the chorus.

"Am I beautiful now or in my youth" is answered in the song, and truthfully. No matter what anti-aging product is being used, the cracks (fine lines and wrinkles) aren't going away. From that realization, there is frustration and panic as she tries to run from the mirror and the truth; she tries to leave the room, but she can't.

Then, after this internal struggle, she realizes this isn't really about beauty or youth; it's a crisis of the search for happiness and what's next in life (the last half of the chorus). So in exchange for the progressive loss of traditional beauty and youth in the aging process, the cracks won't shut up and they are curvy. The trade-off in mid-life for the loss of youth is gaining confidence, being independent, speaking your mind and authentically expressing yourself. You begin to lose external youth, but you can gain sexiness through a new confidence and self-expression.

The verses are well balanced, for a poem, anyway, with seven lines each, and a similar rhythm. I made some other changes to the poem during this process.

To verse 1, I changed "tattooed my face" to "tattooed my skin" in line 4, so there is a similar sound between "skin" and "permission" in line 3. I deleted the poetic alliteration of "squints, smirks, and smiles" in line 5 because it's a tongue-twister for a singer. Line 6 replaces the deleted line 5, and I deleted the words *old* and *inside out* in line 7.

I'd like the song to end on the repetition of that last line, "as sexy as the word itself," if possible. I like the repetition of that phrase to paint a picture of the image (yes, the word sexy is sexy-looking) and the idea that what is sexy is internal, from the "inside out," through self-expression.

I sent all this to Luther in an email and at the bottom noted, "If the repetition of the last line doesn't work structurally, i.e., if a song shouldn't beat the listener over the head with the same line at the end of a song, then I'll make a change there. This was not easy!"

With relief, I hear from Luther: "The changes are working. The chorus is "dead on" for making the big point — good job! With the chorus, now, I can fully get the big idea of the song while the song remains a little interpretive, which I always like. We've got the hook/title showing up boldly with "Mirror Mirror"— bonus! The idea to vamp "as sexy as the word itself" is a cool idea. Elvis Costello uses the end-of-song repeatable line all the time, and it's not always the title or the main hook. Listen to "Alison," in which he vamps "My aim is true" forever at the end or "Watching the Detectives," where he vamps the title until it fades out."

GENRE AND AUDIENCE

Before moving forward, Luther posed two questions to me:

1. Is this song changing for you at all as far as where you see it fitting into some genre? Should it still be slow and jazzy or is it something else?

2. Who enjoys this kind of lyric set and language when they listen to music?

I responded:

Genre: Jazz/blues/soul I think makes sense because art/creativity/self-expression is an expression of the soul, and blues music is about dealing with strife, loss—even though this loss may seem trivial, but a loss of identity really isn't that trivial at all. I am open to other genres because the subject, the "I" in the lyrics and the singer of the song who appreciates "an Etta tune," doesn't have to sing in that genre. Whatever genre or genres we try for this song, I'd like to give the melody a shot. I'm still into repeating the last line of "Mirror Mirror," and I appreciate the Elvis Costello examples you gave me. Since your email, I'm noticing this technique more often, and what I like about it as a music listener is that the repetition of the last line connects the listener more to the message but also to the melody and the song overall. The listener may be singing along and may not want the song to end.

Audience: The lyrics of the song do limit the audience, limiting it to women, although men can also relate to searching for their happiness in mid-life; the chorus makes it bigger than the use of anti-aging products. I'd say the audience is mostly women, age 35+.

GIVING THE MELODY A SHOT

Taking the poem-to-lyrics exercise to the next level, melody writing, was intimidating, but I was open to it because I had a background in music in my childhood and teen years. A young brain is like a sponge, right? Something must have sunk in. In traditional music lessons like I had, in which you're learning an instrument or the theory of music, there wasn't time or the option to just sit back and create an original melody or a complete song.

The first thing I realized was that I couldn't expect a melody to just come out of me, and I wasn't willing to sit at the keyboard, pressing random keys, hoping for something to emerge. I invested in a digital recorder, hopeful that my voice rather than my keyboard would be my instrument, and it was. The creation of three melodies, just the beginning few bars of three separate songs, emerged over a short span of time, the very first of which just popped into my head while watching TV. There was melodic silence in my head for a month after my last mentoring session with Luther, but then, thankfully, three little beginnings to three future songs came to me when my mind was rested.

The intriguing and also frustrating thing about creativity is that none of these melodies were right for "Mirror Mirror." They would be stored for future use and later became my songs, "Get Gone," "Falling" and "Second Best" for a musical play (*see p.439 to read the Mentor Me: Musical Theatre essay*). Time passed and still nothing for "Mirror Mirror."

Detour!

I was stuck with no melody for "Mirror Mirror," but I continued to hum new melodies into my digital recorder. One day in my yard, tapping my foot, I came up with a melody for my future song, "Free" (*see p.439 for the Mentor Me: Musical Theatre essay*). The melody came more easily and more of it (the verse and chorus) emerged at once, followed later by the intro. I then sat down at my keyboard, sang the first note to find the first note on the keyboard and then played and recorded it.

I wanted to write a whole song. I liked this song and didn't want to leave it. Humming was my path to the melody, but nothing was happening. I knew the bridge of this song would get done only if I focused and sat myself down at my keyboard and worked through it. It wasn't fun. It brought back stressful memories of practising for music exams, but it was important enough to me to work through it.

The song got a "thumbs up" after a first listen by Luther, but it was missing a key part of its structure—its skeleton, its bones, its chords. I worried that not having studied music in a long time and not regularly playing would have brought me to a standstill. And it did.

THE SOLUTION: CO-WRITING

It was time to bring in a co-writer, and I decided to go with the third-place winner of our singer–songwriter contest, Rebekah Stevens, because she was up for the challenge and she also fulfilled the "singer" part in singer–songwriter, which I did not.

I passed along my instrumental and vocal melody, lyrics and sheet music to Rebekah. She emailed back her recording of the chords she wrote. Rebekah created the first complete demo of my song, "Free."

That demo helped me connect to other future collaborators, whom you'll read about in the Musical Theatre section of this book: musician and producer, Murray Foster (who came on as a third co-writer on "Free," reconstructing the chords on the bridge and later producing the song) and Julian Troiano, the writer of chords on the rest of my new songs. I met Julian through my voice coach, Ryan Luchuck. Realizing that I wasn't confident in my singing ability, which was so critical to communicating my songs to potential collaborators, I decided I needed to invest in voice lessons. When I mentioned my interest in songwriting to Ryan, he introduced me to Julian.

Lesson learned that, for new songwriters and all songwriters, co-writing is key. Collaboration through mentoring and co-writing is the solution!

P.S. FINAL NOTE ON "MIRROR MIRROR"

"Mirror Mirror" did find its melody, its music. It just took time. Once the melody writing flowed on other songs, a melody emerged for

"Mirror Mirror." In fact, it was the first song Julian and I collaborated on.

Honestly, the lyrics of this song are a real mishmash. I was working with an existing poem whose stanzas became verses, but then I had the freedom of writing a chorus, which looked more like typical song lyrics. I was employing both of the lyric-writing methods Luther had discussed.

The result was that I wrote a melody with a jazzy feel in the verses and a swing feel in the chorus. "Mirror Mirror" is part of the medley we (Murray Foster, Julian Troiano, vocalist Tricia Williams, and I) recorded. Visit www.incommonthemusical.com to have a listen to our music.

SCREENWRITING

SCREENWRITING:
MENTORS AND CONTEST JUDGES

CONTEST JUDGE AND MENTOR,
GENEVIÈVE APPLETON

Photo by Yeliz Atici

Geneviève Appleton (BAAHons Film Production, 1994, MFA Screenwriting, 2003) started her career as an actress in the 80s in film and TV projects such as *Kids of Degrassi* and *Anne of Green Gables, The Sequel.*

She was Associate Producer of the feature film *Wilby Wonderful*, directed by Daniel MacIvor and wrote narration for the travel series *GAP: Great Adventure People* as well as two feature film documentaries, *In the Land of the Moose*, directed by Harold Arsenault, and *Partly Private*, directed by Danae Elon, which won the best New York Documentary at the Tribeca Film Festival.

For her company, White Wave Productions (est. 1992), Geneviève has written, produced, directed and co-edited several films. Her documentary *A Garden's Family* aired on Vision TV and *Actor's Transformation*, featuring the extraordinary work of acting teacher Deena Levy and her students in NYC, premiered at the Female Eye Film Festival and aired on Bravo! Canada.

Her short dance film, *Calling the Minstrel,* was screened at the 2010 Olympics' Cultural Olympiad Digital Edition, the Atlanta Film Festival, and the Izmir International Short Film Festival.

She was invited to screen and give a talk on her documentary about the *East Timor Peace Mission* at the 20th Anniversary Commemoration Ceremony and Conference in Timor-Leste, where it was also shown on East Timor Television. With Colleen Wagner, she co-directed and co-produced the documentary *Women Building Peace* about women in Africa rebuilding their lives and societies after GBV, war and genocide.

Geneviève recently worked as project manager on two AWE Company and Divani Films productions: a virtual reality tour of the City of Toronto's Fort York Museum, and a two-screen, augmented-reality, 3D-animated time travel series for children called *Histronauts*, written, directed and produced by Srinivas Krishna.

She is currently producing the interactive documentary *Biology of Story*, written and directed by Amnon Buchbinder (www.biologyofstory.com), which is launching at South by Southwest Interactive 2016.

Geneviève has taught Screenwriting and Media Production since 2003 at various institutions including the University of Toronto, Bilkent University, Sheridan College, York University, Ryerson University, LIFT, as well as in private workshops.

Biography courtesy of Geneviève Appleton

CONTEST FINALIST JUDGING PANEL: MAUREEN DOREY, ELISE COUSINEAU, BRYCE MITCHELL

MAUREEN DOREY

Photo and biography courtesy of Maureen Dorey

Maureen Dorey is a freelance analyst and story editor and instructor who helps writers find their voices and renew their story inspiration. Her production credits include *Hidden*, written by David Shamoon, directed by Angieszka Holland and produced by The Film Works, nominated for the Oscar for Best Foreign Language Film and three Genies, including Best Screenplay; *Amal*, written by Shaun and Richie Mehta, also nominated for six Genies, including Best Screenplay; and *Blackbird*, written by Jason Buxton and produced by Marc Almon, an Official Selection of the Toronto International Film Festival 2012, winner of the Claude Jutra Award, and nominated for Best Screenplay at the 2013 Canadian Screen Awards. Dorey's television credits include *Moccasin Flats* (Season II) and *Random Passage*, an eight-hour mini-series directed by John N. Smith, produced by Passage Films and Cité-Amérique for broadcast on CBC and RTE (Eire). Other credits include *The War Between Us*, *Lyddie*, and *On My Mind*.

Story Editor Mentor to the Canadian Film Centre's Writer's Lab for the past 14 years, Dorey also teaches in the Film Department at York University and has served as an instructor to LIFT, WIFT, the National Screen Institute, Praxis Film Works, NIFCO and B.C. Film. She acted as story editor on several Canadian Film Centre feature film projects, including *Nurse.Fighter.Boy* (nominated for 10 Genie Awards, including Best Screenplay), *The Dark Hours*, *Siblings* and *Show Me*.

ELISE COUSINEAU

Photo and biography courtesy of Elise Cousineau

Elise Cousineau is the Head of Development and Production Executive at Sienna Films, a Toronto-based independent feature film and television production company.

In addition to managing Sienna Films' slate of television and feature film development, Elise's credits with Sienna include one-hour drama series *Combat Hospital* (2011) for Shaw and ABC, Canada's #1 Original Drama of the Year and Playback Magazine's International Co-Production of the Year; mini-series *Diamonds* (2009), for CBC, ABC and Canal+, which was nominated for nine Gemini Awards including Best Mini-Series; and feature film *How She Move* (2008), which premiered at the Sundance Film Festival and was subsequently distributed by Mongrel Media in Canada and Paramount Vantage/ MTV Films internationally. Upcoming is feature film *Unless*, a Canada-Ireland co-production adapted from the novel by Carol Shields and starring Catherine Keener.

Since beginning work with Sienna Films in 2005, Elise has also participated in various capacities in the development or production of *Titanic* (mini-series 2012, ITV/ABC/Shaw), *The Cry of the Owl* (feature film 2009), *Altar Boy Gang* (mini-series 2007, CBC), *One Dead Indian* (MOW 2006, CTV) and *Weather Report* (documentary 2009).

Elise holds a BFA in Film Production from York University and an Honours BA in Creative Writing & English Literature from Concordia University. She has produced several short films including *Silver Road* (2007), *13.5* (2008) and *The Young Prime Minister* (2009).

BRYCE MITCHELL

Photo and biography courtesy of Bryce Mitchell

Bryce Mitchell is a graduate of Ryerson Polytechnic University Image Arts - Film Studies program and the Canadian Film Centre's Producer Lab.

He has worked in production with Shoes Full of Feet Inc. where he produced the Genie-nominated *At Home By Myself . . . With You*, as well as other notable companies such as Victorious Films (*Twist, Century Hotel*), Northwood Productions (*Cake, Wild Roses*) and Serendipity Point Films (*Barney's Version, Men With Brooms*).

Bryce joined the Meridian team in 2009 as Development Manager under Glenn Cockburn and subsequently took on the role of Agent in 2010. In 2014 he spear-headed the formation of Meridian Artist's Kids and Animation division, now the preeminent destination for directing and literary talent within the sector throughout Canada.

CONTEST INDUSTRY MENTOR, NAVIN RAMASWARAN

Photo and biography courtesy of Navin Ramaswaran

Graduating from the University of Windsor in 2003 with a BA(H) Communication Studies and Visual Arts, Navin Ramaswaran is currently a director and editor represented by studio m, in Toronto, Ontario.

Besides being the creative lead on various TV/web commercials, promo videos and music videos, he is also an award-winning filmmaker. In 2006, Navin wrote, produced, directed and edited *Nara*, his first feature film under his own banner, Splice Films. The film is being distributed worldwide by Echelon Studios.

Many of his newer works have been accepted into multiple film festivals and are distributed worldwide. His current commercial projects include the award winning Coca-Cola Freestyle campaign and the 2015 Lincoln MKC spot. He also edited the viral hit WestJet Christmas Surprise 2014. Navin is currently in post-production for his next feature film *Chasing Valentine*, which he is directing and editing. (*Chasing Valentine* has since had its European premiere at the International Filmmaker Festival of World Cinema in Milan, where it was nominated for seven awards, and its world premiere at the Orlando Film Festival in October 2015.)

He also recently completed *Late Night Double Feature*, a horror anthology, and the award-winning short, *One More for the Road*, produced by Fangoria writer, Kelly Michael Stewart. Navin also directed Season 2 of the web series *Pete Winning and the Pirates* (which is currently nominated for four Independent Screen Awards, including Best Directing) and *The Misfortune of Madeline Moody*, a horror short that premiered in 28 Cineplex Odeon cinemas across Canada in February 2014 as part of distributor Raven Banner's Sinister Cinema Series.

"Navin is a stylish, talented director/editor with a great career ahead of him. He has an amazing visual eye and a solid understanding of story and character," commented Sean McConville, director of *Deadline*.

"It's the calculated chaos that excites me when it comes to filmmaking," says Ramaswaran. Through his passion and drive for filmmaking, Navin believes that he can make an impact in his community and spread awareness on the craft of independent filmmaking.

THE 2015 SCREENWRITER MENTOR EXPERIENCE: INTERVIEW WITH GENEVIÈVE APPLETON AND NAVIN RAMASWARAN

by Amanda Clarke

Conceived by Geneviève Appleton, a director, editor, and producer with White Wave Productions, and sponsored by the founder of Aspiring Canadian Writers Contests (ACWC) Heidi Stock, the 2015 Screenwriter Mentor Experience takes submissions of short film screenplays of up to 10 pages from across Canada. Appleton, who is also the contest's main judge, will create a short list from the entries from which the top three will be selected by a panel of judges which currently include Appleton along with Maureen Dorey, a freelance story editor and screenwriting professor and Elise Cousineau, the Head of Development and Production Executive at Sienna Films. The grand prize winner will receive online script editing sessions with Appleton as well as a mentoring session on how to take a script from the page to the screen with Navin Ramaswaran, an independent director/editor.

"There aren't a lot of opportunities out there really for novice or unproduced screenwriters to submit their works. It's very rare at all that a producer or any other agency will read unsolicited scripts, especially in Canada. Everybody is just so busy trying to get the work in their own portfolios made that they don't really have time to be wading through piles of scripts that may or may not be professional. I'm hoping to bridge that gap and introduce screenwriters to the types of incubator programs that exist and make sure that their script would make a first cut of those types of organizations." This desire to help aspiring screenwriters get their work onscreen led to the creation of the 2015 Screenwriter Mentor Experience.

As the head judge, Appleton is "going to be looking at the scripts from a professional standpoint. Is this a project that I can see on the screen? First of all, is it following industry standards? That's a good indication if the writer is professional or not, or making an attempt to be professional. I'll be looking at it also from a screenwriting perspective as a professor. Does the story work? Does it carry me along? Do I want to keep reading? Do I care about the characters? Is the imagery strong? Because cinema, of course is an image based medium. Is this more of a radio play? Or is it more of a sitcom? Or is it actually a script that will work well on a big screen?" Ramaswaran also stresses the importance of professionalism in the scripts. "Grammar, spelling mistakes, that's my pet peeve. If you've made a single spelling mistake in the script, it's gone unless it's so captivating I can't put it down, but you have to proof your script. Final Draft has spell check." Appleton is also looking for scripts that she "feels are close to being ready to submit for funding and production. I'll hopefully be finding something that I can share with other producers and distributors and help the person find funding."

I'M HOPING TO BRIDGE THAT GAP AND INTRODUCE SCREENWRITERS TO THE TYPES OF INCUBATOR PROGRAMS THAT EXIST AND MAKE SURE THAT THEIR SCRIPT WOULD MAKE A FIRST CUT OF THOSE TYPES OF ORGANIZATIONS.

Once the winning script has been selected by the judges, Ramaswaran steps in to provide feedback on how to develop a 'finished' script for the screen. He emphasizes that "the most important aspect in any art form, but specifically in film making, whether it's writing or directing, is having enough time to develop the script. With a lot of writers, a lot of filmmakers, it's such a rush to get the movie made that often times first drafts get made. It's a whole different thing getting a script ready for production versus something that you're happy with. A lot of people are so protective over their script. They're so hesitant to show other people for feedback and get other people to read it. And I get that, I understand that, but you need to let it go to make it a better product. Writing is very intimate. It's just you and your thoughts essentially, but getting a few people that you trust, writers, mentors, people like that, to read it are a great option to get articulate feedback on your script which is so important."

Ramaswaran continued speaking about working on the script even once filming begins. "Then there's the process when you are making that jump or transition from page to screen. That's a whole other process because, especially on a small budget indie movie, your job doesn't end as a writer. You're still writing and rewriting stuff as actors are cast and locations are found. You're constantly changing things. To tie in with that, there's the collaboration between the writer and the director, the writer and the producers and making all the bridging from one end to the other end of it. It's such an important process that often times people skip little steps that result in sub-par products, sub-par movies. The screenplay is the blueprint. It's the foundation for any movie and if you have a mediocre script your foundation is wobbly to begin with and when you build up on that, it's a disaster."

Appleton also stresses the importance of remembering "that scripts are blueprints for productions. If you don't know how to make a film, then it's going to be hard to write for film. It's one thing to be an audience member and watch, and we learn a lot by doing that, but it's also important to compare what you're watching to the actual script. So go online, there's a lot of databases of scripts and try to find the actual script that was written by the screenwriter (as opposed to a transcript) and then comparing the script to what ends up onscreen and seeing how it was written. In particular scripts are written in a very direct form describing what we see and hear on the screen. They shouldn't be editorializing. They shouldn't be explaining anything because the audience isn't going to have the benefit of having things explained to them. What they see is what they get and they have to figure out and decode the meaning."

THE SCREENPLAY IS THE BLUEPRINT. IT'S THE
FOUNDATION FOR ANY MOVIE AND IF YOU HAVE A
MEDIOCRE SCRIPT YOUR FOUNDATION IS WOBBLY TO

BEGIN WITH AND WHEN YOU BUILD UP ON THAT, IT'S A
DISASTER.

Both Appleton and Ramaswaran agree that mentorship opportunities like The Screenwriting Mentorship Experience are extremely important for aspiring writers. "One of the reasons why [Ramaswaran] said yes to this right away is that I strongly believe in programs like this, you know mentorship and especially practical experience. I went to school for film, but I truly learned by being on set, by talking to other people who do it, by shadowing people, other directors. I think that's an invaluable experience and especially something like this, where you're getting the information from the horses mouth."

Appleton hopes to bring attention to the opportunities there are available for aspiring writers to get their work out there and receive feedback. Incubator programs like Praxis, programs through the Canadian Film Centre as well as continuing education courses at the University of Toronto, Ryerson and York University, which has a dedicated screenwriting program at both the undergraduate and graduate level, are all places for screenwriters to make connections in the industry and get their work out there. A good first step however would be to enter the 2015 Screenwriter Mentor Experience which is accepting entries until June 30, 2015 or to one hundred entries, whichever comes first.

APPLETON SAYS, "REMEMBER THAT THEY SAY NINETY PERCENT OF COMMUNICATION IS NONVERBAL AND NOT TO RELY SO MUCH ON DIALOGUE TO MOVE THE STORY FORWARD. REALIZE THAT PEOPLE SPEAK WHEN THEY HAVE TO SPEAK AND FOR A REASON THAT HAS TO BE AS MOTIVATED AS ACTION. AND THEN TRY TO SUBMIT TO CONTESTS."

The mentor's final words of advice for aspiring screenwriters? Appleton suggests "taking your iPhone or Android or whatever camera you can get a hold of and start rehearsing, preferably with some actors who are trying to break into the industry as well, but even with friends. Working with actual actors who are going to be speaking those lines and acting out those lines, making them come to life. Remember that they say ninety percent of communication is nonverbal and not to rely so much on dialogue to move the story forward. Realize that people speak when they have to speak and for a reason that has to be as motivated as action. And then try to submit to contests."

Ramaswaran believes that "the key is to get your first script made. You meet people all the time who have a script, who have written a script, who are writing a script. There's nothing better than a calling card where you can go to someone and say 'here's my movie. I wrote it, it's great.' That's important because then you have something tangible, it's not just words on paper anymore. Having said that, it's important to go through the proper steps to get there. Go through the proper process of making it. Make sure you have a solid script. Make sure you proof read it. Be patient with it. Step away from it for a couple days or a couple of weeks, then come back and look at it because you'll be surprised how your perception of it is different. Talk to other writers, but remember at the end of the day, it's everyone's opinion versus your work and what you believe in. If you strongly believe in something and the content of the script, then go for it."

Reprint, interview by Amanda Clarke originally published in Toronto Film Scene, *June 23, 2015, thetfs.ca/article/2015-screenwriter-mentor-experience-interview-genevieve-appleton-navin-ramaswaran/*

Interviews with the Screenwriting Contest Winners

Interview with Wendy Chan

First-Place Contest Winner, Screenwriter Mentor Experience, 2015

Photo Credit: Gabriel Lascu

Why did you decide to submit this particular screenplay to the contest?

Posted is the first complete short screenplay that I've written. I developed the idea and wrote the first draft in a creative writing course I took a few years back. I left the draft on top of a seemingly endless pile of works in progress, promising that I would one day return to it. When I came across the contest, I knew that it was the perfect motivation to revisit this piece. I'm constantly trying to discover and refine my voice as a writer, and I think this story is one that closely represents the sorts of stories I like and want to tell—stories that explore the lives of ordinary people and human connection.

What's the backstory to the screenplay?

I've always been a fan of sticky notes (and probably buy way too many). I usually write reminders or to-do lists on them, but sometimes it can get a little overwhelming looking at all these things I have to do. A while ago, I started writing little jokes or motivational quotes to stick amongst my other notes. A lot of the time I forget I have them up, and every time I saw one of the notes, it brought a little smile to my face. Inspired by that, I wanted to write a story about sticky notes, which I thought would make a visually engaging film. All the stories I write tend to be character-driven, so after some brainstorming, I developed the idea for a story about two people who connect based on what is seemingly just a tiny square piece of paper.

When did you start writing?

I've always loved words, even before I could say any words myself. I loved the way they sounded—how certain ones would roll off the tongue while others seem to linger in the air. As soon as I started talking, I learned as many words as I could. I also loved to read—my mom used to catch me up past my bedtime, hiding under my sheets, book in hand. Reading was a way to be surrounded by words and immersed in a new world with new people. The first time one of my teachers told me to write a story and I had the chance to put words to paper, I was hooked. It was so satisfying to take these individual elements and be able to create something from all these ideas that seemed to be just floating in my head.

Was screenwriting your first creative outlet or was it another style of writing? Or another art form?

The style of writing that I started with, and still gravitate toward, is short stories. I tend to write first-person narratives that, again, are heavily character-driven and explore ordinary people in extraordinary situations or extraordinary people in ordinary situations. I write shorter pieces because I constantly have ideas bouncing around in my head, and I like the freedom that short stories give in exploring all these ideas and characters. I started to realize that when I plan and plot stories, I visualize a lot of the story in my head. Even for pieces that are stream of consciousness, I still have a habit of visualizing, for example, how a character would say certain lines or express particular thoughts—and that's what helps me write. I think that's why I started exploring screenwriting—it gives me a chance to express those visuals I have in my head in a medium that's intended for visuals.

Do other forms of artistic expression and/or life experience influence your writing?

I'm influenced by pretty much everything around me, whether it's snippets of conversation (I'm guilty of occasionally eavesdropping), exploring a new neighbourhood or coming across a picture on the Internet. I'm a naturally curious person—I love learning about new and utterly random things. I like trying to make sense of ideas, concepts and behaviour, and the way I do that is through writing. Everything I see and hear around me, even in a small way, piques my curiosity, which in turn influences the stories I want to tell.

Influences—who influenced or encouraged your writing—which writers/authors, filmmakers, other artists, teachers or mentors, loved ones?

I'm fortunate enough to have always been surrounded by people who have been amazingly supportive of my writing. Even when I was eight years old and told my family I wanted to be a writer, they encouraged me to embrace my creativity and fostered my love for words and telling stories. During my bachelor of fine arts degree in the UBC creative writing program, I was surrounded by the most intelligent, creative, and supportive peers and professors. Having the opportunity to learn from writers such as Linda Svendsen, Deborah Peraya, Ian Weir, among others, made me grow immensely as a writer, and perhaps most importantly, made me so excited to write and continue writing.

Tell us about your mentoring experience in 2015 with the contest's industry mentor, Navin Ramaswaran.

It was terrific talking to Navin and learning about how he began his career and all the experiences he's had in the film industry. As my background is in writing, it was really neat hearing the other side of things, from directing to producing to editing and promoting a film. As a writer, I don't necessary know about all these things, so it was interesting to learn about the steps that go into bringing a script to life. Hearing how a film is created made me realize and appreciate the rewarding process that comes from turning a simple idea in your head into a tangible medium that others can see.

How will Navin's advice inform the development of your screenplay into a short film one day?

Navin gave a lot of practical tips on how to begin the process of creating a film, from doing a table read to connecting with others in the industry and finding funding. For a while now, I've wanted the experience of making a short film, but I was overwhelmed and, frankly, a bit terrified about where and how to start. Navin offered a lot of tips and insight on the steps to develop a film, and after talking to him, I'm now motivated and very excited to develop my screenplay into a short film.

Interview with Dawn Prato

Second-Place Winner, Screenwriter Mentor Experience, 2015

Why did you decide to submit this particular screenplay to the contest?

I've always loved the old fairy stories and how you have to be careful what you wish for sometimes. I believed in this short film and thought it was one of my stronger screenplays. The chance for mentoring sessions, as well as winning Stephanie Palmer's e-course, was a big push. I've been following her blog for a while, so I'm overjoyed. I decided to push myself and submit to the contest.

What's the backstory to the screenplay?

Initially, the story was much longer and part of another fantasy world I've been developing. I thought the "careful what you wish for" angle worked, as well as looking at how, a lot of the time, people cause their own problems. They look for the easy way out, not the right way out. While I was developing the story, I listened to *The Erlking* by Franz Schubert, who used Goethe's poem as aid, to achieve the tone I was going for. I've always loved older versions of fairy tales as well—I love Disney, but other collections from the Grimm brothers and Hans Christian Andersen are great. They have a lot of not-so-famous stories that can spark an idea.

When did you start writing?

I started writing when I was very young, before my own writing was all that steady. My mother would buy blank books and write down what I said, and I went from there. I've always been reading as well; my parents were both teachers, and so reading and writing were very important to them. I especially loved series like *The Bailey School Kids*, where real-life people had a bit of a fantasy twist to them.

293

Was screenwriting your first creative outlet or was it another style of writing? Or another art form?

Screenwriting came last for me, actually. I started off with prose, writing a lot of stories and dipping in to fan fiction as well. I drew a lot, too, and I play the piano, but writing was always my go-to outlet. In university, I had the opportunity to take a course on writing for the stage, and that led me to screenwriting.

Do other forms of artistic expression and/or life experience influence your writing?

Music is hugely important for me. If I don't have the right songs while I'm working, the story doesn't feel quite right. Classical, jazz, R&B, pop songs, other instrumental works . . . it has to fit the character in order for me to really get the feel of the writing across.

Influences—who influenced or encouraged your writing— which writers/authors, filmmakers, other artists, teachers or mentors, loved ones?

Where to start . . . my language arts teachers have always been a huge influence for me. I was fortunate enough to have phenomenal teachers all across the board. Mrs. Ferguson in Grade 9, and all of my high school teachers (Hi, Mrs. Dillon-Davis!), especially. Neil Gaiman is a favourite author of mine—the feelings and atmospheres he manages to convey are amazing. My parents, of course, encouraged me even though I'm pretty sure they thought that writing was going to stay a hobby. They still allowed me to pursue it and supported me regardless of what they might have thought, and they continue to do so. I'll always be grateful for that. Sometimes, you just need your mom or dad to tell you what you just wrote is amazing. One last big influence is a friend and writing partner of mine, Jeremy Varner. He's a great friend that calls me out on problems with a story or characters, and it's always a good place to be when someone's honest with you about what you're doing.

You and your fellow contest winners were awarded Stephanie Palmer's e-course, *How to Be a Professional Writer*. What are some key learnings from this course that you will apply to your writing career?

Her e-course is amazing. The tips and pointers about networking and how to find people to connect with really made things clear for me. Setting goals, small or big, and physically writing them down . . . things that seem like they should be second nature by now, realizing that sometimes you have to break things down to the most basic steps in order to really push forward. Even if things get busy and life gets crowded, and you're able to move on to bigger projects, keeping the core of things in mind and keeping them simple—that's what I'm really going to keep in mind while I pursue my career.

Interview with Stefan Cap

Third-Place Winner, Screenwriter Mentor Experience, 2015

Why did you decide to submit this particular screenplay to the contest?

My script is about a boy from a troubled home who gets trapped in a collapsed snow fort and has to tunnel out. When I finished the script, I knew the winter/snow fort setting would probably resonate most with Canadian readers and was on the lookout for a Canadian screenwriting contest. The day after I finished the script, I received an email notice promoting the contest from the Winnipeg Film Group and decided the contest would be the perfect place to submit my story.

What's the backstory to the screenplay?

I grew up in Winnipeg and spent years building and playing in elaborate snow forts.

When did you start writing?

I started writing after leaving a job a few years ago. I was originally focused on short humour pieces and then turned toward screenwriting, as I like the visual aspect of the storytelling for the screen. *The Snow Fort* is the first screenplay I have written.

Was screenwriting your first creative outlet or was it another style of writing? Or another art form?

I have always been into drawing/painting and have also worked sporadically as an actor for several years.

Do other forms of artistic expression and/or life experience influence your writing?

I sometimes draw out scenes I'm writing, sort of like a storyboard. I've also read a lot of scripts as an actor and feel that gives me a sense of what kinds of characters actors like to play and how certain scenes will work in front of the camera.

Influences—who influenced or encouraged your writing— which writers/authors, filmmakers, other artists, teachers or mentors, loved ones?

There are a number of kids' fantasy/adventure stories that I enjoy and that influence my writing (*Bridge to Terabithia, The Dog Who Stopped the War, Stand by Me*, and many others). I am particularly interested in stories that deal with real-life problems using fantasy elements.

Tell us a bit about your mentoring session with contest judge and mentor Geneviève Appleton and the feedback you received that will assist you with a revision of your contest entry or future scripts.

Geneviève was great—she provided valuable feedback on *The Snow Fort* as well as detailed notes on a second short script I wrote, called *The Wish*. I'm working on expanding *The Snow Fort* into a feature-length script and discussed with Geneviève the direction of the story. The short version of *The Snow Fort* ends abruptly in a scenario where it's unclear whether the protagonist survives or not; Geneviève suggested that it may be helpful to provide more resolution in a feature-length piece. She also encouraged me to focus on maintaining and developing empathy for the characters throughout.

Geneviève provided especially helpful feedback on my second script, where I relied heavily on dialogue and scene descriptions to move the story forward. She advised that the dialogue could be streamlined and made to feel more authentic in order to move the plot forward in a more effective way. Geneviève also gave me a list of resources for writers and offered to keep in touch as I work toward completing my feature script. Overall, it was a very helpful and informative experience in which I received detailed feedback and advice on screenwriting.

ADVICE FROM THE FILM INDUSTRY

ADVICE FROM INDUSTRY EXPERT, STEPHANIE PALMER

on being "Good in a Room" and more

Photo and biography courtesy of Stephanie Palmer

Stephanie Palmer worked for Jerry Bruckheimer Films and then for MGM Pictures as Director of Creative Affairs. In that role, she was named by *The Hollywood Reporter* as one of the "Top 35 Executives Under 35." Stephanie now coaches small business owners and creative professionals inside and outside Hollywood on how to effectively pitch their ideas. Visit Stephanie's website at <u>goodinaroom.com/</u>.

~~~

Heidi: I first heard about you and your coaching business when you were a guest on Joke & Biagio's *Producing Unscripted* podcast episode, "Stop Ruining Your Pitches." **What are some common traits or actions among writers who successfully pitch their scripts—those who are "good in a room?"**

Stephanie: The common traits of effective pitchers are that they use the five stages of the meeting technique:

In Stage 1, you build rapport and warm up the room.
In Stage 2, you ask questions and listen, to show respect.
In Stage 3, you deliver the prepared component of your pitch.
In Stage 4, you deliver the "improvised" component of your pitch.
In Stage 5, you ask for one thing, if necessary, and leave on a good note.

Effective pitchers spend time building rapport with the person they are meeting. They prioritize the relationship with the person above the particular pitch. For those who would like to know more, I cover this in more detail in the "Pitch Meeting Structure Used By Hollywood Pros", which you can read here: goodinaroom.com/blog/the-pitch-meeting-structure-everyone-should-know/.

Heidi: After listening to the podcast episode, I bought your book, *Good in a Room*. I've read it twice and I keep returning to chapters and passages that have helped me prepare for meetings with professionals working in and outside the entertainment industry. *Good in a Room* goes beyond instructing readers on how to prepare for a pitch meeting, what to expect in the meeting, how to close, and how to follow up. For me, the added value of your book is your view on the overall process of selling yourself and your ideas and putting it all into perspective. **Please share a bit about the importance of "nurturing your inner circle" and your experience helping your clients "get unstuck."**

Stephanie: For better or worse, screenwriting is a profession where you get told "no" all the time. This is a really challenging aspect of the business for a lot of people, and this is why it is so important to have an inner circle of people who believe in you. This can be friends, colleagues, family members or other people in your life who respect you, like you, and encourage you.

One of the best things about working in Hollywood, or any creative field, is that you get to meet and collaborate with talented people. Seeking out partnerships and building strong professional relationships are key components of having a successful Hollywood career.

As for being stuck, this can be a very valuable clue that there is a flaw or an issue in the project. As much as it may be frustrating, feeling stuck is common and can be incredibly useful. The best way to get "unstuck" is to stop working on the project that is stuck and work on something else. After working on something else and taking a break, it is amazing how often we can get some clarity on the issue, or have a new idea, or a better understanding of what the issue is that is causing "stuckness" so it can be resolved.

Heidi: The top three contest winners of the 2015 Screenwriter Mentor Experience were awarded your e-course, *How to Be a Professional Writer*. **What are some common misconceptions among aspiring screenwriters about becoming a professional writer, and what words of encouragement do you have?**

Stephanie: There are three main misconceptions—that it's easy, it's quick, and you're going to be wildly rich. In my experience, having any one of these three experiences is extremely rare.

As for encouragement, let me speak directly to the serious writers out there. Here is the truth as best I know it: The writers who succeed are not always the absolute best, smartest, or most talented. It's the ones who persevere. If you can stick with it and you have the right information about what to do, you can succeed.

ADVICE FROM INDUSTRY EXPERT, PERRY ZIMEL

The Role of a Manager

Photo Credit: Marni Grossman, marnigrossman.com

Perry Zimel, of Oscars Abrams Zimel & Associates Inc., is an anomaly in his business—he works through lunch and speaks the painful truths up front.

Zimel is a manager representing a list of actors that includes Edward Asner, Lorraine Bruce, Lucas Bryant, Wendy Crewson, Henry Czerny, Megan Follows, Sharon Gless, Leslie Hope, Kristin Lehman, Andrea Martin, Peter Outerbridge and Christopher Plummer.

His director clients include Jerry Ciccoritti, John Kent Harrison, Gail Harvey, Laurie Lynd, Michael Melski and Stefan Scaini.

His writing roster includes acclaimed writers Noel Baker (*Gangland Undercover*); Katie Boland (*Long Story Short*); Susan Coyne, who created the critically lauded Showcase/Sundance Channel series, *Slings and Arrows* and is currently Producer/Writer of Amazon's Golden Globe winner *Mozart In The Jungle*; Katie Ford (*Miss Congeniality* and *Prayers for Bobby*); Mark McKinney (*Less Than Kind*); and Dan Trotta (*Blood and Water*).

"You know what I think is the best part of my job?" Zimel says. "It's the partnerships that I have. I treat each one of my clients like we're partners in a company, so I work with people as opposed to for people."

Clients also include producers Greg Copeland and Karen Wookey, as well as acclaimed film composer, Lesley Barber.

Zimel's first project as a producer was a wheel of six movies for CTV, entitled *Criminal Instinct,* an adaptation of Canadian writer Gail Bowen's popular *Joanne Kilbourne Mysteries.*

Other executive producer credits include John N. Smith's feature, *Geraldine's Fortune*; Anne Wheeler's film, *Suddenly Naked,* which was screened at the Toronto, Vancouver and Berlin International Film Festivals and received multiple Genie Award nominations; and the Allan Moyle–directed feature *Weirdsville,* starring Scott Speedman.

Zimel's CBC musical movie, *Christmas Dreams,* which stars Edward Asner, Tom Cavanaugh, Henry Czerny and Cynthia Dale, airs yearly as an audience favourite on CBC and BounceTV in the U.S. He is now in development on *Queen Bee,* a Jerry Ciccoritti film à la Quentin Tarantino's *Kill Bill,* a CBC half-hour series called *Little Dog,* and a series based on the books *Murder On The Bucket List.*

Zimel divides his time between Toronto and Los Angeles.

~~~

Heidi: As children, we have limited knowledge of the career options that we will have as adults. Only a few occupations came to mind when we were asked in school, "What do you want to be when you grow up?" **What did you dream of becoming one day, and how did**

your find your way to your career as a manager of actors, writers and producers?

Perry: Interestingly enough, I did an oral presentation in Grade 5 French class where the subject was, "What do you want to be when you grow up?" I said a "l'agent du talent." I have been fortunate to have an older sister (Gayle Abrams of OAZ) pave the path ahead of me. I was lucky to know about this profession from a very young age, so it was always a dream of mine. I didn't get here directly but got here nonetheless.

Heidi: It is a unique experience to represent a mix of creative professionals (actors, writers and producers). **How does your experience working with actors and producers, for example, benefit your clients who are writers? And is there a different management approach or style when dealing with clients who work in front of or behind the camera?**

Perry: Representing another individual, the best way for me has been to approach everything without judgement or ego. My job in representing others' interests is to be "reflective light," to hopefully shine what they want/desire in a brighter, more focused way. I love representing every aspect of the industry because my mind is always going a mile a minute. In representing producers, I see what they are buying (from my writers, hopefully) and then I get to deal with the hiring of directors, casting directors, wardrobe people etc. and eventually cast. One feeds the other. One relationship builds on the other. One relationship forms an understanding of what comes next. It gives me a unique perspective on why decisions are being made because I saw where it comes from rather than the "present" reaction to a decision.

Heidi: In my interview with a music manager, I learned that teamwork, communication, honesty and education were essential to creating a good relationship between an artist and a manager and to maintaining client loyalty. **Please share a bit about the importance of honesty, teamwork, communication and education in your client relationships and what additional traits or qualities you might also add to this list.**

Perry: Everyone has heard the saying that we don't learn from our wins but rather our mistakes. Mistakes teach us to take responsibility, teach us to have compassion, etc. No one benefits from having a manager tell them only the great stuff. There are celebrities out there who have never been told, "No, stop, don't..." and have gone off the rails. If you are telling the truth, being what I call a true friend, an artist will grow and learn (as will you). If you are not afraid of losing a client, you will be honest and tell the truth. If you lose a client for telling the truth, both parties are better off.

Heidi: You represent actor Christopher Plummer, who thanked you and his "little band of agents provocateurs who've tried so hard to keep me out of jail," in his gracious and witty Academy Award acceptance speech in 2012. **What are the some of the most rewarding aspects of your job and also some of the most challenging?**

Perry: There is no question that when someone gets up and acknowledges your part in their journey it is fulfilling, but you can't do this job based on thanks. I often say that I am the first person people call when they need something and the last that they thank, so when someone does thank you (like Christopher Plummer), it doesn't go unnoticed. I do my job because I love people. I love the creative aspects of what I do. People think that agents/managers just negotiate. That is one of the smallest parts of the jobs, although I do love negotiating. "Womb-to-tomb management" is my saying. I have seen, experienced and enjoyed every aspect of a person's life by representing their talent. The most challenging aspect of my job would be to make talent feel safe, needed and important during the times they aren't working, and supported and safe when they are working. I once had an assistant say to me, "The work is when they aren't working and not making money!" It is true, it is difficult when someone goes through a dry spell. But if you believe in their talent— you ride it out and it always turns around.

Heidi: You divide your time between Toronto and Los Angeles. For those who don't work in the entertainment industry or for those new to it, what are some common misconceptions about the film and television industry in Canada and in the United States?

Perry: I chose to stay in Canada because I love this country and what it stands for. (Especially the last two years with what is going on around the world). I have been a married gay man for the past 10 years, who goes about my life like everyone else because I live in Canada. I would not have had that "easiness of life" living in the U.S. That and family is part of why I chose to live in Canada. The other part is that I wanted to be involved in a business that was growing, to be seen on the world stage (which we are now).

In terms of the business, two of the biggest differences I can say are:

1. In Canada, most people don't take your call because they are afraid you want something, and in the U.S., most people take your call because they are afraid someone else wants what you have. Neither is the right way of doing business or being supportive. Both come from a place of fear. However, I would rather have someone on the phone than be frustrated that someone doesn't take the call.

2. I would like to say that I understand why the Canadian industry runs the way it does, but I don't. I don't always agree with the reasons why those in the American industry choose what they do, but I always can find a way to understand it. I think Canada needs to take more chances and stop trying to

compete with the U.S. We have super creative and talented people here, and if we trusted the creative more, we would see a better product, that is not only recognized around the world, but also respected in our own backyard.

Heidi: What advice do you have for aspiring screenwriters who are seeking a literary agent?

Perry: I asked my literary associate, Stefan Morris Hogan, this question, and he really hit the nail on the head. This is what we both believe—**be true to your voice**. Write something that is uniquely you. Write what you know. If you want television representation, then write a pilot script and a spec on a show that is out there. Distinguish yourself with reputable competitions. Try and have a short made of one of your scripts with a director/producer as a calling card. Write. Keep writing. What you write now may not get made but it may open a door and may lead to something else. Write. Keep writing!

ADVICE FROM INDUSTRY EXPERT, DIANE DRAKE

to help "Get Your Story Straight" and more

Photo credit: Julie Walke

Diane Drake is an accomplished professional screenwriter, writing instructor, story consultant, speaker, and author. Prior to becoming a screenwriter, Diane served as Vice President of Creative Affairs for Academy Award-winning director/producer Sydney Pollack. Her first produced original script, *Only You*, starring Robert Downey, Jr. and Marisa Tomei, sold for one million dollars, while her second produced script, *What Women Want*, starring Mel Gibson and Helen Hunt, is the second highest grossing romantic comedy of all time. In addition, both films have recently been remade in China featuring major Chinese stars.

Diane is a member of the Writer's Guild of America and has been an instructor/speaker for the Austin Film Festival, the UCLA Extension Writer's Program, the Scriptwriters Network, the Story Development Group, the University Club, and The Writer's Store. She recently released her debut book, *Get Your Story Straight: A Step-By-Step Guide To Screenwriting By A Million Dollar Screenwriter*, (Reel Life

309

Publishing, May 2016), and launched her own online screenwriting course and workshops at www.dianedrake.com.

Biography courtesy of Diane Drake

~~~

Heidi: In the opening chapter of your new book, *Get Your Story Straight: A Step-by-Step Guide To Screenwriting By A Million Dollar Screenwriter*, you write that "stories teach us how to live more fully." **Please share a bit more about why writers write and why we are all drawn to storytelling.**

Diane: I think why one writes can be quite personal, but for me anyway, writing is not only a great excuse to learn, explore and observe, it's also a way to both live more and to try to stay sane. The act of putting one's thoughts/fears/fantasies down on paper helps to both kind of distance yourself from them—see them more objectively—and at the same time, conversely, to vicariously live them.

As an example, I wrote the script for my film *Only You* in a small, characterless apartment on the west side of Los Angeles. I'd been to Italy once before and dreamed of returning. The characters in the movie went to Positano because I wanted to go to Positano. I got to live their fantasy adventure in my mind as I wrote it, and then I got to live it—not to mention hang with Robert Downey Jr.—in reality. As the saying goes, it doesn't get much better. Finally, if you're really lucky and work really hard, you and your work get to add meaning and enjoyment to the lives of others. That's a pretty great reward.

Heidi: In *Get Your Story Straight*, story structure is discussed in detail with examples from well-known feature films. Discuss how critical structure is to storytelling in film.

Diane: Structure is the mostly invisible (to the layperson, anyway) but critical underlying framework of a film. The current conventions of movie three-act structure have their original basis in Aristotle's Poetics theory of beginning, middle, end. This seems so obvious to us now, but that's probably because it's the main way stories have been told for the last few thousand years.

I liken a screenwriter's understanding of story structure to a musician's understanding of the fundamentals of music. Most people can't necessarily tell you where a piece of music might be off key, or where the rhythm is wrong, but they can *feel* something isn't right.

Same goes for stories. If the story isn't set up in the first act, developed in the second and resolved in the third; if the first act goes on for too long; if there aren't enough turning points; if the protagonist is too passive or the story isn't so much resolved in the end as simply stops, most movie-goers may not be able to pinpoint exactly where things went off the rails, or where they became disinterested, but usually the problem is at least partly structural in nature.

Heidi: You are the screenwriter of two popular romantic comedies, *Only You* and *What Women Want*. Romantic comedies have changed in recent years. **What advice do you have for screenwriters who enjoy writing in a particular genre, if that genre undergoes a shift in tone or temporarily wanes in popularity?**

Diane: As much as I'd like to say to write whatever is in you, if your goal is to sell your work to someone who's willing to spend a considerable amount of money to produce it, I think you also have to keep one eye on the market. That said, the market is always changing. The sitcom, for example, has been written off a few times in my lifetime, and then something comes along and changes the game and it's reborn. The latest example of this is *Modern Family*. I also think the changing world of television itself—and by this, I mean anything you can watch via the Internet as well, and all the new companies offering streaming original programming—has created all kinds of new opportunities and markets. The entertainment business is a dynamic beast; it helps to stay aware of the trends.

Heidi: How did your experience as Vice-President of Creative Affairs for Academy Award–winning director and producer Sydney Pollack inform both the writing and later the development of your feature films?

Diane: I really can't say enough good things about my experience with Sydney in terms of how grateful I am to have had it and how it prepared me to become a writer. He was a brilliant man—complicated, inspiring and extremely demanding. He was always raising the bar on himself and on those around him. It was a challenging environment to work in, but it drove me, and we had a great camaraderie among the people there.

Also, of course, I read a ton of scripts—I had access to some of the best material and writers in town. I was able to see and read what was working and what wasn't; what was selling and what wasn't. I also got to see, first hand, how subjective the game is, how often one person in the office might love something and another not, so I think it helped me handle criticism of my own work a bit better. I also learned the validity of the aphorism about "killing your darlings." You can't get too precious about something if it's detracting from the whole.

Heidi: As an educator, you have taught in the classroom, online and at retreats. Do you have any tips for students to help them decide what type of learning environment works best for them?

Diane: One thing that surprised me about teaching online was that I felt I kind of got to know my students better than I did in the classroom. I've spoken with other instructors about this phenomenon and many of them felt the same way. Something about communicating one-on-one via the written word over time allows you to develop a certain rapport that can sometimes be more difficult to create given the time constraints of an in-person classroom environment. On the other hand, I think the classroom experience can also be helpful because of the student interaction, though I do make an effort to really encourage that sort of thing among my students online as well. And, speaking for myself, anyway, I love retreats, as you really get to immerse yourself in the subject and experience for a day or more at a time. I think they're all valuable; just depends on the student.

Heidi: In *Get Your Story Straight*, you encourage content creators to embrace both the process and the competition. What advice do you have for new screenwriters who are discouraged by their progress or intimidated by the competition?

Diane: I think it's the nature of the game to get discouraged from time to time. Screenwriting is a deceptively difficult craft, and a certain amount of "failure" is simply inevitable, even for the very best among us. My dad used to point out to me how hard it must be to hit a baseball if a .300 batting average was considered a good one—that means you're missing at least two out of three times!

Screenwriting is equally hard, if not harder, statistically speaking. So I think it's important to just keep moving forward and accept the setbacks as both the cost of being in the game and as opportunities to learn.

Be sure to savour every little victory, every draft—every line!—you're proud of, and every time you finish something, remind yourself what an accomplishment that is, how few people even get that far. As for competition, viewed in the right light, it can be a good thing; it can fuel you and make you believe that if others around you are succeeding, so can you. It tells you that it's possible, that there is opportunity out there. Regardless, remember that you're learning and growing creatively every time you're up at bat, and no one can take that from you. I tell my students and clients that I wish them every success, but even more than that, I wish them fulfillment and joy in the process.

Screenwriting: Essays

Beyond Writing:
How to Get Your Short Film Made

by Navin Ramaswaran

Photo courtesy of Navin Ramaswaran

Skill Development—The Value of Collaboration

The value of collaboration between filmmakers is unparalleled. One of the best decisions I made after writing the first draft of *Chasing Valentine* was to bring another writer on board. As this project was so close to me, I needed an outside perspective. I knew my strengths (overall plot, interesting characters, interesting scenes or scenarios) and my weaknesses (structure, pacing and a tendency to overwrite). Enter Neal Schneider, a wiz when it comes to structuring and pacing a screenplay. Neal's strengths filled in gaps that I couldn't on my own,

315

and at the end of the day we had a solid foundation to effectively write our feature.

Initially, we worked on scenes individually, keeping an open dialogue about the work we had each done. Once we had a draft that we agreed upon, Neal took over as the main writer. We maintained a discussion throughout the process and I provided notes while Neal executed the writing.

This collaborative process continued on set—I was directing and didn't want to stretch myself too thin by also having to focus on rewrites and things that could be handled by another individual. Neal was always on set to take care of any writing needs, while I focused my attention on directing.

Chasing Valentine was the toughest production for me to date. As is known to happen on a micro budget indie set, so many things didn't transpire the way they were meant to or went completely wrong. I was certainly kept on my toes coming up with a plan B or C if I didn't already have one in my back pocket. However, the post-production process was the complete opposite; it was one of the smoothest and most satisfying experiences of my career.

I edited the movie myself and assembled a small group of people I trusted to view the first cut that I was happy with. This tightly knit group consisted of my producer, cinematographer, co-writer, two colleagues and a good friend—a wide range of people with varied levels of involvement; some had worked on the project intimately, while others were viewing the film with fresh, unbiased eyes. These were people I trusted to provide articulate and honest feedback. The results were amazingly helpful in shaping the final movie. Elements that I was unsure of were made clear by their feedback, while certain things that I hadn't noticed were brought to my attention. Of course, the positive elements were also highlighted.

What interested me the most was what a group of people who had never watched this movie would think of it. After compiling notes based on the feedback of those who had seen the first cut, I went through and selected the points that I agreed with and that I thought would help shape a better version of *Chasing Valentine*. After editing a new cut of the movie, I took the next step and had a test screening for 40 people—mostly people I did not know and who had no information about the movie besides the synopsis and an early poster. This was basically a larger version of my first private screening.

Once again, this was such an asset in shaping the final cut of the movie. From the feedback of the test screening, I learned that the movie was slightly too long, and one particular sub-plot was confusing. I took some time off from working on the movie and after a few weeks went back to work on the next cut, this time with a friend who is also an editor. By this point, the length of the film had to be trimmed down, but I had seen the movie so many times that I was finding this to be a difficult task. I invited a friend and fellow editor, Mike Donis, to work on this part of the project with me. Having a fresh pair of trained eyes at this point was what the movie needed. The cut that came out of this stage essentially became the final cut of the movie that is now being released. It was quite the process, one that I would apply to all my future projects.

As you can gather from my experience, filmmaking is one huge collaborative medium, from pre-production right into post-production. The key is for the *right* people to provide input, and there must always be *one* clear vision (i.e., the director's). Otherwise, you'll surely be on the express route to disaster!

BEYOND WRITING—HOW TO GET YOUR SHORT FILM MADE

I would never recommend tackling a feature film to first-time filmmakers. Make your mistakes on short films first—it's the best film school you can go through. I made my first short for a film class, but those that followed were self-financed. This is how most filmmakers who are starting out do it. If you efficiently budget your movie and fit production within two to three days, you can get away with pooling together a modest budget to get it made yourself. The key is getting the right collaborators on board—a good DOP, first AD, and PM—people who are good at what they do and believe in your project enough to come on board for an honorarium. I volunteered on other filmmakers' sets and banked those favours for when I needed to crew up my own film.

Another avenue is crowdfunding. Although this option is pretty saturated at this point, if you have a large following or interest for your project, it is possible to tap into that demographic to raise the budget for your first short film. Keep in mind that running a crowdfunding campaign is a full-time job; do your research and assemble a team of reliable people to back you up.

There are also several government funding options. In Ontario, for example, avenues such as the Ontario Arts Council, Bravo Fact and Toronto Arts Council are some of the available funding sources you can apply for.

Getting Seen—Distributing Your Film, Networking, and the Possibility of Feature Filmmaking

Once your short is made, the next step is to get it seen by a public audience. Film festivals are key to the lifespan of a short film, as this is where you create a buzz for the film. Allocate at least 10% of your budget for submission fees and have a solid game plan; research each festival on your list and make sure you're submitting to the ones that screen your genre. It never hurts to send a friendly note informing the festival programmer of your film. You may be able to save money on submission costs by requesting a fee waiver. As much as you can, tour with your film. Festivals are the best way to network with other filmmakers and create ongoing relationships with festival programmers—if they meet you, chances are they'll remember your name the next time you submit.

Once you've finished your festival run, you should attempt to have your short distributed. There are specialty channels and distribution companies that acquire shorts for broadcast or digital consumption (ShortsHD, Ouat Media, etc.). Never make your film available for free online—no distributor or film fest will want something that people can readily obtain.

Shorts are often also used as a pitch for a larger project, like a feature or series. I made a short called *Seek* that was a prologue for my main character in *Chasing Valentine*, which I used to pitch the feature. This garnered interest from potential financers and showed crowdfunders what I was capable of producing with a small budget, and in return, this helped get *Chasing Valentine* off the ground. It's one way to stand out from the plethora of filmmakers with a script looking to get their feature made.

Making a feature film is no easy task, but it can be an extremely rewarding experience. Ensure that you go into it only when you're 100% confident in your project. Make a few shorts first and get all the rookie mistakes out of the way. Once you do that, a feature is basically a larger version of a short—bigger budget, longer schedule, larger cast/crew and wider scope.

When all is said and done, enjoy the process. There will be ups and downs, but we're not saving the world here—we're creating entertainment. If we can't have some fun while doing that, what's the point? Now get out there and make your first film!

Visit Navin's website at www.navinr.com.

Mentor Me: An Inside View of Sessions with Script Consultant, Stéphanie Joalland

by Heidi Stock

This is the third inside view of mentoring sessions in this book. It is literally, "mentor *me*," as I am the student. These sections are included in the anthology to give you a sense of the experience and benefits of one-on-one mentoring with a poet, songwriter, screenwriter or producer. It is meant to give the reader a sense of what private mentoring sessions may be like for you. Every mentor and every student is as unique as the relationship between them.

My Mentor—Stéphanie Joalland

Photo credit: Tania Diez, www.taniadiez.co.uk

Stéphanie is originally from France, but she now divides her time between London, U.K., and Berlin, Germany, and writes and consults globally.

320

Stéphanie began as a reader for the French studios TF1 International and Canal+, evaluating hundreds of English language scripts from all over the world, which allowed her to gain a deep understanding of storytelling. She then worked as a story editor for TF1, where she developed dozens of international animated European and North American co-productions, such as Emmy-nominated *Pet Aliens*. She also worked as a TV screenwriter in the French film industry and created, among others, an animated TV show, *Valerian and Laureline*, for Luc Besson (Europa Corp). She then moved to America to study producing, directing and screenwriting at UCLA, where she graduated in 2008.

With her British partner, Sean McConville (writer/director of *Deadline*, starring Brittany Murphy and Thora Birch), Stéphanie now has a London, U.K.-based production company, Frenzy Films. She's currently developing film and TV projects as a writer–director and as producer. Her recent feature-film debut, *The Quiet Hour*, a sci-fi thriller starring Dakota Blue Richards (*Skins*, *The Golden Compass*) and Karl Davies (*Game of Thrones*), played at over 20 international festivals. It was nominated for best British film at the Raindance Film Festival and Best International Film at the Sofia International Film Festival, was showcased at Newport Beach Film Fest and won Best Feature at the Kansas City Film Festival. *The Quiet Hour* was released in September 2015 in the U.K. and is now sold all over the world.

Stéphanie works as an advisor and mentor in the Raindance MA Film Program, in association with Staffordshire University in the U.K., and has also worked as a script consultant for Raindance Canada. She is an alumna of Berlinale Talents and IFP Emerging Narrative in New York.

Biography courtesy of Stéphanie Joalland

~~~

GETTING STARTED

For our first mentoring session, Stéphanie requested to review a current outline of my short film screenplay for which she would provide a script consultation. I sent her a four-page outline of all scenes for this future 10-minute film. The scenes were a compilation of action and bits of dialogue from my short stories as well as voice-overs of some of my poems. It was as unusual as it sounds, but in the heart of the outline, I had three scenes showing the journey of two characters, Faith and Joe. I learned that was something I could use.

SOME USEFUL BITS AND PIECES

Stéphanie read the outline and commented:

"Your outline is beautifully written; however, I must say that at the moment, it reads very much like an experimental film or a stream-of-consciousness narrative that would work better as a play or as a video installment. To be perfectly honest, I'm not sure that it would make sense to work with a script consultant on the current version as it's too different from the cinematic language script doctors and screenwriters are used to, and it's more akin to theatre, indeed.

That being said, I think there's a story there that could be told in a more traditional way. There's something very moving and powerful about your idea of a woman, Faith, who struggles to come to terms with the tragic death of her brother, Joe, who was found dead on New Year's Day. You could make her a poet so that you can use a lot of your own poetry (as part of the narration, though, as opposed to the poems being extraneous to the story). However, it would imply narrowing down the story to its essence, clarifying it, and completely rewriting it so that it's more akin to a short film with a beginning, a middle and an end as opposed to a juxtaposition of poetic vignettes, and I don't know if that's something you'd like to do?"

Up for the Challenge

Sure, that's something I'd like to do! I was just pleased something promising emerged from this outline and that my mentor supported the inclusion of poetry, which I had hoped for but didn't expect.

The mentoring journey took place over a three-month period and included reading scripts and books on screenwriting, watching short films, creating a step outline and writing a first draft and then the final draft.

The Beginning, Middle and End

Working with the three "useful" scenes in my original outline to find the beginning, middle and end, the structure of my short film script became the following:

Sequence 1: We meet Faith on New Year's Day. She's aloof, disconnected from the rest of the world, alienated and seeks solace in her poetry (used in a voice-over).

Sequence 2: We flash back to what happened to her brother, Joe, on New Year's Day last year.

Sequence 3: We see her connecting to a little boy, which shows that she has finally started to overcome her grief and guilt.

Stéphanie explained that the three sequences will show how Faith can't forgive herself for what happened to her brother and how she ultimately overcomes her grief, which is her "transformational arc." The fact she overcame her grief would be shown through a scene in which we see her connecting with a stranger at the end of the film.

Moving Forward with Some Small Changes

After that mentoring session, I reviewed the three sequences and told Stéphanie the following:

Sequence 1: I wonder if we can start with the entertaining and more dramatic scene of Joe on the street because of that article you sent that recommends having an opening scene that pulls the viewer in. That scene ends with him dying and saying, "You came," and that scene can flow into an office scene in which Faith is in a daydream, staring at a photo of her and Joe in the nativity scene play. Her co-worker says twice to her, "You came; you came," until she comes out of her daydream. "What?" "You came to work this morning. I thought you were getting ready for tonight with what's-his-name." Faith answers, "Georg," and when we see her arrive at home, we see that Georg is her cat. We'll have a couple of young office workers snicker at her because her sweater is on inside out. Embarrassed, then annoyed, she is rude and dismissive to a begging homeless man who sits in front of her church.

Sequence 2: When she arrives at her apartment door, we'll have a neighbour yell in the next apartment, "He's an asshole," and when she closes her door, we have a brief flashback scene to an argument in which Joe yells at Faith, "He's an asshole," referring to their Dad. Joe leaves Faith because he refuses to get back on the meds he recently stopped taking; he claims that medication stifles his creativity. He leaves, and that will be the last time they see each other.

She undresses out of her work clothes and when putting her sweater on a shelf in the closet, she knocks over a jewellery box with photos of her and Joe. She also finds a note that says, "Remember, kiddo [she's the younger sibling], you are beautiful from the inside out." Maybe there would be a brief flashback to the nativity play in the church as children, where he is coaxing, encouraging her to get on stage, but she has performance anxiety. In reaction to the old note from her brother, she cries a bit, but smiles, looks at herself in the mirror and writes the beginning of a poem. Here we learn that Faith writes poetry and has a bit of a creative side that her brother wanted to encourage.

Sequence 3: Faith decides to get dressed up instead of spending the evening in front of the TV. This is a step forward for her to want to get out in public and go to church to pray for her brother's soul. This also works well because this day, New Year's Eve/Day, is a day of obligation in the Catholic Church and the Solemnity of Mary/Feast of Mary (and Faith played Mary in the nativity play). She hasn't been to church in a long time, which we learn from some snide comment from a member of the congregation. But we see that Faith handles the remark in stride; it doesn't affect her, like the snickering office workers.

Before the church service, Faith watches a young boy being disciplined by his mother for touching the nativity play figurines near the altar. At the coat check, she meets the boy, who looks up at her lovingly and won't let go of her hand. He'll be named Angelo for angel because he is a key step toward her final transformation. When she leaves the church, she will give some change to the homeless man who she'd dismissed earlier. This time, she'll see the face of her brother Joe in this man. He'll say, "Happy New Year" to her before she blinks to see Joe's face disappear and the face revert to that of the homeless man. Regardless, she'll smile and walk away. The film can end there.

FROM SEQUENCE TO STEP OUTLINE

With some changes to the originally planned sequences, I created the following draft of my step outline.

Scene 1. Joe, homeless, manic and ranting on a street corner in the financial district of a large city on New Year's Eve, 2001, is found dead by EMS workers on the morning of New Year's Day.

Scene 2. Joe's sister, Faith, finishes her workday at noon on New Year's Eve, 2002, and is seen staring at a photo of herself and Joe as children in a nativity play. She comes out of her daydream when she's visited by a co-worker, who asks about her plans for the night, and when she gets up to leave, young office workers snicker at her because her sweater is on inside out.

Scene 3. She leaves the office, located in an urban, upper class neighbourhood, where she is passed by nannies pushing double strollers and a caregiver with an elderly woman wearing a mink coat.

Scene 4. Embarrassed about her inside-out sweater, then annoyed, Faith is dismissive to a homeless man who sits on the steps in front of the church in her urban, lower-middle-class neighbourhood, which is noisy and strewn with litter.

Scene 5. At her apartment door, Faith hears a neighbour yelling and cursing, which triggers a memory of an argument she'd had with her brother, Joe, at her apartment, when he'd left last year on Canada Day. It was the last time they saw each other. She comes out of her daydream when her cat, Georg, greets her.

Scene 6. In her bedroom, Faith changes out of her work clothes and, after pulling a box labelled "New Year's Eve" from the closet, a jewellery box falls down and out spill photos of her and Joe as well as an encouraging handwritten note from him. She sits down in front of her mirror to read it. Inspired, she writes a couple of lines of a new poem.

Scene 7. Faith moves to her living room with the box containing her annual party items for a night home alone on New Year's Eve: party hat for her and a child-size hat for her cat, confetti, glitter nail polish and a grooming brush, *The Sound of Music* DVD, one tin of gourmet canned cat food and a mini-bar size bottle of Irish Cream. The DVD player won't work and the cat refuses to join her in the living room when she calls him.

Scene 8. Faith finds the cat asleep on her bed, and nearby on the dresser is the new poem and Joe's note. She picks up the note and reads it again. She returns to her closet, redresses in her career clothes, finds her full-length coat, puts it on, and leaves the apartment.

Scene 9. In her coat, she receives positive attention from a couple of strangers. She enters the church where she had passed by a homeless man that afternoon.

Scene 10. As she walks down the aisle of the church, a woman snickers to another person about Faith's lack of attendance over the past year and Faith ignores her. Faith kneels to say a prayer for her brother but is distracted by a young boy who is being disciplined by his mother for playing with the nativity play figurines in front of the altar.

Scene 11. At the end of the service, Faith walks to the coat rack, and after putting on her coat, the boy appears beside her, takes her hand, and they make eye contact. She smiles. The boy's mother is calling him, but he ignores her until Faith breaks eye contact with him.

Scene 12. Faith leaves the church and is ignored by the homeless man who had asked her to spare some change earlier in the day. She approaches him now and gives him some money. When he looks up at her, she sees the face of her brother for a few seconds until she blinks. The homeless man thanks her and wishes her a Happy New Year. She does the same to him.

STEPPING TOWARD THE FIRST DRAFT

It took a while to get to this point, but the steps toward it were necessary and eased the writing of the first draft. (*Also read about the importance of outlines in the writing of a musical theatre play, in my interview with Elise Dewsberry on p.402.*)

Originally, I set the story in the year 2001. My story was about loss and grief in an urban setting, and 2001 being the year of the 9/11 attacks, it provided a solemn backdrop to my little story on a grand scale. Not being a filmmaker, I didn't take into account all the considerations and complications of setting this film in the past, even if it was just 15 years ago. So the change was made to set the story in the present day.

Another issue that my mentor raised about my first draft was that I underwrote character descriptions and sometimes character reactions, too. This is also not helpful to a director.

The big challenge for me was creating a beat (through an action or a reaction) to help the reader of my screenplay clearly understand Faith's decision to get dressed and go to church. Those actions lead to her transformation, and it was critical to understanding Faith on the page, and hopefully in time, Faith on the screen. This missing beat was a note I received from both my mentor and an external reader. (*You can have look at the first draft of this screenplay on p.337.*)

Getting a Second and Third Opinion

My mentor, Stéphanie, did refer to script "doctors" rather than script consultants in our first chat, so it was fitting that she suggested it would be valuable to seek another opinion. She requested that I send my first draft screenplay to two readers for notes. In month two of our three-month mentoring period together, we were too close to the story and external feedback was welcomed.

Stéphanie created the following questions for the readers:

- How would you sum up the story in a few lines?
- What's the theme of the story, in your opinion?
- Was the story clear? If not, what felt confusing to you?
- Do you find the protagonist relatable?
- Is there any moment in the script that felt unnecessary?
- Is there any moment in the script you didn't buy?
- What did you think about the dialogue?

- Did you like the use of the poem as a voice-over?
- Did you like the ending?
- Do you have any further ideas or notes?

Below is some of the feedback on these questions I received from the readers that was helpful in considering changes for the screenplay's final draft.

How would you sum up the story in a few lines?

Reader #1: On New Year's Eve, Faith's brother dies, homeless. She must find a way to reconcile her memories of him, including her guilt at perhaps not helping him enough. What place can faith now have in her life?

Reader #2: On the holidays, a nebbish woman finds new confidence when she remembers the belief that her deceased, albeit mentally ill, brother had in her.

What's the theme of the story?

Reader #1: Faith, in the Christian sense (the love of humankind: faith, hope and charity. Charity begins at home. *Caritas*: love, dearness.)

Reader #2: Don't judge a book by its cover.

Was the story clear?

Reader #1: Yes, in general.

If not, what felt confusing to you?

Reader #1: Why does Faith search for her rosary when she's at the subway? Was she searching for change but found her rosary instead, which made her reconsider and not take the subway? If she was searching for her rosary instead of change, then why did she go to the subway in the first place? A detail, but important, as it marks her turning point.

Do you find the protagonist relatable?

Reader #1: Yes. I especially like her crazy turnaround when she dresses up and swishes out of her apartment. It makes her three-dimensional. Although I'm a little confused as to why she does this. Is it just a "to hell with it" moment?

Reader #2: The story needs context to make her relatable. She's sheepish at work, but judgmental and angry on the streets. Interesting. But what the heck made her that way? Why is she sheepish? Why is she alone with her cat? I like where you're going with a complex character, but you need to flesh out the gaps so I can connect. What's her internal problem? What sets her back?

Is there any moment in the script that felt unnecessary?

Reader #1: "Stifling my creativity" seems a little wooden and out of place. Would he say this? Or would he say something like, "...these goddamn pills. I can't write! I can't..."

Is there any moment in the script you didn't buy?

Reader #1: Occasionally, the prop symbolism seems a little heavy-handed—the figurines, for instance. Perhaps on screen this wouldn't stand out as much (I'm reading it as a text). For example, the recurring figurine of Mary—on screen, would it be the same one from scene to scene, or a different one? Reading it, I pictured the same object. Then there's the rosary; that could be one too many religious icons for me. Perhaps she should stick the figurine of Mary in her pocket and not have any rosary? (Just a suggestion. Feel free to ignore it.) It occurs to me that maybe the "props" tip the balance because there's such heavy symbolism all the way through the text: Faith/faith; Mary, Joseph/ little boy at the end; nativity/family; church at beginning/end.

What did you think about the dialogue?

Reader #1: Good; the characters came alive.

Reader #2: Tighten. Tighten. Tighten. Dialogue is one of the most difficult areas of screenwriting. Say the words out loud. Get in the emotional state of the character—how would it sound then? For example, "You need your meds, Joe. Look how upset you are without them." Maybe this line could be, "You're upset. You need something." Because you're already talking about meds, you don't need to repeat that part. And remove first names (e.g., Joe) as much as possible. Nobody says someone's name unless they're patronizing, really angry, trying to control them, and so on.

Did you like the use of the poem as a voice-over?

Reader #1: Yes, I really did. It gives the script, and the protagonist, another dimension. I guess I read it as a song rather than a poem, but perhaps that's because *The Sound of Music* is mentioned. But I don't think it matters.

Did you like the ending?

Reader #1: Yes, although I'd also be happy with a little less resolution and the neat circling back to the beginning. I think struggles with memory, loss, guilt and faith cannot easily be put in place. Sometimes, they do not live comfortably side by side. Faith (in the religious sense) can give some ready-made answers, but I find there's also something eerie in this, as well as being reassuring. I'd be okay with a screenplay showing this.

Reader #2: I like the idea that she goes to church for the first time in a long time and sees a homeless man that reminds her of her dead brother, but the story requires more of a major arc to make an impactful ending.

Do you have any further ideas or notes?

Reader #2: The neighbour scene: When the neighbour yells, "He's an asshole," it's a plot invention for the next scene—kind of like during a fight, when a sword falls out of the sky and they use it to kill the villain. Now, these sorts of fabrications happen all the time in scripts, but you have to "trick" the audience into thinking it happened for some other reason. Like with the sword, maybe you set up a beat where a skinny kid is carrying a ton of weapons across a bridge and is about to drop everything. Then it makes sense when the sword drops.

In this case, you could add some more dialogue before the neighbour says the triggering line. For example, the bellhop says "They're at it again." Then, when she gets to the door, she hears a woman say, "He's just a friend!" Then the man says, "He's an asshole!" So it makes the audience relate to a jealousy situation—it's realistic. So we think it's clever that the next scene relates, not that it was placed there just for the purpose of the script.

I read the notes of the readers but was advised by my mentor to take a break from the script for a few weeks. That break allowed me to see what resonated in the creation of my final draft.

(Also read about the importance of external feedback and taking a break from your script in an essay by Navin Ramaswaran on p.315.)

CREATING THE FINAL DRAFT

In our last mentoring session, I kept in mind my mentor's advice that "at the end of the day, script assessments are always very subjective and, unless readers give you the same recurring notes, which means there might be an objective issue, the rest is often down to subjectivity and personal taste. So it's good to keep an open mind, yet it's important to stick to the choices you feel strongly about."

So, I stuck with the choices I felt strongly about and worked on addressing the feedback from the external readers that would impact my final draft. My revisions are noted in *italics* below each reader's notes.

Was the story clear?

Yes, in general.

If not, what felt confusing to you?

Why does Faith search for her rosary when she's at the subway? Was she searching for change but found her rosary instead, which makes her reconsider and not take the subway? If she was searching for her rosary instead of change, then why did she go to the subway in the first place? A detail, but important, as it marks her turning point.

Correct! Faith at the subway did not make sense, so I no longer have the subway as a setting in the final draft. The original poem has Faith searching for change at the subway, but I realized that the poem did not need to stay as it was, word by word, to be included in the screenplay.

Do you find the protagonist relatable?

Yes. I especially like her crazy turnaround when she dresses up and swishes out of her apartment. It makes her three-dimensional.

333

Although I'm a little confused as to why she does this. Is it just a "to hell with it" moment?

This was the missing beat also noted by my mentor! Why does Faith leave her apartment? To fix this, I added the action of the framed photo of her and Joey in the nativity play falling out of her purse when she stumbles over it. Then, I added a line spoken confidently to herself, "Okay for you, Joey," before she gets dressed to go out.

The story needs context to make her relatable. She's sheepish at work, but judgmental and angry on the streets. Interesting. But what the heck made her that way? Why is she sheepish? Why is she alone with her cat? I like where you're going with a complex character, but you need to flesh out the gaps so I can connect. What's her internal problem? What sets her back?

Exactly! A complex character. I haven't figured her out yet, either. Much more needs to be done in future drafts, but this time, I tried to remedy this a bit by showing her reading material as a way of revealing her emotional state and her way of being in the world. Before the female co-worker surprises Faith by dropping by her cubicle, Faith puts the photo of her and her brother in her purse and then pulls out a book, The Highly Sensitive Person: How to Thrive When the World Overwhelms You, *and turns to a bookmarked page.*

Is there any moment in the script that felt unnecessary?

"Stifling my creativity" seems a little wooden and out of place. Would he say this? Or would he say something like, ". . . these goddamn pills. I can't write! I can't . . ."

Agreed. I removed "stifling my creativity" and used an "I can't" statement instead. I went with, "I can't act, sing. I can't think!"

Is there any moment in the script you didn't buy?

Occasionally the prop symbolism seems a little heavy-handed—the figurines, for instance. Perhaps on screen this wouldn't stand out as much (I'm reading it as a text). For example, the recurring figurine of Mary—on screen, would it be the same one from scene to scene, or a different one? Reading it, I pictured the same object. Then there's the rosary; that could be one too many religious icons for me. Perhaps she should stick the figurine of Mary in her pocket, and not have any rosary? (Just a suggestion. Feel free to ignore it.) It occurs to me that maybe the "props" tip the balance because there's such heavy symbolism all the way through the text. Faith/faith; Mary, Joseph/ little boy at the end; nativity/family; church at beginning/end.

Yes. In my attempt to find that beat to make sense of the turning point, when Faith leaves her apartment to go to church on the anniversary of her brother's death (also a day of religious obligation in her faith), I added more prop symbolism. Not the way to go, so changes in recurring symbolism were made in the final draft.

What did you think about the dialogue?

Good; the characters came alive.

Tighten. Tighten. Tighten. Dialogue is one of the most difficult areas of screenwriting. Say the words out loud. Get in the emotional state of the character—how would it sound then? For example, "You need your meds, Joe. Look how upset you are without them." Maybe this line could be, "You're upset. You need something." Because you're already talking about meds, you don't need to repeat that part. And remove first names (e.g., Joe) as much as possible. Nobody says someone's name unless they're patronizing, really angry, trying to control them, etc.

I tightened up the dialogue a bit. I deleted Faith's reference to her brother by his first name and deleted the first line, "You need your meds, Joe," altogether.

Do you have any further ideas/notes?

The neighbour scene: When the neighbour yells, "He's an asshole," it's a plot invention for the next scene—kind of like during a fight, when a sword falls out of the sky and they use it to kill the villain. Now, these sorts of fabrications happen all the time in scripts, however, you have to "trick" the audience into thinking it happened for some other reason. Like with the sword, maybe you set up a beat where a skinny kid is carrying a ton of weapons across a bridge and is about to drop everything. Then it makes sense when the sword drops.

In this case, you could add some more dialogue before the neighbour says the triggering line. For example, the bellhop says, "They're at it again." Then, when she gets to the door, she hears a woman say, "He's just a friend!" Then the man says, "He's an asshole!" So it makes the audience relate to a jealousy situation—it's realistic. So we think it's clever that the next scene relates, not that it was just placed there for the purpose of the script.

It was a poorly crafted plot intervention so I decided to remove the neighbour scene. For Faith to flash back to a memory of her brother did not require another character to utter a phrase that her brother used. It was the anniversary of her brother's death and throughout the day she had been thinking of him. That seemed to me to be enough for her to recall that memory.

The final draft of my short film screenplay, *Happy New Year*, appears on the pages following the first draft, although it is certainly not "final." There are many more revisions that this screenplay could and deserves to go through to improve on the notes provided by the readers and my mentor, as well as any future notes it receives.

SCREENPLAY DRAFTS FROM MENTORING SESSIONS

HAPPY NEW YEAR, FIRST DRAFT

By Heidi Stock

FADE IN:

EXT. TORONTO - DOWNTOWN - STREET - MORNING - DECEMBER 31

A homeless man, JOE MCLEISH (33), paces in front of a Nativity Scene and a coin collection box.

Two HOMELESS YOUTH, a male and a female teenager, sit on steps across from Joe.

> MALE TEENAGER
> (points at Joe)
> Look it's Jesus! Hey Jesus, you're a week late!

The female teenager laughs.

> JOE
> Blasphemy! I am not Jesus. I am Joseph, the father of the Son of God!

The teenagers laugh.

> (CONTINUED)

Three men stroll by carrying food, beer and liquor.

                    JOE
              (speaking to the three men)
          My brethren, wisemen, come, bring an
          offering to our unborn saviour. In
          Christ you will never die.

The men ignore Joe and walk away.

A couple walk by, affectionately touching one another.

                    JOE
              (points at the couple)
          Fornicators!

The homeless youth laugh.

                    JOE
              (points at the homeless youth)
          Thieves!

Two men dressed in business suits pass in front of Joe.

                    JOE
          Moneylenders!

The male homeless youth waves goodbye to Joe, then gives him the finger, takes the female youth by the hand, and they walk away.

                              (CONTINUED)

Joe meekly waves goodbye back, then coughs and spits up blood. He buckles at the knees, sits, gasping for air and shivering.

EXT. STREET - MORNING - JANUARY 1

Three male EMS workers walk to Joe's frozen dead body lying behind the Nativity Scene.

The figurine of Mary is in his hand.

> EMS WORKER #1
> (to his co-workers, sarcastic)
> Happy New Year...

EMS Worker #1 picks up a wallet lying near Joe's body. He opens the wallet and removes a driver's license card.

> EMS WORKER #1 (CONT'D)
> ...Joseph McLeish, 1981. Huh. Like me. 33 years old. Okay. Let's go.

The EMS workers lift Joe.

The figurine of Mary drops to the ground.

They place Joe in a body bag and close it - seen from the POV of the body bag.

> JOE (V.O.)
> (in a peaceful voice)
> Wisemen, you came.

INT. OFFICE, MORNING, ONE YEAR LATER

FAITH MCLEISH (34), plain appearance, at her
desk, holds and stares at a photo of a boy and
girl in a nativity play in a picture frame
labelled, Faith & Joey McLeish, Christmas
1989.

A stylish, stunning female CO-WORKER (22)
passes co-workers, drinking and eating with
party hats on, and walks up to Faith's desk
and peers around the cubicle wall.

          CO-WORKER
You came...

Faith, surprised, drops the frame, then sets
it upright.

          CO-WORKER (CONT'D)
Careful Faith. Too much coffee?
    (sighs)
Anyway, I was saying, you came to
work this morning? I thought you'd be
at home getting ready for some poetry
thingy. Night class.

          FAITH
What? No. It's a holiday. Anyway I
said I may not be in today because I
have plans tonight
    (pauses)
with
    (pronounced Gay-org)
Georg.

               (CONTINUED)

                    CO-WORKER
          Gay-who? That's your guy's name?

                    FAITH
               (pauses)
          Yes, he's Austrian.

                    CO-WORKER
          That doesn't sound Australian to me.

                    FAITH
               (frustrated)
          No not Australian, Austrian. German.
          They speak German in Austria. Anyway
          I came in and now...

Faith looks at the clock on her computer
screen which reads 11:55 AM 2015-12-31.

                    FAITH (CONT'D)
          ...now I have to go.

Faith turns off her computer, grabs her coat
and hurries away.

                    CO-WORKER
               Wait!

Faith turns and looks back at the co-worker.

                    CO-WORKER
          Your sweater.
               (mouths the words)
          It's on inside out.

                                        (CONTINUED)

> FAITH
> (annoyed)
> What?!

> CO-WORKER
> Inside out!
> (loudly)
> Your sweater is on inside out.

Other co-workers laugh and Faith walks to the exit.

> CO-WORKER (O.S.)
> (daftly)
> Happy New Year!

EXT. UPTOWN - YONGE/ST.CLAIR - AFTERNOON

Faith leaves the office building, nearly loses balance when a nanny barrels past with a wide double stroller. Faith regains balance and is nearly tripped by another caregiver protecting a path for an elderly woman dressed in a mink coat who is using a walker.

EXT. STREET - AFTERNOON

Faith stumbles trying to pass chatty, elderly women walking contently with their shopping bags. Faith shakes her head, steps onto the street but a bike courier forces her back on the sidewalk. An old homeless man sits on church steps.

(CONTINUED)

HOMELESS MAN
(to Faith)
Spare some change?

FAITH
(quietly)
No.

HOMELESS MAN
(oblivious, repeats again)
Spare some change?

FAITH
No! No change!

HOMELESS MAN
Jesus!

Faith pauses, surprised at her anger, swiftly walks away.

HOMELESS MAN
(mutters)
Jesus, Mary and Joseph!

INT. FAITH'S BUILDING - AFTERNOON

Faith stands outside her apartment door.

MALE NEIGHBOUR (O.S.)
(yelling)
He's an asshole!

She cringes. Faith opens the door, closes it, then leans against it, drops her purse, squats, bows her head, and closes her eyes.

FLASHBACK

INT. FAITH'S APARTMENT - JULY 1, THE PREVIOUS
YEAR - AFTERNOON

Faith enters her apartment to find Joe in her
living room, half-dressed, shirtless with
just boxer shorts on. The A/C unit in the
window is on full blast.

            JOE
        (yelling)
    He's an asshole!

           FAITH
    What? Who? Who are you talking about?

           JOE
    Who else?! Jack.

           FAITH
    You mean Dad?

           JOE
    He's not my Dad! Not yours either.
    Stop calling him that.

Joe starts pacing manically.

           JOE
    He's trying to kill me and it's not
    the first time. He locked me up...with
    all those crazy people.
    Now...

(CONTINUED)

Joe ruffles through a duffle bag and pulls out a pill bottle.

> JOE (CONT'D)
> ...now...he's poisoning me with these goddamn pills. Stifling my creativity. I can't...

Joe smacks himself on the head with his palm three times.

> JOE (CONT'D)
> ...think. I can't think!

> FAITH
> (raising her voice)
> You need your meds Joe. Look how upset you are without them.

> JOE
> Upset?! Who cares about upset? Upset is real. I'd rather be real. I'd rather be living than numb.

> FAITH
> (pleading)
> That's the thing Joe. You can't live without the pills!

> JOE
> I can't?! 33 years and I'm still here. 33 years and I'm still me.

Joe picks up his duffle bag and heads for the door.

(CONTINUED)

                    JOE
          (sarcastically)
     Thanks for your support Sis! Oh, and
     Happy Canada Day!

END FLASHBACK

INT. FAITH'S APARTMENT - AFTERNOON

Faith raises her head and wipes tears off her
face. She sees her cat, GEORG, nearby.

                    FAITH
     Come here sweetie.

Faith stands up and walks to the cat and pats
him.

                    FAITH
     Thank God for you Georg. You are my
     good little boy, aren't you?

INT. FAITH'S APARTMENT - BEDROOM - AFTERNOON

Faith removes her work clothes, puts on
pajamas that are lying on her bed, folds the
cashmere sweater she's wearing and puts it on
a shelf in her closet.

She reaches for a box labelled New Year's
Eve. When she removes it, another box falls,
out of which falls a journal.

                              (CONTINUED)

She opens the journal. Inside are poems from her childhood and a note that reads, REMEMBER SIS, YOU ARE BEAUTIFUL FROM THE INSIDE OUT - JOEY. She half-smiles and then moves the box to the bed.

INT. FAITH'S APARTMENT - LIVING ROOM - EVENING

Faith sits on her couch and sets the box labelled New Year's Eve on the coffee table.

She removes two party hats (adult and child), confetti, a nail file, nail polish, a cat grooming brush, The Sound of Music DVD, a catnip treat, and a mini-bar bottle of Irish Cream.

> FAITH
> Georg! Come on. It's show time.

The cat doesn't join her.

Faith walks to the DVD player (its clock reads 7:30), turns it on, presses the eject button but the drive won't open.

She tries to pry it open with the nail file but it doesn't work.

Faith sits back down on the couch and reaches for a pen and a To Do list notepad sitting on the side table.

(CONTINUED)

She writes #1 Buy DVD Player, #2 Buy more Irish Cream.

She stops writing, taps the pen three times on the notepad and then writes #3, pauses and glances around the room.

She starts to write beside #3, INSIDE OUT, THIS BLACK CASHMERE SWEATER AND NOW THE WORDS I CAN'T CONTAIN.

She stops writing, startled by a noise from the bedroom.

> FAITH
>
> Georg?

INT. FAITH'S APARTMENT - BEDROOM -EVENING

The cat plays with the old note from Joey (Joe) and the box is turned on its side. Faith walks in the room, pulls the note away and Georg jumps off the bed.

Faith finds a rosary on the bed as well as old photos of Joey in the spot where the cat was lying. She picks up both, places them on her dresser next to mini figurines of Joseph, Mary and Jesus.

(CONTINUED)

She pauses, focusing on the figurines, then goes to her closet, puts her work clothes back on, fixes her hair in the mirror. She digs further back in her closet and removes a dry cleaning plastic cover off a winter dress coat.

She faces the mirror and puts on the coat.

> FAITH (V.O.)
> I have a coat named Darling with faux fur collar and cuffs, three-quarter length black.

Faith removes a box from the closet and puts on a wool hat.

> FAITH (V.O.)
> When matched with a wool hat on a crisp winter day

Faith puts the rosary in her pocket and leaves the room.

INT. FAITH'S APARTMENT - LIVING ROOM - EVENING

Faith walks into the room and puts on high heel boots.

> FAITH (V.O.)
> She is all Hollywood glamour

Faith walks to the table and picks up The Sound of Music DVD.

(CONTINUED)

>   FAITH (V.O.)
>   elegant, like the Baroness with her

Faith puts the DVD down, picks up a purse,
and pats the cat.

>   FAITH
>   (mimics the voice of the Baroness
>   character from The Sound of
>   Music)
>   Auf Wiedersehen Darling

INT. FAITH'S BUILDING - HALLWAY

Faith locks her apartment door and dashes
down the stairs.

>   FAITH (V.O.)
>   And she is Darling and not St.
>   Clair West, her original nickname,
>   to honour the silver-haired dames
>   donning the real thing, not this
> $160 version, $80 on sale.

EXT. STREET - NIGHT

Faith passes by a young man in labourer's
clothes.

>   FAITH (V.O.)
>   She passes by the construction worker

>   LABOURER
>   Smile, darlin', it's a holiday

EXT. SUBWAY ENTRANCE - NIGHT

Faith goes into the subway entrance to rummage through her purse for her rosary.

> FAITH (V.O.)
> She fumbles for change at the subway

> TRANSIT WORKER
> That's OK, darling, no need to pay

Faith shakes her head to imply no to the transit worker, checks her coat pockets, finds the rosary, then exits.

EXT. STREET - NIGHT

Faith smiles and walks confidently.

> FAITH (V.O.)
> I could get used to being part of this entourage. Sometimes a gal just needs a little attention. Even if it is for strangers.

Faith runs up church steps.

> FAITH (V.O.)
> Even if it is for her coat.

Faith opens the church door.

HEIDI STOCK

INT. CHURCH - NIGHT

Faith walks down the aisle and passes by an elderly female member of the congregation at the end of a pew.

> FEMALE CONGREGATION MEMBER
> Is that Faith McLeish?
> (to her neighbour judgmentally)
> Haven't seen her in a while.

Faith selects a pew near the front and kneels. She wraps her rosary in her hands, begins to bow her head, then stops when she hears a thump at the altar.

She makes eye contact with a toddler boy who fell in front of the Nativity scene display. Faith lowers her head to pray.

INT. CHURCH - LATER THAT NIGHT

DISSOLVE TO: She raises her head as altar boys and the priest walk down the aisle to the church lobby.

Faith walks slowly to a crowded area of multiple coat racks.

She puts on her coat and looks down to find the toddler boy holding her hand and looking up at her. He doesn't smile but looks intently.

Faith half-smiles at the boy.

(CONTINUED)

                    BOY'S MOTHER (O.S.)
        Angelo?

The mother finds her son and Faith.

                    BOY'S MOTHER
        What's gotten into you today?
            (to Faith)
        I'm sorry.

                    FAITH
        Don't be. No need to apologize.

The boy releases Faith's hand.

EXT. CHURCH - NIGHT

Faith exits the church and on the steps sees
the old homeless man from earlier that day.
His head is down and he is silent.

She approaches slowly, squats down, and
places $20 in his palm.

He looks up and she sees the face of Joe in
his.

She shakes her head, blinks, and then Joe's
face disappears.

                    OLD HOMELESS MAN
        Thank you. Happy New Year.

                    FAITH
        Happy New Year. Thank you.

Faith walks down the street.

FADE OUT.

Happy New Year, Final Draft

By Heidi Stock

FADE IN:

EXT. TORONTO - DOWNTOWN - STREET - MORNING - DECEMBER 31 SUPER: NEW YEAR'S EVE 2014

A homeless man, JOE MCLEISH (33), oddly charismatic, more showman than homeless man, paces in front of a Nativity Scene and a coin collection box.

Two homeless youth, a female and a MALE TEENAGER, sit on steps across from Joe.

>   MALE TEENAGER
>   (points at Joe)
>   Look it's Jesus! Hey Jesus, you're a
>   week late!

The female teenager laughs.

>   JOE
>   Blasphemy! I am not Jesus. I am
>   Joseph, the father of the Son of God!

The teenagers laugh.

Three men stroll by carrying food, beer and liquor.

(CONTINUED)

                    JOE
            (to the three men)
My brethren, wisemen, come, bring an
offering to our unborn saviour. In
Christ you will never die.

The men ignore Joe and walk away.

A couple walk by, affectionately touching
one another.

                    JOE
            (points at the couple)
Fornicators!

The homeless youth laugh.

                    JOE
            (points at the homeless youth)
Thieves!

Two men dressed in business suits pass in
front of Joe.

                    JOE
Moneylenders!

The male homeless youth waves goodbye to Joe,
then gives him the finger, takes the female
youth by the hand, and they walk away.

Joe meekly waves goodbye back, then coughs
and spits up blood. He buckles at the knees,
shivers, and gasps for air.

EXT. STREET - MORNING - JANUARY 1

Three male EMS workers walk to Joe's frozen dead body lying behind the Nativity Scene.

> EMS WORKER #1
> (to his co-workers, sarcastic)
> Happy New Year.

EMS Worker #1 picks up a wallet lying near Joe's body. He opens the wallet and removes a driver's license card.

> EMS WORKER #1 (CONT'D)
> Joseph McLeish, 1981. Huh. 33, like me. Okay. Let's go.

The EMS workers lift Joe, place him in a body bag and close it - seen from the POV of the body bag.

> JOE (V.O.)
> (peaceful)
> Wisemen, you came.

INT. OFFICE - MORNING - ONE YEAR LATER SUPER: NEW YEAR'S EVE 2015

FAITH MCLEISH (35), unkept, with a plain appearance and modestly dressed, at her desk, holds and stares at a photo of a boy and girl in a nativity play in a picture frame labelled, FAITH & JOEY MCLEISH, CHRISTMAS 1989.

(CONTINUED)

Faith hugs the frame and puts it in her purse from which she pulls out a book, THE HIGHLY SENSITIVE PERSON: HOW TO THRIVE WHEN THE WORLD OVERWHELMS YOU, and turns to a bookmarked page.

A stylish, attractive, expressive female CO-WORKER (22) passes co-workers, drinking and eating with party hats on, walks up to Faith's desk, and peers around the cubicle wall.

> CO-WORKER
> You came.

Faith, startled, drops the book on her desk, then quickly turns it face down.

> CO-WORKER (CONT'D)
> Careful Faith. Too much coffee? You need to chill like us interns.
> (sighs)
> I thought you'd be at home getting ready for some poetry thingy. Reading. Whatever.

> FAITH
> What? No. It's a holiday. And I said I may not be in today because I have plans tonight
> (pauses)
> with
> (pronounced Gay-org)
> Georg.

(CONTINUED)

>   CO-WORKER
>   Gay-who? That's your guy's name?
>
>   FAITH
>   (pauses)
>   Yes, he's Austrian.
>
>   CO-WORKER
>   That doesn't sound Australian to me.
>
>   FAITH
>   (frustrated)
>   No not Australian, Austrian. They
>   speak German in Austria. Anyway I
>   came in and now...

Faith looks at the clock on her computer screen which reads 11:55 AM 2015-12-31.

>   FAITH (CONT'D)
>   ...now I have to go.

Faith turns off her computer, grabs her book, purse, and coat, and hurries away.

>   CO-WORKER
>   Wait!

Faith turns and looks back at the co-worker.

>   CO-WORKER
>   Your sweater.
>   (mouths the words)
>   It's on inside out.

                                   (CONTINUED)

                    FAITH
    What?!

                    CO-WORKER
    Inside out!
        (loudly)
    Your sweater is on inside out.

Other co-workers laugh and Faith walks to the
exit.

                    CO-WORKER (O.S.)
        (daftly)
    Happy New Year!

EXT. UPTOWN - YONGE/ST.CLAIR - AFTERNOON

Faith leaves the office building and nearly
loses balance when a nanny barrels past with
a wide double stroller. Faith regains balance
and is almost tripped by another caregiver
walking arm in arm with an elderly woman
dressed in a mink coat.

EXT. STREET - AFTERNOON

Faith stumbles trying to pass a row of chatty,
elderly women staggering with overloaded
shopping bags. She nervously quickens her
pace, steps onto the street, but a bike
courier forces her back on the sidewalk
behind the women taking up the full width of
the sidewalk.

An OLD HOMELESS MAN sits on church steps.

                              (CONTINUED)

>   OLD HOMELESS MAN
>   (to Faith)
>   Spare some change?

>   FAITH
>   (quietly)
>   No.

>   OLD HOMELESS MAN
>   (oblivious, repeats again)
>   Spare some change?

>   FAITH
>   No! No change!

>   OLD HOMELESS MAN
>   Jesus!

Faith pauses, surprised at her anger, swiftly walks away.

>   OLD HOMELESS MAN
>   (mutters)
>   Jesus, Mary and Joseph!

INT. FAITH'S BUILDING - AFTERNOON

Faith opens her apartment door, closes it, then leans against it, drops her purse, squats, bows her head, and closes her eyes.

FLASHBACK

INT. FAITH'S APARTMENT - JULY 1, 2014 - AFTERNOON

Faith enters her apartment to find Joe in her living room, half-dressed, shirtless with just boxer shorts on. The A/C unit in the window is on full blast.

> JOE
> He's an asshole!

> FAITH
> What? Who are you talking about?

> JOE
> Dad!

Joe starts pacing manically.

> JOE
> He's trying to kill me again. Look at these!

Joe ruffles through a duffle bag, pulls out a pill bottle, and rattles it in front of Faith's face.

> JOE
> He thinks I should take them, but I stopped! I can't act, sing. I can't...

Joe smacks himself on the head with his palm three times.

(CONTINUED)

                    JOE (CONT'D)
          ...think!

                    FAITH
          But look how upset you are without
          them.

                    JOE
          Upset?! Who cares about upset? Upset
          is real. Upset is alive!

                    FAITH
          Alive? You can't live without the
          pills!

                    JOE
          I can! And I can find another place to
          live too.

Joe picks up his duffle bag and heads for the
door.

                    JOE
          Thanks for your support Sis! Oh, and
          Happy Canada Day!

END FLASHBACK

INT. FAITH'S APARTMENT - AFTERNOON

Faith raises her head and wipes tears off her face. She sees her cat, GEORG, nearby.

> FAITH
> Thank God for you Georg. You are my good little boy, aren't you?

INT. FAITH'S APARTMENT - BEDROOM - AFTERNOON

Faith puts her purse in front of her bed, removes her clothes, puts on pajamas lying on her bed, folds the cashmere sweater and places it on a shelf in her closet.

She reaches for a box labelled NEW YEAR'S EVE. When she removes it, another box falls, out of which falls a journal.

She opens the journal. Inside are poems in a child's handwriting surrounded by crayon sketches. Faith smiles, closes the journal, and moves the box to the bed.

INT. FAITH'S APARTMENT - LIVING ROOM - EVENING

Faith sits on her couch and sets the box labelled New Year's Eve on the coffee table.

She removes two party hats (adult and child), confetti, a nail file, nail polish, a cat grooming brush, The Sound of Music DVD, a catnip treat, and a mini-bar bottle of Irish Cream.

(CONTINUED)

                    FAITH
          Georg! Come on. It's show time.

The cat doesn't join her.

Faith walks to the DVD player (its clock
reads 7:30), turns it on, presses the eject
button but the drive won't open.

She tries to pry it open with the nail file
but it doesn't work.

Faith sits back down on the couch and reaches
for a pen and a To Do list notepad sitting on
the side table.

She writes #1 Buy DVD Player, #2 Buy more
Irish Cream.

She stops writing, taps the pen three times
on the notepad and then writes #3, pauses and
glances around the room.

She starts to write beside #3, INSIDE OUT,
THIS BLACK CASHMERE SWEATER AND NOW THE WORDS
I CAN'T CONTAIN.

She stops writing, startled by a noise from
the bedroom.

                    FAITH
          Georg?

INT. FAITH'S APARTMENT - BEDROOM -EVENING

The cat plays with items from the box that is now turned on its side. Faith walks in the room. Georg jumps off the bed.

Faith sits on the bed, finds a rosary hanging out the box, and picks up an old shrivelled note.

> FAITH
> Remember Sis, you are beautiful from the inside out - Joey

Faith stands up, takes one step, and knocks over her purse with her foot. The framed photo of her and Joey falls out. She puts the note and the picture frame on her dresser.

> FAITH
> (confidently)
> Okay. For you Joey.

Faith walks to her closet, puts her work clothes back on, fixes her hair in the mirror. She digs further back in her closet and removes a dry cleaning plastic cover off a winter dress coat.

She faces the mirror and puts on the coat.

(CONTINUED)

> FAITH (V.O., RECITING A
> POEM)
> I have a coat named Darling with faux
> fur collar and cuffs, three-quarter
> length black.

Faith removes a box from the closet and puts on a wool hat.

> FAITH (V.O.)
> When matched with a wool hat on a
> crisp winter day.

Faith picks up the rosary, puts it in her pocket, grabs her purse, and leaves the room.

INT. FAITH'S APARTMENT - LIVING ROOM - EVENING

Faith walks into the room and puts on high heel boots.

> FAITH (V.O.)
> She is all Hollywood glamour.

Faith walks to the table and picks up The Sound of Music DVD.

> FAITH (V.O.)
> Elegant, like the Baroness with her

Faith puts the DVD down and pats the cat. She mimics the voice of the Baroness character from The Sound of Music film.

> FAITH
> Auf Wiedersehen Darling.

INT. FAITH'S BUILDING - HALLWAY

Faith locks her apartment door and dashes
down the stairs.

> FAITH (V.O.)
> And she is Darling and not St.
> Clair West, her original nickname,
> to honour the silver-haired dames
> donning the real thing, not this
> $160 version, $80 on sale.

EXT. STREET - NIGHT

Faith passes by a YOUNG MAN in labourer's
clothes.

> FAITH (V.O.)
> She passes by the construction
> worker.

> YOUNG MAN
> Smile, darlin', it's a holiday.

Faith smiles and walks confidently.

> FAITH (V.O.)
> I could get used to being part of
> this entourage. Sometimes a gal just
> needs a little attention. Even if it
> is from strangers.

Faith runs up church steps.

> FAITH (V.O.)
> Even if it is for her coat.

Faith opens the church door.

INT. CHURCH - NIGHT

Faith walks down the aisle and passes by an ELDERLY WOMAN at the end of a pew.

> ELDERLY WOMAN
> Is that Faith McLeish?
> (to her neighbour judgmentally)
> Haven't seen her in a while.

Faith selects a pew near the front and kneels. She wraps her rosary in her hands, begins to bow her head, then stops when she hears a THUMP at the altar.

She makes eye contact with A TODDLER BOY who fell in front of the Nativity scene display. Faith lowers her head to pray.

INT. CHURCH - LATER THAT NIGHT

DISSOLVE TO: She raises her head as altar boys and the priest walk down the aisle to the church lobby.

Faith walks slowly to a crowded area of multiple coat racks.

She puts on her coat and looks down to find the toddler boy holding her hand and looking up at her. He doesn't smile but looks intently.

Faith smiles at the boy.

(CONTINUED)

> BOY'S MOTHER (O.S.)
> Angelo?

The MOTHER finds her son and Faith.

> BOY'S MOTHER
> What's gotten into you today?
> (to Faith)
> I'm sorry.

> FAITH
> Don't be. No need to apologize.

The boy releases Faith's hand.

EXT. CHURCH - NIGHT

Faith exits the church and on the steps sees the old homeless man from earlier that day. His head is down and he is silent.

She approaches slowly, squats down, and places $20 in his palm.

He looks up and she sees the face of Joe in his.

She shakes her head, blinks, and then Joe's face disappears.

> OLD HOMELESS MAN
> Thank you. Happy New Year.

> FAITH
> Happy New Year. Thank you.

Faith walks down the street.

FADE OUT.

MUSICAL THEATRE

MUSCIAL THEATRE: INTERVIEWS

INTERVIEW WITH
LANDON BRAVERMAN AND JOSEPH TREFLER

LANDON BRAVERMAN

Photo and biography courtesy of Landon Braverman

Landon Braverman is a New York City–based composer, originally from Vancouver, Canada. With bookwriter/lyricist collaborator Derek P. Hassler, he has created the new musicals *Queen of the West* (winner of Best Score and Best Musical at the Manhattan Theatre Mission), *Picture Perfect* (Prospect Theatre Company), and *Choices* (various off-Broadway, Top 10 Finalist Ken Davenport Short Play Competition). Their most recent project, *The White Rose*, was workshopped at

Millikin University and with New York Theatre Barn. Their music has been featured in concerts at Lincoln Center, 54 Below, NYMF and in other venues across the world.

As an active music copyist, Landon has worked alongside various Broadway and Tony Award winning composers. Recent projects include the Broadway premieres of *Amazing Grace* and Jason Robert Brown's *Honeymoon in Vegas*, starring Tony Danza. With Grammy Award winning Sh-K-Boom/Ghostlight Records, he assisted on the recordings of various new musicals including *Bring It On* and *Giant*.

Landon is the Co-Founding Artistic Director of the Canadian Musical Theatre Writers Collective (www.cmtwc.com), a national organization devoted to supporting and promoting the work of new writers at home and abroad. For CMTWC he produced *Blame Canada!*, a widely acclaimed sold-out concert series seen around the world.

Landon holds a BA and BMus from Mount Allison University, and an MFA from New York University's Graduate Musical Theatre Writing Program (Tisch). He is a proud member of ASCAP and the Dramatists Guild.

www.bravermanhassler.com

JOSEPH TREFLER

Photo and biography courtesy of Joseph Trefler

Joseph Trefler is a New York–based composer–lyricist, originally from Toronto, Canada. He has written a number of musicals, including *Lady Late Nite* (short film musical distributed by Ouat Media), *A Ladylike Murder* (premiered at the Isabel Bader theatre in Toronto in 2012) and, most recently, *Men With Money* with bookwriter-lyricist Bill Nelson (to be produced in Queens, NY in November 2016). He composed the score for *The Music Box*, a short dance film that was shown on Air Canada flights. He is a winner of the 2015 NMI New Voices Project (sponsored by Walt Disney Imagineering Creative Entertainment). His new musical, *The Unusual Engagement Of Chester Pringle*, written with bookwriter–lyricist Jonathan Pearson and bookwriter Seth Tucker, was presented at the Wild Project in New York City in July 2014, winning Best Short Musical in the Fresh Fruit Festival. Recently, a concert of Joseph's songs was performed at Lincoln Center's *Broadway's Future Songbook* series.

Joseph is a Co-Founder and Artistic Director of the Canadian Musical Theatre Writers Collective (CMTWC), which has over 180 members and growing. He was a juror for the 2014 Playwrights Guild of Canada Tom Hendry New Musical Award. Joseph received his

HEIDI STOCK

Bachelor of Music from the University of Toronto and his MFA from the Graduate Musical Theatre Writing Program, Tisch School of the Arts, New York University.

www.josephtrefler-composer.com

~~~

Heidi: What was your path from a personal interest in musical theatre to professional career?

Landon: Musical theatre has been a part of my life for as long as I can remember. When I was six years old growing up in Vancouver, I did a summer performance intensive called *Gotta Sing! Gotta Dance!*, which immersed me in the genre. Soon after, I landed my first professional acting gig and never looked back. I moved into the writing and producing side of the business during my undergraduate years at Mount Allison University. I taught myself piano and found a new passion for creating original work. I was lucky enough to have the opportunity to write and produce a few original shows in my years there, which led me to New York City, where I now reside.

Joseph: I got hooked on *Wicked* in high school. I must have listened to the cast recording a thousand times—literally! I was obsessed. Halfway through high school, a good friend of mine suggested we write a musical together, so we did! I never stopped writing after that.

Heidi: What makes musical theatre such a popular form of theatre entertainment and, among its biggest fans, a passion or even an obsession?

Landon: Beyond the sheer entertainment value that comes from combining story with music, dance, and various elements of spectacle, I think musical theatre is popular because it has the ability to connect with people of all ages in a deeply personal and emotional way. It does this while transcending all boundaries. It's one of the most universal art forms in modern existence. It may be a form of escape, but it's deeply rooted in our inner reality. It is also exceptionally flexible; it has the ability to transform with the times, meaning it's constantly surprising us and staying relevant.

Joseph: I think there's something visceral about musical theatre. I once read (I can't remember where) that words make you think thoughts and music makes you feel feelings, but the combination of words and music can make you feel a thought. In other words, when we experience musical theatre we're experiencing it on an intellectual level and an emotional level simultaneously. That has tremendous power. It draws people in.

Heidi: Theatre, like film, is highly collaborative in nature. Please talk a bit about the importance of—and your own experience with—collaboration among members of a creative team in the early phases of writing a new musical.

Landon: I always joke that writing musicals is a form of alchemy. Getting a musical to truly work and become that magical everlasting piece of art is one of the toughest things to achieve. It is this way *because* it is so highly collaborative. Every element is equally important, and when one falters from that central vision, the whole piece suffers.

I am lucky to have an excellent collaborator—lyricist and bookwriter, Derek P. Hassler. We met while studying at NYU and have been writing together ever since. Our collaboration is a marriage. It has its ups and downs. But the most important thing is that when all is said and done, we have the same impulse and vision for the piece we are writing. He may write the words and I the music, but we work hard to make it feel like it's one voice moving seamlessly through space and time. It takes a lot of back and forth in person and through emails.

Joseph: Writing musicals is, in my opinion, the most highly collaborative of art forms. Everything—book, lyrics, music, set, lighting, etc.—has to work together as one entity to tell the story. If

377

even one element is off it can ruin the moment. That's what makes creating musicals so challenging. But when they *do* come together you get something that transcends the individual elements—something magical.

This melding of different elements is what I strive for in my own work. My collaborators and I work mostly via email, but we may exchange a hundred emails over the course of writing a single song. The high degree of back and forth allows us to create something that feels like it was written by one person. I like to think of it as melding my brain with my collaborator's brain. It's very intimate and, when successful, it's an extremely gratifying kind of collaboration.

Heidi: What were (or still are) some of the challenges of creating original musical theatre productions in Canada? And how are organizations like Canadian Musical Theatre Writers Collective (CMTWC) and other Canadian organizations or individuals addressing these challenges and helping musical theatre creators?

Landon: I think we are on the cusp of a new renaissance for Canadian musical theatre. There is an exciting dialogue happening from coast to coast. Nevertheless, we still have a ways to go to achieve our goal of a vibrant scene, where a consistent array of high-quality new works are being developed, produced and entering the repertory.

The major issue is the lack of infrastructure and knowledge on how to properly develop new musicals. We have a wealth of raw writing talent, but little knowledge on the specific craft elements of writing musicals. This needs to be improved first and foremost if we want to create pieces that will last at home and abroad. Next, since 99% of our theatre works under the not-for-profit model, we need funding bodies to recognize the importance of new Canadian musicals and start channeling money into its development. Lastly, we need theatres and producers across the country to commit to the development *and* production process. One last caveat: in the long term, we need to create an infrastructure that will allow new Canadian shows to be recorded and licensed so that they can have a life after their original premiere.

CMTWC is working to help change the dialogue in the country and lobby for more development. We have had great success around the world shining a light on the work we already have through our series of cabaret concerts called *Blame Canada!* In regard to the writers, we are working to help emerging talent reach their full potential by launching the CMTWC Writers Workshop, a new intensive focused on the craft of writing music and lyrics for the genre. This course will be taught by Canadian musical theatre legend Leslie Arden. We are also working to create a book writing course. Many of our collaborators, like Acting Up Stage, Touchstone Theatre, the Charlottetown Festival and the Canadian Music Theatre Project (CMTP) are committing major resources to both the development and production of new works. This is a major and very exciting step forward, and the fruits of these labours are already starting to be seen in the public eye. The best example is *Come From Away*, which began at CMTP and will be at Mirvish later this year before heading to Broadway.

Joseph: The main challenge for Canadian musical theatre is the lack of infrastructure. First, writers don't have anywhere in Canada to study the craft of musical theatre writing, so they are at a major disadvantage when competing with trained writers from abroad. Second, there are very few places in Canada dedicated to developing new musicals, so Canadian musicals rarely make it to the level of being production-ready. Third, when a great new Canadian musical is created despite the above obstacles, Canadian producers are usually unwilling to take a risk on an unproven commodity. That's why fantastic new Canadian shows like the Broadway-bound *Come From Away* (by Irene Sankoff and David Hein) have American premieres before Canadian ones, which is frustrating.

I like to refer to the above three steps (education, development and production) as "the pipeline." All three need to be in place for Canadian musical theatre to be successful. CMTWC is working to make the pipeline a reality. Last year, we partnered with Theatre 20, Leslie Arden and Jen Shuber on Composium, a training course for musical theatre writers. CMTWC is starting our own musical theatre songwriting course this coming fall and planning to add a book writing course in the near future. Other organizations, such as the Canadian Music Theatre Project (created by Michael Rubinoff) and Acting Up Stage (created by Mitchell Marcus), are focusing on developing new musicals. (*Come From Away* is one of CMTP's major success stories.) The hope is that, with these elements in place, we'll see an explosion of new, well-crafted Canadian musicals in the next few years. The challenge will be to get Canadian producers to commit to commercial productions of those shows.

Heidi: Are Canadian musicals (specifically English language Canadian musicals) distinct? Do they have a unique perspective or voice when compared to musicals written and created in the United States or in the U.K.?

Landon: I don't think so. The canon is too small to truly see a trend or to try to compare it with other countries. This is not necessarily a problem; however, it does bring up the challenge of having the U.S.—and thus, Broadway—south of the border. It's easy and common for Canadian writers to compare—to build up expectation based on what they see so close by. In my opinion, the sooner this stops, the sooner our work will thrive. We have to understand that we are not, and never will be, the U.S. or Broadway. Their business model and demographics are inherently different.

The most important thing is to find stories that are engaging and tell them in a well-crafted way. If they happen to cross over to an international stage, that is wonderful. If not, it's no problem, either.

Joseph: It's difficult to talk about trends in Canadian musical theatre because there have been so few commercially successful Canadian musicals. My sense is the answer is no, Canadian musicals don't currently have a unique voice compared to musicals created in the U.S. or the U.K. However, I don't think that lack of a unique voice is necessarily a problem. Recently, there was a CBC interview with writer Madeline Ashby, who encouraged Canadian artists to focus more on creating "good art" as opposed to "good *Canadian* art." I agree with her. I think Canadian musical theatre writers should focus on telling the stories they want to tell, as well as they can, without worrying about how "Canadian" the stories are. I think any art created by a Canadian artist inherently has a Canadian perspective simply because it was created by a Canadian.

Heidi: What advice do you have for aspiring writers of musical theatre?

Landon: First and foremost, learn the craft. Even the most groundbreaking shows in the canon are rooted in the great rules of our genre. It's why they work. Also, make sure you are writing about something you are truly passionate about. Musicals take a long time, so you need a project that can keep you excited through the inherent ups and downs of development. Lastly, remember that it's a small business, and one with room for so many ideas. Don't let rejection and other stresses get you down. Keep writing. Stay passionate. Remain focused on the end goal. The rest will come, I promise!

Joseph: Learn your craft. If you have the opportunity to take a course in musical theatre writing, do it. Study musicals that you love and figure out what makes them tick. Most importantly, just keep writing!

CONVERSATION WITH MICHAEL RUBINOFF

Photo and biography courtesy of Michael Rubinoff

Michael Rubinoff earned a BA in political science and an LLB (Valedictorian) from Western University (formerly the University of Western Ontario [UWO]). While at Western, he served on the university's Board of Governors and two terms as Legal Society President. In 1997, on a platform highlighting post-secondary school issues, he ran for Member of Parliament in the riding of London North Centre and was one of the youngest candidates in the country. Prior to being called to the Ontario Bar in 2002, he launched M. Rubinoff Productions Inc., a commercial theatre company producing mid-sized theatre in the City of Toronto.

Recent producing credits include the Canadian premieres of the off-Broadway plays *Love, Loss, and What I Wore*, co-written by Nora Ephron and starring 21 of Canada's most notable actresses, and *Dog Sees God: Confessions of a Teenage Blockhead*, which starred Canada's most notable young actors. His productions have earned one Dora Mavor Moore Award for excellence in Toronto theatre and six nominations for other awards.

Michael is a 2004 graduate of the Commercial Theatre Institute Intensive Producing Program, in New York and was President of

ScriptLab, a not-for-profit organization in Toronto with a commitment to the development of the works and the artists of Canadian musical theatre. He is President of the Toronto Alliance for the Performing Arts and chair of their Commercial Theatre Development Fund.

He is the producer of Theatre Sheridan's six-show season and produced the 2012 transfer of Theatre Sheridan's production of *RENT* to the Mirvish-owned Panasonic Theatre. In 2011, he established the Canadian Music Theatre Project, at Sheridan, Canada's incubator for new musical theatre works by Canadian and international artists.

As a producer, he continues to develop new works. As a lawyer, he practiced commercial real estate law and entertainment law, with a focus on live theatre.

~~~

Heidi: What was your path from a personal interest in theatre to a professional career as a producer and then Associate Dean, Department of Visual and Performing Arts at Sheridan College?

Michael: I like to say that I was a child actor of no significance. I did some film and television as a kid and always loved the theatre. For me, it was *Les Misérables* at the Royal Alexandra Theatre when I was 13. I was just mesmerised by the power that show had emotionally, and that left quite an impression. I think for those in musical theatre it always starts with a show. I did musicals in summer camp, but I went off to university to pursue other passions and specifically went to law school.

In my last year of law school, I had a summer job lined up at a law firm and an articling job and decided to produce and direct musicals at the University of Western Ontario, where I did a production called *Blood Brothers*. I was really interested in commercial theatre, the business of theatre, which is not very prevalent in Canada. Canada is 99% not-for-profit theatre. You have the Mirvishes, who are really the drivers of commercial theatre, and I was most interested in that. I did a lot of research, met with major producers of musical theatre around the world and practiced law for about a year or two. Then I pursued producing theatre full time for a couple of years, which was a challenge.

I went back to law, but parallel to practising law (and about 15–20% of my law practice was entertainment law, specifically in live theatre), I continued to produce, and that led to an opportunity at Sheridan, going on almost six years ago. I had always cast students from Sheridan in my musical productions. I always attended their shows. I chaired the Professional Advisory Committee for the Music Theatre Performance Program, and when the person who'd had my job before me was promoted to Dean, I was asked if I would be interested in taking on her job as Associate Dean. I left a Bay Street law firm and came to Sheridan.

Heidi: What makes musical theatre such a popular form of theatre entertainment and, among its biggest fans, a passion or even an obsession?

Michael: A couple of things. I think a good musical has to have a compelling story and there has to be a compelling reason to musicalize that story. When those two factors come together, it arouses a passion and an emotion unlike any other medium. I think the fact that it's also live—there's something about sitting with people in a room and watching people on a stage that's very live, that's very real, that evokes emotion in a way that other mediums can't. Subsequent to that, especially in musical theatre, you do have a chance to listen to recordings of this music that recaptures some of those emotions, and it allows you to be a bit more interactive in the process, whether you sing well or you don't sing well, or you sing publicly or you sing privately. Music has always captured us in various forms, but when it's part of telling a compelling story, it's an emotional response that lasts.

Heidi: Joseph Trefler, Co-Founder of the Canadian Musical Theatre Writers Collective, told me that the Canadian Music Theatre Project (CMTP) at Sheridan College is "arguably the most important new initiative in Canadian musical theatre." Please talk a bit about the beginnings of the CMTP, from concept to creation in 2011.

Michael: I've been engaged as a producer for almost 15 years, and part of that has been the development of new musicals, which became a significant interest and practice of mine. One of the major problems in Canada is that musical theatre is an American art form, adopted by the British and certainly adopted by Canadians, but it's not inherently a Canadian art form.

As a result, there has been no infrastructure (not only no infrastructure but no institutionalized infrastructure) to develop new musicals in this country. Our theatre companies aren't doing it (I believe they should be at the forefront of it), and I think part of that is because the development of a musical is much more expensive than many other things in entertainment because you need time, musicians, actors who can sing, writers and composers. You need a large group and infrastructure to hear the work, because only if you can hear it can you rapidly respond and make changes.

There's a quote that's been attributed to Arthur Laurents and to Andrew Lloyd Webber and Stephen Sondheim: "Musicals aren't written, they're rewritten." This is quite true. There was no infrastructure in Canada providing that opportunity because you need to fail. You need the opportunity to say that song doesn't work, that lyric doesn't work, we need to bring in a new song, and to be able to work quickly to do that.

So when I came to Sheridan, I had a skill set as a producer, and I was coming in at a very important time for Sheridan's Music Theatre Performance Program, which up to that point had a 40-year history as a diploma program. Sheridan then received the approval to transition the program from a three-year advanced diploma to a four-

385

year baccalaureate degree, an Honours Bachelor of Music Theatre Performance.

Within that development, there was a mandate that in the fourth year of the program, students had to work on a capstone project. That's an opportunity to apply the skills you learned in the previous three years to some project. I believed this was the perfect opportunity to create an incubator to develop new musicals, because we could fund it as an academic program and an academic requirement (thereby institutionalizing it) so it wasn't something that would not be there year over year. Even though our students are not age appropriate, they have a level of skill, talent and intellect that makes them useful to the writers.

We could bring in professional writers, pay their fees, and could bring in a professional director and musical director. Through the Canadian Music Theatre Project, they get five weeks to develop. The focus is on development, not on product. It's all on revising and reworking and at the end of it, the only public part is a 45-minute presentation at music stands. Then, from there, we have a recording studio. We are able to record demos for the writers so they can share their work with other producers. Also as part of our program, we have a six-show season that our third- and fourth-year students perform in. We began to program one of those new musicals into our season so that we could give it some production value, some additional development. In the very short period of time we've been doing this, I'm very proud. We've had a great deal of success.

Heidi: One of the most recent successes of CMTP is *Come From Away*, a musical by Sankoff and Hein. Please talk a bit about this collaboration and the steps to bringing this production from an incubator to Mirvish Productions in November/December 2016 and then to Broadway in spring 2017.

Michael: It's still surreal as you say that to me! *Come From Away* was my idea. Soon after 9/11, I read these incredible stories about what happened in Gander, Newfoundland and the surrounding towns. As I said to you at the outset, you need two things. You need a compelling story and a compelling reason to musicalize it. The Celtic sound out in Newfoundland and Labrador is just infused in the culture and the blood of those people. It is incredibly moving, spirited, beautiful music that I believe is very Canadian. I believe that the story is so compelling that if it was told as a musical, there might be something that was very special.

I had looked for writers for years. Nobody had taken me up on the idea. And then about a year before I arrived at Sheridan, I went to see *My Mother's Lesbian Jewish Wiccan Wedding*, which Sankoff and Hein had written, and I was completely floored by it. It had authenticity and integrity, and it was a great, true story based on David's life and his mom's. I wrote them on Facebook and said, "Let's go for dinner and just chat." We went for dinner (three hours—it was wonderful), and at the end of it I said, "I'm trying to find people to write this musical about what happened in Gander on 9/11." Well, they took me up on it just as I was going to Sheridan. It was the first project that I committed to at the incubator. We did a 45-minute workshop of it at books and stands. It was enthralling. It was very special. I immediately committed to doing a full production at our studio theatre to give it more development.

Subsequent to that, it was selected as one of the shows for the 2013 National Alliance for Musical Theatre in New York. They put on a festival; it is *the* festival for musical theatre in the world. A committee chooses eight shows a year. I'm on that committee now. They are presented in 45-minute readings by Broadway talent. It's a by-invitation, industry-only festival. *The Drowsy Chaperone* was presented at that festival. *Come From Away* was as well, and that is where commercial producers saw the show and optioned it to take it on the journey it is on now. *Come From Away* had a premiere last summer at the La Jolla Playhouse in San Diego and opened at the Seattle Repertory Theater.

We're in rehearsals right now in Washington, DC, where we will open at the Ford Theatre on September 7 before coming to Toronto and then Broadway.

Heidi: In *The Globe and Mail* in October 2015, J. Kelly Nestruck wrote about the emergence of original musical theatre nationwide. In your opinion, what can be done to support this trend? Do we need more incubators, more commercial producers, or private investment from companies or philanthropists?

Michael: I think we need our theatres to take the risk and bet on our writers. To do that, they need investment from companies and philanthropists to support what is a very, very expensive undertaking. However, if you look at American and British theatres, you can see there's an economic argument. The Royal Shakespeare Company heavily invested in *Matilda the Musical*. It's become a huge success, providing a very significant revenue stream back to the theatre company. We've seen the public theatre being involved in a number of musicals, specifically *Hamilton*, and they have economic interest in *Hamilton*. I believe that we have the talent. We have talented writers and actors; we have people who can create the type of musicals that can be exported internationally. They can provide revenue streams, attract more donors and more corporate investment, but we are not taking the risk to do it.

It's slowly changing. One of the musicals we developed, *Prom Queen*, will have its world premiere at The Segal Centre in November. Another musical we developed about Terry Fox will have its premiere at Drayton in October. We saw *Les Belles-Soeurs* at the National Arts Centre and it will be at the Charlottetown Festival and the Citadel Theatre. But we're not doing enough of it and we're not institutionalizing it, so there's ongoing development. At the end of the day we need theatres to commit.

Heidi: What advice do you have for musical theatre writers about planning, budgeting and fundraising, if they want to self-produce and get their show on stage, for example, at a Fringe festival?

Michael: To me, it's less important getting on stage than getting developed. It's one of the hardest things to do and I think most writers underestimate that. They get a Fringe slot, they say, "Hey, let's write a musical," and they just throw it out there. I think they have to pay more attention to:

- Do they have a good idea?
- Do they have a reason to musicalize it?
- Do they have a strong outline?
- How discerning are they in the process?
- Who are they getting advice and guidance from?
- What is the right time to present the piece?

So many people produce musicals that aren't ready to be seen by an audience and it is detrimental to the writers or to the piece. The emphasis should always be on development. As much as it is a dream of mine to produce shows that I hope go to Broadway, you don't sit there saying, "A show about a small town in Eastern Canada on 9/11 is going to be the next Broadway hit." You just don't know. You need to really focus on telling a good story and the way that you're telling it, continuing to revise and rewrite and being your own harshest critic. I've never met a successful writer who is completely satisfied with what they've written. They're reluctant to share with an audience until they believe that there's something of quality.

I would say to writers that planning, developing and rewriting are the most important things, and how you find development opportunities to support that.

If you are going to present something publicly, why are you doing that? The idea of putting something out in public and someone walking by and saying, "I'll write a cheque to produce that,"—it just doesn't really exist.

But if you develop it and bring people in at the right time, there may be opportunities to get to the next level. I certainly believe that the National Alliance for Musical Theatre (the NAMT Festival) is one of the greatest platforms in the world in terms of propelling your new musical to interest commercial producers or regional theatres.

And musicals are a lot of work! Although *Come From Away*, from our first workshop to Broadway, will be five years, that is record fast time. Very rare. Usually eight to ten years. It just takes time. It takes time to get the writing done, get the money together and find development opportunities. Again, it's just so striking to me how many people want to go public. It really destroys things. Sometimes people want to go public with the first draft. You just have to be really smart about it.

Recommended Additional Reading

J. Kelly Nestruck, "A Homegrown Musical Theatre Movement Emerges Across Canada", *The Globe and Mail*, October 2, 2015.

Michael Rubinoff, "Commercial Producing," *The New Indie Theatre Producer's Guide*, edited by Sandra Lefrançois, published by the Toronto Alliance for the Performing Arts in partnership with Theatre Ontario, 2011 edition.

Interview with
Irene Sankoff and David Hein

Photo and biography courtesy of Sankoff and Hein

Irene Sankoff and David Hein (book, music and lyrics) are a Canadian husband-and-wife writing team and the recipients of the Bryden Ones-to-Watch Award.

Their first musical, *My Mother's Lesbian Jewish Wiccan Wedding* (based on David's mother's true story), was the hit of the 2009 Toronto Fringe Festival and was picked up by Mirvish Productions, extended five times, and has now earned rave reviews and multiple Best Musical awards at the New York Musical Theater Festival and across North America, with Sankoff and Hein performing in most productions.

Their second musical, *Come From Away*, just enjoyed a record-breaking, critically acclaimed world premier co-production at the La Jolla Playhouse in San Diego and Seattle Repertory in Seattle, with direction by Chris Ashley (*Memphis, Xanadu, Rocky Horror*). *Come From Away* tells the true story of when 38 planes from around the world were diverted to Gander, Newfoundland on 9/11. Developed at The Canadian Music Theatre Project at Sheridan College, and at

Goodspeed Musicals, it has won Best Musical awards in Seattle and San Diego and was included on The Best Theatre of 2015 list by the *LA Times*. This fall, it will be presented in Gander, Newfoundland and Toronto, and in the spring of 2017, it will transfer to Broadway.

Their current show, *Mitzvah*, tells the story of a family whose son has autism, as he approaches his Bar Mitzvah, set against a backdrop of stories from autism's history and the recent neurodiversity movement. It was recently developed at the Finger Lakes Musical Theatre Festival, the Rhinebeck Writers Retreat, TheatreWorks SV and the Jewish Plays Project with director Marc Bruni (*Beautiful: The Carole King Musical*). Created with support from the Ontario Arts Council, *Mitzvah* was commissioned and is now being developed by Yonge St. Theatricals.

~~~

Heidi: What was your path from a personal interest in musical theatre to a professional career?

Irene: Sometimes I don't know how I got here. I kind of took the long way around. I've loved musicals since I was a kid. I was always sure being in the arts was what I wanted to do. I majored in dance and minored in drama in high school. However, my father always encouraged me to do other things since being in the arts is such an unstable proposition. So at his request I took an aptitude test before applying to university, and the result was a 98% match to the performing arts. The guidance counsellor had never seen a result come up with that much of a match for anyone in anything.

I still did a double major in psychology and creative writing in university, but then afterward got an MFA in acting while performing in New York. I have had other more mainstream careers to support my creative pursuits until very recently, when *Come From Away* was picked up by commercial producers, and the demands on our time actually don't even allow for day jobs. And thankfully we no longer need day jobs. I think having other jobs and meeting people in the "real" world has helped keep me connected to the people who make up our audiences, which helps to create work that resonates. And really, having also worked in more traditional fields, I am truly best suited to the work and lifestyle of the arts.

David: I didn't grow up on musical theatre but loved theatre in general. I grew up watching Shakespeare on the Saskatchewan and 25th St. Theatre in Saskatoon, and then I acted in plays throughout high school in Ottawa, which somehow led to me getting a BFA in set and lighting design at York University. (Irene and I actually met on the first day of school.)

After school, I designed over 60 shows in New York and Toronto but continued to write songs throughout. I've been a songwriter and been in bands for as long as I can remember, so eventually I got out of the "lucrative" theatre design business and got into the "lucrative" singer–songwriter business, putting out a couple of albums and touring across North America a few times.

But when I was a singer–songwriter and Irene was acting, we both had day jobs and we barely got to see each other. So one summer, we decided to write and perform a musical together, mostly so that we could actually spend time together. We applied to the Toronto Fringe Festival and wrote *My Mother's Lesbian Jewish Wiccan Wedding (MMLJWW)*, based on my mom's true story. And suddenly we were sold out. Then, Mirvish picked it up for a run at the Panasonic. And suddenly we were musical theatre writers.

Come From Away is just our second show. *MMLJWW* continues to get produced across North America—and we're just starting to figure out our new career. As a side note, one of my former day jobs was in marketing and graphic design. It started as a temp gig, but turned into designing posters and CD cases for our first show. Irene and I both gigged as standardized patients for medical schools, working with tons of other artists and learning communication skills. And I was also a clown for a flower shop.

Heidi: Theatre, like film, is highly collaborative in nature. Please talk a bit about the importance of—and your own experience with—collaboration among members of a creative team in the early phases of writing a new musical.

Irene: At first, it should just be the authors in the room. If you get too many opinions too early in the process, it kind of kills your creativity and can send you down a path that you ultimately don't find interesting. So although workshops and readings are great, they shouldn't come too early in the process.

You have to implicitly trust your collaborators and be able to be very, very frank with them, and they should be able to be frank with you as well and say things you may not want to hear. It probably goes without saying, but having the right people on your team in terms of personality, vision and communication skills and temperament can make all the difference in the world.

David: I think it's probably different writing with your spouse, but there are a lot of good lessons that we've learned along the way. We have rules like, don't talk in generalities and don't discuss things when hungry, tired or grumpy. But also, recognize that you and your partner in crime are both aimed at the same thing—making the best show possible—and they may not agree with you all the time, but that's a good thing. I can't tell you how many times I've thought A, and Irene's thought B, and the best answer was actually C, which we came up with together. Of course that doesn't mean we didn't have to argue our way through it—"Writing is fighting"—but it's also a lot of fun. Beyond working together, we've learned quickly that working with nice people trumps almost everything else. Life's too short. And making "plays" can be a lot of hard "work." For me, it comes back to why Irene and I started working together—because we loved each other and wanted to spend more time together. That's what gets you through.

Heidi: What were (or maybe still are) some of the challenges of creating original musical theatre productions in Canada? And how are initiatives like the Canadian Music Theatre Project and other Canadian initiatives or individuals addressing these challenges and helping musical theatre creators?

Irene: Musicals need time to develop. Time and, frankly, money. Making a musical is a huge investment in time and money for all parties. And there are so many things that can stall the process, from waiting on people's schedules to loss of funding to legal tie-ups. Michael and the folks at CMTP really understand that and don't rush the process, even though it takes a while to show people the pay-off. If there is a pay-off. And there isn't always—most of the time there isn't. But that doesn't mean people in Canada should stop making musicals, even if multiple shows don't get past the development stage.

We were invited to a writer's retreat in Palo Alto, California, and one of the things they assured us of was that it was a work session; we'd present something for investors at the end of the week, but even if we ended up throwing out everything we wrote—even if we ended up throwing out our entire concept—that was fine. It's Silicon Valley; they understand the importance of failure. They are used to seven different start-up ventures failing before one hits. Not everything you attempt is going to work. But you still need to make the attempt *and* be smart enough to abandon it if it's not worth pursuing.

David: I think the challenges of writing new musicals in Canada may be the same as writing new musicals anywhere. You need time, you need actors, musicians, directors, a chance to share it with an audience, a chance to record. I feel like you'll hear a lot about how theatres in Canada don't produce enough new musicals in their seasons—and I feel that—but I also feel like that's understandable. Musicals are expensive and require much more development than plays. What we need is more investment in development of new works—workshops and readings—and investment in getting audiences excited about those workshops and readings. That's exactly what CMTP is doing.

Heidi: Are Canadian musicals (specifically English language Canadian musicals) distinct? Do they have a unique perspective or voice when compared to musicals written and created in the United States or in the U.K.?

Irene: Good musicals are good musicals. It doesn't matter where they were written or who wrote them. Identifying something as Canadian or American or Australian is just another way of defining "us" and "them." I like being surprised by where something came from or who created it after I've enjoyed the work. It shouldn't define whether I'll see it or participate in its development.

David: It's hard to define exactly what a Canadian musical is. I think *Come From Away* fits the bill since it's written by Canadians, developed in Canada, and about a true Canadian story, but there shouldn't be anything wrong with working with collaborators from abroad, developing shows elsewhere, or telling others' stories. There have been some attempts to group Canadian humour as "spectator humour," but I'm not even sure that's true. And I could try to find some roots between Canadian music in Great Big Sea, The Tragically Hip or Blue Rodeo, but I'm not sure how much they share with Drake or Arcade Fire. At the end of the day, trying to define a "Canadian" piece of art may be as hard as trying to define what makes a "good" piece of art.

Heidi: What makes musical theatre such a popular form of theatre entertainment and, among its biggest fans, a passion or even an obsession?

Irene: For me it was stories about people overcoming insurmountable odds to be the best person they could be. I think there's something in that that appeals to a lot of musical theatre fans.

David: People will always say that musical theatre is dying, but if anything, it feels more relevant and popular than ever. It's one of the only art forms that combines visual design, music, acting, dance and storytelling (something for everyone!), created by hundreds of people—over years of development. It's the ultimate group marathon sport. And it's magic for so many reasons: it's a group experience which feels rare these days; each performance is unique and when a run finishes, the show may never be seen again; and finally because it happens eight shows a week, filled with theatrical magic—even with our own shows. I still watch them, wondering, "How did they do that?" Great musicals entertain, educate and inspire, and you become obsessed when you see something great.

Heidi: From Fringe to Broadway—you are an inspiration! What advice do you have for aspiring writers of musical theatre?

Irene: See as many shows as you can and dissect them. What makes them work? What makes them not work? Be ruthless with yourself and with your work. It should never just be "good enough."

David: Here are nine random bits of advice (or mistakes we've made):

1. Be nice. People want to work with people who are nice.

2. Do your research. Your show isn't right for every festival, theatre, director, and researching them will help you stand out.

3. It never hurts to ask. Write to people and ask for their advice, or ask them whatever. Just don't harass them, and make sure you're asking something worthwhile.

4. Write a show that you think is important. If it does well, you're going to be spending years with it, so you have to love it and think it's going to change the world. Plus, that helps you talk to others about why they should help you with it.

5. Start with the story. A show without a good story is rarely good, regardless of how good a composer or lyricist you might be.

6. Canada, like any country, is filled with interesting stories, but

397

no one knows our stories except us, which means you've got an advantage. Tell them.

7. Sometimes you need to write something bad just to write something. Then, once you've written more, or during a workshop, or on "perfectionist Tuesday," you can make it better. But writing something bad is better than writing nothing at all.

8. Only compare yourself to others if it inspires you. If it's driving you crazy, take a break from Twitter.

9. Agents, websites, social media, meeting someone famous— nothing will serve you better than being nice and writing a good show. And Canadians are all already nice.

Interview with Susan Dunstan

Photo and biography courtesy of Susan Dunstan

Susan Dunstan is a musical theatre performer for the following select shows/workshops: *Come From Away* (Broadway); *The Lion King* (US/Tour), *Kinky Boots, Priscilla Queen of the Desert, Lord of the Rings, The Lion King* – Shenzi (Mirvish), *South Pacific* (Drayton), *Annie Get Your Gun* (Massey Hall), *Ragtime* (Livent), *Somewhere in the World* (Canada Girl) and *The Princess and the Handmaiden* (The Charlottetown Festival).

When not performing in a show, Susan can be found at the dog show with her Champion Dobermans and Standard Poodle or teaching at her private voice studio.

www.susandunstan.com

~~~

Heidi: What was your path from a personal interest in musical theatre to a professional career?

Sue: I always knew I wanted to have a professional musical theatre career. Even when I was small. I had CDs of *Miss Saigon* and *Les Misérables*, *Cats* and *Phantom of the Opera*. My mom took me to see *Cats* in Thunder Bay, Ontario where I grew up and it was amazing. I did all of the musical shows in elementary school and throughout high school. I auditioned for a professional show called *Spirit of a Nation* when I was still in high school and I left high school early to join that tour. I went straight from that tour to Sheridan College where I studied musical theatre.

Heidi: What makes musical theatre such a popular form of theatre entertainment and, among its biggest fans, a passion or even an obsession?

Sue: Well it is still an analogue art form. You can't stream it, you can't stop and rewind it, you have to be present for it. I think the element of singing and dancing is also very special. It heightens the show as well as lessens the pool of people who are capable of doing it, which once again makes it more special.

Heidi: What are your favourite musical theatre songs to perform?

Sue: I like all varieties of musical theatre from traditional old-school songs to modern contemporary pop musical theatre. One of my favourite shows is *Godspell* and another favourite of mine is *Into the Woods*.

Heidi: Please talk a bit about the importance of—and your own experience with—collaboration among the cast and the whole team of a musical theatre production—whether big or small.

Sue: The show I am currently working on, *Come From Away*, is a huge example of a collaboration. There are 12 actors on stage. It is a true ensemble piece, but this ensemble is made up of all principal actors. This is also a piece that tells the story of love and generosity, so the interpersonal relationships between the cast are very important to fuel the storytelling. The creative team and the producers have been so open, welcoming, loving, supportive and generous. Whoever leads the team sets the tone for the work environment. It is important if you want a good show to make sure whoever is leading has the right energy.

Heidi: What advice do you have for aspiring musical theatre performers?

Sue: Learn your craft. Go to school or take classes. If you don't get into one school, take more classes and try again. Don't forget to build a life outside of performing. Friends and family and hobbies and pets are the things you will need when trying to build a career. Sure you have to be focused, but not so focused that you forget that there is more to life than work.

INTERVIEW WITH ELISE DEWSBERRY

Photo and biography courtesy of Elise Dewsberry

Elise has been involved in the development of new works for over 40 years—as an actor–singer, as a director, as a dramaturge and as a writer.

While living in Toronto, Elise served as the Assistant Artistic Director of the Muskoka Festival, the coordinator of the festival's annual Musical Theatre Writer's Colony, the Associate Dramaturge of the Canadian Stage Company, the Resident Dramaturge of the Smile Theatre Company, and she was the co-founder of Toronto's Script Lab.

Elise spent many years touring Canada with *Nine Months*—a one-woman musical that she commissioned from writers Carl Ritchie and Stephen Woodjetts. Elise and Carl also co-wrote *Any Body Home?*, which was produced by the Cordova Bay Theatre in Victoria, British Columbia and published by Dramatic Publishing.

Elise joined the Academy for New Musical Theatre as Associate Artistic Director in 2003, joined Founding Artistic Director, John

Sparks, as Co-Artistic Director in 2010 and became Artistic Director of New Musicals Inc., in 2013.

Elise also serves as a Los Angeles Ovation Award voter and is the author and evaluator of the Book Lab and the Outlining Lab, offered online through www.writingmusicaltheatre.com.

~~~

Heidi: What was your path from a personal interest in musical theatre to a professional career?

Elise: When I was only 10 years old, I took an after-school drama class (in Toronto) and immediately fell in love with the idea of acting, and made up my mind it was what I was going to do with my life. I studied speech arts and drama at the Royal Conservatory and joined every local community theatre group that would take young adults. When I was thinking about college, I found the Boston Conservatory of Music and discovered that they had a bachelor's degree in drama—musical theatre. I had actually never thought of combining acting and singing until that moment (although I was a soloist in the church choir, and studied singing privately), but it sounded good to me! Turned out I loved it—and I haven't really gotten away from musical theatre since.

After Boston, I began my career in Toronto, then moved to New York for a while, and then came back to Toronto (before eventually winding up in Los Angeles). But it was while doing summer stock theatre outside of Toronto (at the Muskoka Festival in Gravenhurst) that I was exposed to new musicals through their development program— and then I was really hooked. I apprenticed as a dramaturge at the Canadian Stage Company, founded the development company Script Lab, and wound up as Artistic Director of New Musicals Inc., in Los Angeles.

Heidi: Theatre, like film, is highly collaborative in nature. Please talk a bit about the importance of—and your own experience with—collaboration among the members of a creative team and cast in the early development phase of workshopping and getting a new musical ready for the stage.

Elise: Theatre is indeed collaborative—and I would venture to say that musical theatre is the most collaborative art form of all. Obviously, there is a collaboration at the beginning, with the book writer, lyricist and composer. This early collaboration is crucial and can be very difficult to navigate because the whole team has to be very clear about what they are trying to write if the various elements are to come together cohesively. Then, adding the rest of the collaborative team—the dramaturge, director, music director and cast—continues the process. Any writer or writing team benefits greatly from getting outside feedback and particularly from hearing their work brought to life by actors. I am a great believer in the writing team having at least a table reading of their first draft as early as possible, and they should ask their cast (as well as their dramaturge and director) for feedback. At New Musicals Inc., we do many table readings and staged readings as a regular part of the development process and find them to be invaluable.

Heidi: You've worked as a producer, teacher and performer in musical theatre, in both Canada and the United States. Do you see differences in musical productions in the two countries in terms of the perspective or voice of the writer and also the opportunities available or the challenges of producing new musical theatre?

Elise: That's a very interesting question! I would say that, unfortunately, developing new musicals is an expensive and difficult endeavor no matter where it is happening. There are likely officially more opportunities in the United States, but there is also more competition as there are so many people writing musicals. The government funding in Canada is much better relative to the United States, but it still isn't enough to meet the need. Regarding actual productions and the voice of the writers, I don't honestly see a difference. Good storytelling is good storytelling, and good craft is good craft.

Heidi: I was a student of your Outlining Lab through New Musicals Inc.'s Academy for New Musical Theatre. The course mantra (if you will) is "Don't start writing until your outline is rock solid." Please speak a bit about the importance of a "rock solid" outline before a writer of musical theatre begins to write the show's book.

Elise: As you can see from my lab "mantra," I firmly believe that a rock solid outline is vital to the early development of a new musical. I think outlines are also useful for plays, but a play can be written without a detailed outline. I don't think that works for a musical, for at least three important reasons. One is that, whereas writing a play is usually a solitary endeavor, writing a musical is collaborative. So without an outline, the team can't be sure they are all on the same page. Also, because the story of a musical will need to be told at least partly in song, it is important to make sure that the story is going to support the *need* for songs. The songs of a musical generally allow us to track the journey of the lead character as he or she pursues his or her main goal. So the story needs to evolve in a way that keeps that journey heightened enough to necessitate the character(s) bursting into song. And finally, once the musical is further along, it gets much more difficult to make revisions that involve songs that have already been written. It is far more efficient to work out as many details of the logic of the plot *before* the songs are written.

Heidi: New Musicals Inc. (NMI) not only offers in-person and online study but also develops and produces new musical plays. Please speak a bit about the development and production opportunities available to NMI students.

Elise: As you have mentioned, New Musicals Inc. has several different avenues for the development of new musicals and the study of the craft. For book writers, lyricists and composers who want to hone their skill set, we offer the online labs through our sister site, www. writingmusicaltheatre.com. For musical theatre creators who want to put their skill set to use in a collaborative environment (and to look for potential new collaborators), we have our Core Curriculum that follows the same structure originally created by the famous Broadway conductor, Lehman Engel. Participants are put on a new collaborative team every month and given assignments that are then critically reviewed by the staff. The final assignment is an original, 15-minute musical, which NMI produces in an LA theatre. The only other place in the world that offers this program is the BMI Lehman Engel workshop in New York.

Once participants have completed the Core program, they can be invited to join our ongoing Writers' Workshop that meets monthly to allow our members to present whatever they are working on for critical feedback.

For musical theatre creators who have completed a new musical, we offer critical feedback at various levels, from an overview evaluation to a detailed analysis to a staff table reading. Any new musical submitted for this kind of dramaturgy is automatically also entered into our annual Search for New Musicals, the winner of which receives a workshop with our Academy Repertory Company and a concert reading in Los Angeles.

We also offer a kind of à-la-carte menu of dramaturgical services, by the hour or by the project, to try to support the needs of different projects at different stages of development. One of the more popular new programs is the Sandbox, which is literally self-designed by the participants to meet their current needs.

We also produce occasional concert readings as well as the biennial STAGES Musical Theatre Festival, where we present staged readings of five to eight new musicals. There is currently no official submission process for the STAGES Festival, but we always look at the Search submissions for possible shows for the festival.

We have produced three world-premiere productions and hope to do more in the future. At this time, our funding doesn't allow for regular productions, and we have so far needed to restrict our choices to musicals written by members of our ongoing Writers' Workshop.

Heidi: In your opinion, what makes musical theatre such a popular form of theatre entertainment and, among its biggest fans, a passion or even an obsession?

Elise: There is just no denying the power of music to capture and enthrall us! If you watch a small child reacting to music with a strong beat, you will see how primal and instinctual it is. Music has the ability to evoke powerful emotions. And when you combine music with storytelling, there's nothing quite like it. We love to laugh, and a well-crafted comedy song can make us laugh even more than a stand-up routine. We all love to be moved and there is nothing quite so moving as a heart-felt ballad. For many years, there was kind of a stigma attached to the idea of people bursting out into song, and musicals were marginalized and musical theatre lovers considered to be geeks. But shows like *American Idol* and *Glee* have re-exposed television audiences to the power of music, and recent great movie musicals like *Chicago* and *Moulin Rouge* have all helped to make musicals cool again. Thank goodness!

Heidi: What advice do you have for aspiring writers, performers or producers of musical theatre?

Elise: My best advice is: get out there and do it. Find yourself a community and do as much musical theatre as you can. If you are a book writer, lyricist or composer, write as much as you can and make sure you get feedback, readings and exposure in any way you can.

Submit to contests, festivals and fringe festivals. Consider writing short-form musicals for the internet; I think that's going to become more and more of a great way to get exposure and experience for writers and performers. That can work for producers as well; try the internet, fringe festivals and readings to get started and to make connections. The one thing I would say *not* to do is to write a new musical and then spend the next 10 years or more of your life trying to get that one piece produced. I'm not suggesting you give up on it, but I am suggesting you keep on writing more. You can pursue the development of one piece while you are writing the next, and you will learn more and make more connections while you are doing it.

Interview with Jennifer Ashley Tepper

Photo and biography courtesy of Jennifer Ashley Tepper

Jennifer Ashley Tepper is the Director of Programming at Feinstein's/54 Below and the author of *The Untold Stories of Broadway* book series. As the leader of Feinstein's/54 Below's creative team, Tepper has curated or produced over 1,500 shows, ranging from musicals in concert, to original solo acts, to theatrical reunions, to songwriter celebrations and beyond. On Broadway, Tepper has worked on shows in directing, producing and marketing capacities, including *[title of show]*, *The Performers*, the 2011 revival of *Godspell* and the 2013 revival of *Macbeth*. In addition, she is the co-creator of the Bistro Award–winning concert series, *If It Only Even Runs a Minute*, now in its sixth year. Tepper also frequently collaborates on shows and concerts with the group known as Joe Iconis & Family.

As a writer, Tepper has authored two volumes of *The Untold Stories of Broadway* series, published by Dress Circle. For these books, Tepper interviewed 250 theatre professionals about the Broadway theatres themselves and their stories of working in each house. *NBC New York* has called the books an "inspiring must-read." Tepper was recently named one of the 10 professionals on *Backstage Magazine*'s 1st Annual Broadway Future Power List. According to the article, "Proving herself both a zeitgeist predictor and theatrical historian with her eclectic programming, Tepper is leading the conversation on contemporary musical theatre."

~~~

Heidi: What was your path from a personal interest in theatre to a professional career?

Jennifer: I became obsessed with theatre at a young age, while growing up in Boca Raton, Florida. I spent my childhood studying cast recordings, reading books about theatre, seeing local and touring productions and learning everything I could about Broadway from afar. I moved to New York at the age of 18 to attend NYU, and from then on, the city was my campus. I had several internships during college, including at the York Theatre and the Rodgers and Hammerstein Organization. During my senior year of college, I interned with Jeff Bowen and Hunter Bell, writers of the musical *[title of show]*. When that show moved to Broadway during the summer after I graduated, I became the assistant to Michael Berresse, the director on the production. I spent the next two years working a variety of freelance jobs in the theatre as well as day jobs, from assisting director Michael Greif, to PAing a variety of readings and workshops, to nannying, to tutoring, to assisting producers.

During this time, I also began to create my own work, including creating the concert series, *If It Only Even Runs a Minute*, celebrating underappreciated musicals, which has now won several awards and is in its sixth year, and collaborating with musical theatre writer Joe Iconis on his shows and concerts. In 2010, I began working full time for producer Ken Davenport and eventually became his Director of Marketing and Communications, working on shows including Broadway's *Godspell* revival and *Macbeth*, starring Alan Cumming.

410

At the same time, I was still working on my own projects, and in 2013, I became the author of *The Untold Stories of Broadway* book series when the first volume was released by Dress Circle Publishing. That same year, I also transitioned jobs and became the Director of Programming at Feinstein's/54 Below. As the leader of Feinstein's/54 Below's creative team, I have curated or produced over 1,500 shows, ranging from musicals in concert, to original solo acts, to theatrical reunions, to songwriter celebrations and beyond.

Heidi: What makes musical theatre such a popular form of theatre entertainment and, among its biggest fans, a passion or even an obsession?

Jennifer: Musical theatre is a fusion of so many different artistic elements, from music, to storytelling, to dance, to design. It is the ultimate "mutt" of entertainment, and thus it has this unique way of reaching people's hearts. Any musical is naturally the result of hundreds of different people working together to create one thing, and that also makes it special. And because you can endlessly see different versions of the same show, as well as enjoy both live versions and recordings, musical theatre inspires obsession because there's always more to take in—no show is ever completely "done."

Heidi: You are Director of Programming at Feinstein's/54 Below and Co-Creator of the *If It Only Even Runs a Minute* concert series. Please talk a bit about the opportunities both give to writers of musical theatre.

Jennifer: As the Director of Programming at Feinstein's/54 Below, I love being able to work with theatre writers of all different ages, backgrounds, styles, races, career points and so on. From evenings that give emerging writers a platform, to concerts that celebrate established writers, our programming gives all theatre writers and audiences a chance to relate to their audiences on their own terms. I've also made it a priority to present musicals in concert, from brand

411

new work, to underappreciated shows of the past that deserve a new chance, to hit musicals seen in a new way. *If It Only Even Runs a Minute* purely embraces short-lived shows of the past and we invite writers of these shows to share stories and songs from their musicals. We've been able to give new life to many shows that have not been heard since their original productions, and we've inspired new audiences to learn about shows that they hadn't heard of previously.

Heidi: In your TEDx Broadway talk, you speak about the loss of Broadway's smaller and mid-size theatres in the 1980s and the predicament of finding theatre space for new productions. What are some of the positive changes you've seen in recent years, and what more can be done?

Jennifer: We're living in an amazing time for Broadway theatres. We have a new Broadway theatre reopening this season after 50 years of disuse—the Hudson. It's been reported that the Shuberts are building a new Broadway theatre on 8th Avenue between 45th and 46th Streets. These are positive changes and because of the increasing demand for Broadway theatres, it looks like we'll continue to see new spaces popping up over the next decade. One of my hopes for a positive change is that theatres like the Edison and the Mark Hellinger (now the Times Square Church) will return to use as Broadway houses. I also hope that we'll see off-Broadway spaces landmarked and prioritized as viable and worthwhile venues to protect for years to come.

Heidi: In November 2016, Volume 3 of *The Untold Stories of Broadway* will be released. Please talk a bit about this book series concept and how it came to be.

Jennifer: I've always had a love for the Broadway theatres themselves and how the physical spaces have impacted the art form overall, our community and the shows inside of them. Brisa Trinchero and Roberta Pereira, who founded Dress Circle Publishing, invited me to pitch them a book in 2013 and *The Untold Stories of Broadway* was the idea I put together. For the series, I have interviewed over 250 theatre professionals, from actors, to directors, to writers, to producers, to all of the people who aren't interviewed as often, including doormen and women, ushers, box office treasurers, dressers and so forth. Each book contains eight chapters that each take you through the history of one Broadway theatre chronologically, using the personal stories and memories of people who have worked there as well as many discoveries I myself have made about the theatre and the shows it's housed. The third volume will include the Belasco, Broadhurst, Edison, Lyric, Majestic, Schoenfeld, St. James and Walter Kerr Theatres, and I'm so excited for it to be released!

Interview with Louise Pitre

Photo and biography courtesy of Louise Pitre

Receiving a Tony nomination for her Broadway debut in the smash hit *Mamma Mia!* was a highlight for Louise Pitre, Canada's first lady of musical theatre, in a career that spans theatre, television and concert stages across North America and Europe.

In addition to headlining the Toronto, Broadway and U.S. touring company casts of *Mamma Mia!*, Louise is known for her signature performances as Fantine in *Les Misérables* (Toronto, Montreal and Paris), the title character in *Edith Piaf*, Mama Rose in *Gypsy* (Chicago Shakespeare Theatre, Gary Griffin director) and Joanne in *Company* (again with Gary Griffin). She also earned rave reviews for leading roles in *Annie Get Your Gun*; *Song & Dance*; *Jacques Brel Is Alive and Well and Living in Paris*; *I Love You, You're Perfect, Now Change*; *The World Goes 'Round*; *Blood Brothers*; *Tartuffe*; *Who's Afraid of Virginia Woolf?*; *The Roar of the Greasepaint, The Smell of the Crowd*; *Applause*; *The Toxic Avenger*; and *A Year With Frog and Toad*. In 2014, she premiered in the new Asolo Rep Theatre production of *Luck Be a Lady* (created and directed by Gordon Greenberg), and in 2015, she originated the role of the snake in the world premiere of *The Little Prince* (by James D. Reid and Nicholas Lloyd Webber) at Theatre Calgary, for which she won a Critter Award.

In September 2009, Louise made her Carnegie Hall debut, singing the role of Ulrika in the concert version of the musical *Kristina* by ABBA's Benny Andersson and Bjorn Ulvaeus, which she reprised at Royal Albert Hall in April 2010.

In 2013, Louise premiered her self-penned one-woman show *On The Rocks* at Theatre Passe Muraille in Toronto, with original songs by Louise Pitre, W. Joseph Matheson and Diane Leah.

Louise has guested with orchestras across Canada and the U.S. and appears in concert regularly throughout North America, with accompaniment ranging from big band to solo piano.

Her small screen appearances include Lifetime's *A Christmas Wedding*, *Recipe for a Perfect Christmas*, *Merry Matrimony*, *MVP*, *Flashpoint* and the CBC biopic *Celine*, in which she played Celine Dion's mother, Thérèse. She was the host of *Star Portraits* on Bravo! for its two seasons. She was chosen to be one of the three judges for Andrew Lloyd Webber's CBC series *Over the Rainbow*.

Louise is the winner of a National Broadway Touring Award, a New York Theatre World Award, a San Francisco Theatre Critics' Award, a Betsy Mitchell Award and four Dora Mavor Moore awards, all for best performance by a leading actress in a musical.

Since earning her Honours BA in Music Education (piano) from Western University (formerly the University of Western Ontario [UWO]), Louise has become the proud recipient of honorary degrees from the Royal Conservatory of Music and Humber College, along with a Doctorate of Music from Western University.

She has released five solo CDs: *Shattered*, *All of My Life Has Led to This*, *Songs My Mother Taught Me*, *On the Rocks* and an all-French CD, *La Vie en Rouge*. She is heard as Fantine in the Paris cast recording of *Les Misérables*, and as Ulrika in the Benny Andersson/Bjorn Ulvaeus musical *Kristina* cast recording, live at Carnegie Hall. She and W.

Joseph Matheson and Diane Leah, recorded their original wartime musical *Could You Wait?*, which premiered at Theatre Orangeville.

~~~

Heidi: What was your path from a personal interest in musical theatre to a professional career?

Louise: I did not have a path, really. I saw my very first show when I was in high school. It was *Godspell*, at the Bayview Playhouse in Toronto. We had taken a bus from Welland, where I was living. It blew my mind. I remember turning to my girlfriend and saying, "I want to do *that!*" but I did not do a show until my fourth year university. I knew nothing about musical theatre. It was a review called FLICKS (skits and songs and dance). I could not believe I got it! It turned my head around, and I decided not to go to teacher's college and pursued theatre instead. I was in my fourth year at Western—piano major/music education Honours BA. I moved to Toronto and worked as a secretary for three years while trying to figure out how to get into this business.

Heidi: What makes musical theatre such a popular form of theatre entertainment and, among its biggest fans, a passion or even an obsession?

Louise: It is the ultimate complete entertainment to me—theatre/music/dance/design. It speaks to your mind (although sometimes the books are not exactly life-changing), but it also grabs your heart when a song starts because speaking is just not enough to convey the emotion of the moment. It is an all-encompassing couple of hours where you can get lost in the dream and the reality and the music.

Heidi: Which musical theatre songs inspired you as an audience member and which ones do you love to perform and why?

Louise: "I Dreamed a Dream" inspired me. A friend put some headphones on my head one day years ago and said, "You have to hear this." I could not believe it! It made me go audition for *Les Miserables*— and I got the part. That was a huge shift in my career. I still love that song because you know this woman by the end of the song. You know what she has gone through. I love "Welcome to the Theatre," from *Applause*. Another winner! I love "Send in the Clowns." It is one of the most complete and perfect songs. "The Man That Got Away" is another favourite. Harold Arlen is one of my heroes. But perhaps my all-time favourite song to sing is "Ne Me Quitte Pas," the Jacques Brel song that is the most perfect one-act play in a song. The images are simply stunning. I am talking about the French version, of course.

Heidi: Like film and television, theatre is highly collaborative. Please talk a bit about the importance of collaboration among members of the cast and the team of a musical theatre production.

Louise: To me, musical theatre is the ultimate collaboration. Nothing works wonderfully if one element goes awry. The lighting can make or break a production or a number. The costumes either make you believe or take you out of the story or scene if they are not right, natural or believable. The sound can make or break the best singing or speaking. The set either helps you fly or makes you clunk. And if one member of the ensemble is not present or believable, the lead is automatically brought down a notch or two, because the audience's eye wanders and scans the stage and will pick up on untruths, which will ruin the effect. The production can only be as good as the weakest element of the whole.

Heidi: At the moment, you are in rehearsals for *Joni Mitchell: River* **at The Grand Theatre. Tell us a bit about the production.**

Louise: It is an all-sung show. One song after another. I have never really sung any Joni Mitchell. I do not own any of her recordings. I knew the famous songs; that's it. So this is a challenge; mostly because her songs are not standard melodies. They are meandering lines that jam a lot of words in a few beats. It is more like a stream of consciousness. I take it as being conversational. We are doing different takes on a lot of songs. That is fun. Greg Lowe, our musical director, is the most phenomenal guitarist I have ever worked with. It is worth doing this show for that alone. He uses 18 guitars in this show, each guitar tuned differently. Joni Mitchell had this special way of tuning guitars differently for some songs. It is a really terrific aspect of this show. Allen MacInnis created this show because he heard an interview with Joni saying that in a perfect world her songs would be sung by actors! The idea is to really hear the words and the story. She was not exactly the best enunciator.

Heidi: Three years ago, you premiered your one-woman show, *On the Rocks.* **What advice do you have for musical theatre performers who want to explore writing in addition to performing?**

Louise: It was a mountain to climb. I bravely—or stupidly—suggested writing my own show when Theatre Passe Muraille asked me to do something at their theatre. I am proud of it. It was a very gruelling but rewarding exercise. I would suggest getting a good dramaturge. Jen Shuber helped me shape it and give it an arc, a flow it would not have had otherwise. It certainly makes you appreciate just how difficult it is to come up with a script. I would also advise someone to stay away from producing it yourself. I would not do that again. I pulled it off, but the pressure of that aspect of it was an anxiety I wish I had not had to deal with.

Interview with Robyn Hoja

Photo and biography courtesy of Robyn Hoja

Robyn Hoja is an innovator and a creator with a passion for bringing people together. While her 21-year-old heart has settled in theatre, she always finds herself surrounded by people from many industries and all walks of life.

Currently in her fourth and final year at Ryerson University, studying Creative Industries, Robyn will be sitting as the President and Artistic Director of the Ryerson Musical Theatre Company and just completed a contract working as a marketing assistant at Mirvish Productions.

~~~

Heidi: What was your path from a personal interest in musical theatre and the performing arts to the founding of the Ryerson Musical Theatre Company (RMTC)?

Robyn: Growing up in Peterborough, Ontario, a town bursting with arts and culture, I was immersed in the world of musical theatre, performance and dance from a very young age. After being a part of many musicals, plays and dance competitions and assisting with drama camps, in my final two years of high school, I eventually stumbled into the Trent University theatre student group, the Anne Shirley Theatre Company (ASTC), which was putting on *Legally Blonde*. I was thrilled to be a part of this production that had students from all different programs at Trent collaborating on this musical, and as soon as I accepted my offer to Ryerson University for Creative Industries, I couldn't wait to join the musical theatre extracurricular that my new school offered. However, once arriving, I soon found out that this student group did not exist. I knew that I couldn't be alone in hoping for a musical theatre extracurricular—nearly everyone I had talked to mentioned being a part of their high school pit band, or painted sets for their shows, or shone in the ensemble. There was a clear want and need for this to exist, so I decided to put the wheels into motion and get RMTC off the ground.

Heidi: What I admire most about the company is that it provides an opportunity for participation in theatre by students whose academic focus is not theatre. It's a chance for creative expression by students who may just enjoy the art form.

Robyn: Absolutely! A lot of the success of RMTC stems from the collaboration of students from all programs across Ryerson. Watching students from Political Science, Radio and Television Arts, Journalism and Business Management all learn a piece of choreography together is really fascinating. Everyone is able to bring something different to the table from their different learning styles, and when you top that with different past theatre experiences, it makes for a very cool dynamic.

Heidi: In your opinion, what makes musical theatre such a popular form of theatre entertainment and, among its biggest fans, a passion or even an obsession?

Robyn: Theatre as a whole offers an escape from reality. It transports you, similarly to movies and books, into a different timeline and a new narrative that lets you take a break from your life and be drawn into a new story. But with theatre, it is all living and breathing right in front of you. What makes musical theatre really stand out, I believe, is the fluid coordination of the blocking, the score, the vocals and the choreography. There are always going to be fans of acting, or dance or music, but the mastery of the three brings these audiences together and has the ability to wow them in ways they couldn't have imagined.

Heidi: Theatre, like film, is highly collaborative in nature. Please talk a bit about the importance of—and your own experience with—collaboration among members of different teams, for example the executive and production teams of RMTC.

Robyn: What is really great about the RMTC is that we work without a hierarchy. If any section of our group was missing, we could not function. We are all on the same line and need each other in order to operate. This is what I think really drives the collaborative (and supportive) nature of RMTC and really how it thrives. I've learned that it is most important that your team feels they have the ability to accomplish what they can do and that they have a team surrounding them that wants them to be successful. With our production team, there has to be a lot of "big picture" talks to ensure that the overall vision of the production is being met, while with our executive, it is more focused on "what's next" and always ensuring that what we are doing now is putting us in a good position for the next two, five, 10, 20 years.

Heidi: What advice do you have for aspiring musical theatre performers and also aspiring theatre producers?

Robyn: Just try. The world of theatre is for trying, for experimenting, for failing, for succeeding and most importantly for learning. Never did I think that at 21 I would have created a 90+ person student group and, without the glimmer of the "what if" mentality, I don't know if RMTC would be here today.

Learn more about RMTC at www.ryersonmt.ca and on social media (@ ryersonMT)

INTERVIEW WITH JULIAN TROIANO

Photo and biography courtesy of Julian Troiano

Julian Troiano has been surrounded by music his entire life, starting with his uncle, Hall of Famer Domenic Troiano. He continued on this path by teaching himself piano and performing with several bands through his teen years.

Julian graduated from Metalworks Institute's Music Performance and Technology Program in 2014 with a full-ride scholarship. Experienced in film composition and songwriting, as well as live and in-studio performance, Julian makes a living in the industry by performing, co-writing songs and producing artists.

Julian is a product representative for Roland Canada and is an active Youth 4 Music Ambassador for the Coalition for Music Education.

~~~

Heidi: When did you start writing songs?

Julian: I wrote my first complete song when I was 18. I started writing a little later than a lot of singer–songwriters.

At 15, I started to teach myself piano to accompany myself as a singer because a musician once told me that if you want to be communicating with other musicians but can't do something instrumentally as well, then it limits you in a lot of ways. I mainly learned by ear, and I had just enough theoretical knowledge that I could fill in some of the gaps to learn songs and perform.

Heidi: What was your first song and the inspiration for it?

Julian: Part of my first song was written in my parents' basement when I got my first keyboard. It was the first time I remember coming up with a melody and thinking, "I'm going to keep working on this!" I had been taking singing lessons with Ryan Luchuck (*see p.237*) for a year, and he took me under his wing and essentially became my musical mentor. We threw ideas back and forth and then we completed the song together. We also recorded an EP together a couple of years ago.

That first song was called "Be Me", based on one of my biggest struggles, a friend's influence over me. It was one of those situations that you don't know is bad until everything spills over into your life. He influenced me to not be myself. It made me self-conscious and a copy of him instead of me. It's funny to see how you wrote when you were younger. There's less of a filter and judgment on songwriting structure.

Heidi: Was songwriting your first creative outlet?

Julian: I think music (playing and singing) was my first creative outlet. Initially, with songs, lyrics were the last thing I listened to. I liked the melody and the soundscape and the instruments. I remember sometimes listening to a song and I had no idea what it was about because I enjoyed the musicality of it so much. Writing was more of an advanced outlet. I had to kind of try it, as it didn't come naturally to me right away.

Heidi: Do other forms of artistic expression and life experience influence your songwriting?

Julian: Life experience, absolutely. There were times when I didn't write for a year and I'd get upset with myself and then I realized that I had to live and go through things to cultivate ideas and to understand more about life. I feel that as we grow and learn as people, we become more advanced as musicians and creators. It all works together. If you were secluded in a room for your whole life, I don't think you could write. You need either life experience or to be extremely empathetic and tap into other peoples' lives and experiences to write.

As far as being inspired by other art, I'm inspired by scores for fantasy-type movies like *The Lord of the Rings* and epic musical films like *Guys and Dolls* and *West Side Story*, with those classic, amazing songs, and also Gershwin's *Rhapsody in Blue*. With musicals, I feel more emotion than with any other artistic medium. There's just something about music combined with acting and a story that touches me more than any TV show or movie ever could.

Heidi: Who influenced or encouraged your writing?

Julian: As a personal mentor, definitely Ryan Luchuck. Influence-wise, Stevie Wonder and Jason Mraz. I listened to Jason for about a year, for hours every day, and even found every single live performance of his. His lyrics are so clever and he has a very unique writing style. I also love Elton John and Billy Joel.

Heidi: What tips do you have for new songwriters on making the most out of a co-writing session or an ongoing collaboration with another songwriter?

425

Julian: Transparency. Always be very up front on what the writing share is. If you don't iron that out right away, you can definitely get into tense situations. If you're in an ongoing writing relationship, it's usually 50/50 even if one person does more, because you're going to make up for it in the next song. (You also want to write with someone who is pushing to do their best, too.)

Explore all aspects of songwriting, but don't feel pressure that you have to excel at all of them. Sometimes there's more advantage to developing the areas you're already strong in so you can be a more effective co-writing partner. I know some people like writing by themselves, but I like bouncing ideas off of someone else. I find if I'm writing by myself I'll throw away so much stuff but if I'm with someone else, they'll say, "No, that's a good idea" or vice versa.

Heidi: What advice do you have for new songwriters and musicians about trying to make a living in music?

Julian: Being diverse with musical skills, being open to things changing and knowing that you want to go in a certain direction. You may not know exactly where you want to end up, but if you're sticking to it, then that is super-exciting in itself! Having a diverse skill set (recording software, teaching, performing, etc.) will help greatly in making a living along the way.

I'm super grateful that I'm able to do music. At one point, I didn't know which role in music I enjoyed more, which is why I kept doing all of them. That worked to my advantage because it gives me a bit of experience and knowledge in each area. This is especially important for writers because initially there's not going to be any money or income from writing. You need to be doing other musical things to survive at the same time so you don't have to go work somewhere you don't want to work while writing.

CONVERSATION WITH SONGWRITER–
PRODUCER, MURRAY FOSTER

Photo and biography courtesy of Murray Foster

Murray Foster is a musician, songwriter, director, teacher and entrepreneur.

Murray spent thirteen years as the bass player for the Newfoundland band Great Big Sea, and prior to that was a founding member of the Toronto group Moxy Früvous. Murray is currently a songwriting professor at Seneca College. In 2015, a song he wrote for the band Fortunate Ones, called "Lay Me Down," spent three weeks at #1 on the CBC Radio 2 Top 20. Murray also plays upright bass in the jazz trio, The Lesters.

In 2013, Murray became a founding member of the Toronto Music Advisory Council (TMAC), which advises Toronto City Council on how to improve the city's music ecosystem. Through this involvement, Murray has recently incorporated a non-profit called Toronto Music City to partner with the City of Toronto and Daniels Developments in order to improve music education across Toronto and build affordable housing for musicians.

Murray recently wrote, directed and scored a feature-length film called *The Cocksure Lads Movie*, which played at film festivals in Madrid and Shanghai and won the Special Jury Prize at the Niagara Integrated Film Festival in 2015. The movie was released across Canada in August 2015 and on iTunes in November 2015. From 2014 to 2016, Murray was Executive Director of Our Place Initiative, a non-profit organization dedicated to improving civic engagement across Toronto.

Murray's other ventures include founding the Toronto Songwriting School (www.torontosongwritingschool.com) and Choir Nation (www.choirnation.ca), which brings choir singing to corporate employees across Canada. He is also President of the Board of Directors of The Urban Orchestra, which performs orchestral music in unconventional urban venues.

~~~

Heidi: What are some of your earliest memories of artistic expression?

Murray: Earliest memories? Well I played one of the three wise men in kindergarten in a nativity play. I guess that's my earliest; it's not my best, but it's my earliest memory. In terms of creativity, I started playing music when I was 10 or 11, piano and guitar. I spent a lot of time learning, listening to Q107 radio station, and learning Led Zeppelin songs like "Stairway to Heaven" on guitar, which I think is a great education for young people. I also spent a lot of time playing Dungeons & Dragons. It's not music-related, but I think it's a great outlet for creativity and a great sort of training ground for an imaginative mind. It's a fantastic game.

Heidi: What role has collaboration with co-writers and fellow performers played in your career?

Murray: It's something that I'm doing more and more these days, and I think it is sort of an emerging trend in the music world, certainly in the pop sphere. Most of the songs you hear on the radio are co-writes, and that system has been very formalized. In Toronto, in LA, in Nashville, you meet another songwriter and you co-write, and the royalty system is all well established. It's a larger part of every songwriter's world to co-write. For me, specifically over the last two or three years, I've worked with a number of artists. My most successful collaboration was with the Fortunate Ones, a duo from Newfoundland. They opened up for Great Big Sea a few years ago and we ended up talking. They hung out at my house, with no intention of co-writing, and within three days we had written three of the songs on their first album. That's been one of my most fruitful ones, and that song, "Lay Me Down," went to #1 on CBC Radio 2. It's more and more a part of every songwriter's life.

Heidi: What advice from your past collaborators or mentors do you still follow today?

Murray: One piece of advice I received about co-writing is to always keep it moving forward. If you're working with an idea and there's a three-minute or five-minute gap where no one's speaking and no new ideas are being put forward, the idea will just sort of die. So I think it's just important to keep a momentum, a creative momentum, and finish the song or even sketch out the song, but get it done in that one burst of creativity and energy in one session. You can come up with an idea and the other person is like, "No, it's not great" and then they come up with an idea and you say, "No, that's not great", and then you're both sort of silent for three minutes, and then it's like "OK, time to go home." It's important to say yes to ideas for sure, but it's also important to keep the momentum going and the energy up in the session.

Heidi: As a songwriting teacher, what makes a productive relationship between an instructor and a student?

Murray: I think there are just some students who are open to exploring and open to learning, trying new things, and as an instructor, that's what you're looking for. There are students who come across as kind of grumpy, and you teach them stuff and you're trying to convey that excitement to them, and they're just not buying it. They are too cool to take a chance creatively and that's a real buzzkill in terms of a classroom or a relationship. You want students who are keen to take a chance and try new things—you know, take some risks.

Heidi: Same question, but in your role as a producer this time—what makes a successful relationship between a producer and an artist?

Murray: For me, the best collaborations in the studio are when the best idea wins. It's not about who owns the idea, but when everyone in the room says, "That's the best way to do it—that's the best way to go." What really stifles a creative process in the studio is when people start treating their ideas like their children—very protective. Their idea of winning is having more of their ideas on the CD than anyone else. For me as a producer, when I go into a situation with a band, they've often been doing arrangements, song structure and lyrics a certain way for a long period of time. You know, you write them in wet concrete and eventually the concrete sets and it's not necessarily the best version of that song but it is the one they've gotten used to. As a producer, you come in there with the dynamite and sometimes, you have to dynamite the concrete and say, "I know you've been doing it this way for a year and a half, but this bridge doesn't work, and your second verse is too long, and your second chorus is too long, so we've gotta change it." And you hope that they are receptive to that, to changing stuff that they've gotten really used to.

Heidi: The music industry has changed since you co-founded your first band around 1990. What are some of the pros and cons of starting a band or being a solo artist today?

Murray: Well, on the con side, it is much, much harder to make a living because CD sales don't really exist anymore and radio royalties have shifted a lot to streaming, and streaming pays almost nothing. If you think of the three traditional streams of revenue for an artist, a musician—CD sales, radio play and live performance—really, only live performance is going to be paying you any money. For most musicians these days, you have to do other things. You have to be a producer, engineer or teacher, or something like that. You have to have five things on the go that make you a bit of money to support your career as a musician. That's the big downside.

The big upside is that recording technology is much cheaper and so, in my house, for a few thousand dollars, I have a system that can do professional recordings. That was not at all available 20 to 25 years ago. You can make a really good-sounding record for $10,000. Book the studio for two or three days, do the drums, then tracks, then do all the vocals at home, and all the over-dubs, and that's a great luxury.

The upside of streaming is that so many people have access to so much music now through YouTube and streaming sites. There are fewer gatekeepers. You can access your audience really immediately, which is great, but it also means that record companies are less and less apt to support you. A lot of functions by record companies (funding for videos and CDs) have vanished. Now you have to be the musician, band leader, promotion company, bank (you have to crowdfund) because there's no label money. The opportunities for a young genius in his or her bedroom to make a splash are probably bigger than they were, but they have to do all of it themselves. They have to learn social media, crowdfunding, all of that stuff, and it's often outside of the wheelhouse of a musician. A musician should just be a musician because that's what they're good at. But these days, you have to be good at this crazy array of other skills. I'm sure there are amazing musicians in North America who, because they can't do social media very well or don't have this other skill set, will never be professional musicians. Whereas 25 years ago, they'd be discovered by a record company and they would be supported and nurtured.

Heidi: Your creative career path over the past five years has been winding and diverse. Was it all a wonderful surprise to you, getting into teaching and filmmaking? And did you find that your skills and experience in music prepared you for this new, creative direction?

Murray: With the film, *The Cocksure Lads*, if I'd known it would take four years to complete, it would have been much more daunting. I jumped into it with that sort of naive sense of "how long's this gonna take, you know—five weeks?" and then four years later you have the movie. It's sort of my naïveté that carried me into that forum, that genre. I learned tons and tons, some of it obviously related to filmmaking but other stuff just like life lessons in terms of putting together a project, running a project, dealing with people and stick-to-itiveness. For something that I kind of stumbled into, it has paid a lot of dividends. And being a musician provides you with the really valuable skill set of being comfortable in front of people, which is not something every person has.

Musical Theatre: Essays

Collaboration, Community, from Page to Stage

by Marion Abbott

Photo and biography courtesy of Marion Abbott

Marion Abbott is a proud graduate of the Musical Theatre Performance Program at Sheridan College and has achieved her ARCT in Piano Performance and Grade 10 Voice from the Royal Conservatory of Music. As a performer, Marion has appeared in such shows as *Bye, Bye Birdie*, *Drood* and *Into the Woods*. For 10 years, Marion ran Marion Abbott's Performing Arts Studio in Brampton, Ontario. The studio produced over 30 productions, including *All Shook Up*, *Seussical*, *Mousetrap* and *Zombie Prom*, and the students performed at Walt Disney World, Orlando, Florida, in 2009 and 2011. Marion works for Drayton Entertainment as a musical director for *Aladdin: The Pantomime* and for the Drayton Youth Program. She is the founder of The Spirit of Maud Theatre Company, Plain Stage Theatre Company and The Women of Musical Theatre Festival. In 2014, Marion created The Confidential Musical Theatre Project, and it made its world debut in Toronto in July, with *Sunday in the Park with George*. Within the first two years, the concept was franchised in 15 cities in both Canada and the United States. The Confidential Shakespeare Project and The Confidential Opera Project are both sister companies, operating in Toronto. In her (very!) spare moments, Marion is a voracious reader and a huge film buff; Walt Disney is her personal hero and she enjoys reading about his life and legacy. Marion is married to Italian visual artist Giancarlo Piccin and they have a son, also named Giancarlo. They are certain he will grow up to be an accountant.

~~~

The Way Back to Creativity

In 2013, I hit "artistic burnout." I was teaching and leading music and generally working in my field, but I was feeling incredibly unhappy and unfulfilled. I had no idea what I wanted to do, but I knew that my heart yearned for more and that I was meant to *do* more.

So I worked for Target and had a year-long adventure in retail! And I loved it. It taught me the value of leadership and what my own capabilities were in that area. I learned how a store was built and how the mighty retail machine works. Sadly, Target was unsuccessful in Canada. Before Target Canada closed, I left, but not without a renewed sense of self and clarity that comes after a "famine."

Six months after leaving, I came up with the concept for The Confidential Musical Theatre Project and, with that journey, made my way to exactly where I'm supposed to be. That time of "artistic famine" gave me a fierce love and appreciation for all of the opportunities currently afforded me, and working in retail full time gave me a unique understanding of that world and the struggle most artists have with balancing their artistic journey with the need to work a "joe job." At the time, it was pretty awful to live through, but I'm forever thankful for my artistic burnout and that chapter of searching and yearning.

The Need to Showcase Aspiring Talent

As long as I can remember, I have *loved* putting people in shows.

My senior kindergarten report card actually says, "Marion loves to perform and direct plays. Due to this ability, she has organized her peers into dramatic roles, which they demonstrate before the class."

When I started The Confidential Musical Theatre Project in Toronto, I didn't realize how few opportunities there were for musical theatre artists to get to perform on a regular basis, and then I learned that the same was true for so many performing artists. The Plain Stage Theatre Company and The Confidential Shakespeare and Opera Project were born out of that realization.

I believe that all artists deserve a chance to show what they can do, to use their skills and feel validated by the response of a live audience. I have a burning passion within me to create as many opportunities for as many artists as possible, as quickly as possible. That passion powers me through every project, every meeting, every email, every phone call. I don't know how else to describe it. I love that quote from the musical *Hamilton*, where they describe Alexander Hamilton by saying, "Why does he write like he's running out of time?" My passion for all artists to have an opportunity has led me to produce shows as though I'm running out of time, and I'm loving it! All of it! Meeting new artists excites and inspires me. As my work grows and I'm able to include even more artists—directors, musical directors, stage managers, technicians—I just get more and more inspired to do more. Phew! I'm all fired up just writing about it! As my personal hero, Walt Disney, once said, "The way to get something done is to stop talking and get busy doing."

435

THEATRE: A PLACE FOR COLLABORATION AND COMMUNITY

The challenge of theatre is that it is a team effort, a community effort. The beauty of theatre is that it is a team effort, a community effort.

The Confidential Musical Theatre Project proposed a unique question: can a cast of performers, who only met each other 60 minutes before the performance, create believable relationships? Will the audience actually believe that they're married? Best friends? Colleagues who've worked together for years? And the answer to that is a resounding yes.

By taking away the rehearsal process, the artists are solely dependent upon each other to tell the story of the musical. All barriers usually created by experience, equity standing and good old theatre gossip are stripped away by this desperate need for each artist to give his or her best in order for all of them to succeed. And the results have been magical. The arts can survive only if we support each other. My personal motto is that I want to work only with artists who are kind, reliable and generous. Talent is talent and it will always find its "stage." But kindness, reliability and generosity are what I think are key to creating great theatre and great community.

FROM PAGE TO STAGE: GETTING YOUR SHOW PRODUCED

There are those pieces entitled "Everything I needed to know about life, I learned in kindergarten." Well, for me, everything I needed to know about producing, I learned by running a performing arts studio for kids. My studio used to put on three recitals, two musicals, two plays, a music marathon, multiple solo concerts and various special events every year.

And I learned and learned and then learned some more about everything from casting to show rights to venue choices to dealing with actors from these hectic (crazy! insane!) years. Oh, the stories I could tell! A few of my personal favourites include a fire, a snowstorm, an actor going home sick 10 minutes before a performance, a flooded theatre and taking 14 teenagers to Disney World to perform. Buy me a drink and I'll share them all!

And believe me when I say that not all of my producing efforts were successes. Like the time my six actors marched on stage for a performance, only to find three audience members in attendance. Or the time I ignored my gut, cast the most talented actor in a leading role (rather than the most generous) and paid for it in a myriad of ways, right up until the end of the closing night party.

I feel that producing is a juggling act. You juggle booking your venue with obtaining your show rights, with your director's recent day job schedule change, with your stage manager's need for exact dates and times. You juggle your dreams for your leading lady with her recent family emergency and the need to let her go and recast a week before opening. And you juggle your need for downtime with the need to advertise and encourage your artists and sit in on rehearsal and and and—. And boy do I love to juggle! I love and embrace it all.

If I Had to Give Producing Advice, I'd Say Three Things:

1. **Momentum is everything.** Set your date and go, go, go! As long as you keep your end goal date open, you'll never reach opening night. If you don't have your next production date in mind once you get your first one rolling toward opening night, you'll disappoint both your patrons and your artists. If you don't keep your timelines tight, you'll lose the interest and commitment of your artists. Momentum is *everything*.

2. **Less is more.** Don't try to achieve more than you can afford. No story was ever ruined by the lack of pyrotechnics or massive set pieces. Keep the focus on your actors and the text of the story they're telling. Less is more every single time. If

437

you have a budget of millions—awesome! But still, spend it wisely, because less is always more. Always.

3. **Own it. Own it all.** If you felt strongly about a casting decision, own it. Don't waver. If fewer than half of what you were hoping for show up to watch your show, own it. Don't make excuses and try to pretend it didn't happen. Your artists need a strong leader at the top. If you waffle all over the place and try to act on all the advice and opinions you're given (and believe me, you'll be given a *ton* of advice and opinions, whether you ask for it or not!), you will not be effective. Make your choices, do your work and own it.

Mentor Me: An Inside View of Sessions with Singer–Songwriter Julian Troiano and Producer Murray Foster

by Heidi Stock

This is the fourth and final inside view of mentoring sessions in this book. It is literally, "mentor *me*," as I am the student. These sections are included in the anthology to give you a sense of the experience and benefits of one-on-one mentoring with a poet, screenwriter, songwriter or producer. It is only a sense of what private mentoring sessions may be like for you. Every mentor and every student is as unique as the relationship between them.

Getting Here

Sessions with Julian Troiano (co-writer) and Murray Foster (producer) evolved out of my songwriting mentoring sessions with Luther Mallory (*refer to p.258 to read the Mentor Me: Songwriting essay and p.423 and 427 for interviews with Julian and Murray*).

Songwriting mentoring with Luther involved two very specific challenges: to turn one of my poems into lyrics and then to put those lyrics to song. The first challenge was accomplished. My poem, "Mirror Mirror," was turned into lyrics with Luther's instruction and after writing a chorus. But I was distracted by the melody that emerged, which didn't suit "Mirror Mirror's" lyrics, intended genre or overall "vibe." I was all right with this, though. Studying creative writing over the past six years, I was used to distraction, detours and the unexpected, especially when trying to force the writing process on a particular piece.

I worked on the second challenge, lyrics to song, with co-writer Rebekah Stevens (*refer to p.229 to read Rebekah's interview*), but not on "Mirror Mirror," as we'd planned. Instead, we focused on the song

439

"Free." I wrote the melody and lyrics, emailed them to Rebekah with a scratch vocal, melody track on keyboard, lyric sheet and sheet music. Remotely and independently, Rebekah wrote the chords for the song and created a demo. It was a treat for me to hear my song performed by a more polished musician and singer.

I was a bit self-conscious about the vocal recording of the melody I'd shared with Rebekah. Realizing that I would like to collaborate with a co-writer on future songs, I invested in voice lessons to learn to communicate my songs with more confidence. Through my singing teacher, Ryan Luchuck (*refer to p.237 to read Ryan's interview*), I was introduced to singer–songwriter Julian Troiano, who, like Rebekah, could do chord arrangement for my melodies but could also engineer and edit tracks.

GETTING STARTED: CO-WRITING COMPOSITIONS FOR A MUSICAL PLAY

All my songs have this in common—they are written:

- With my voice as the instrument (and then mapped out on my Yamaha keyboard)
- While moving (either standing or walking, whether indoors or outdoors)
- With the image of a character performing on stage

When writing melodies, I always envision an actor–singer and his or her movement on stage. Mind you, these performers are faceless. Not everything is clear to me, but I have a sense of the age, gender and personality traits of the characters these performers are portraying. Being able to conjure up persistent images of characters in my imagination as the melodies developed through my voice was a sign to me that all these songs were connected to one another and to the stage as a musical play.

Between December 2015 and February 2016, Julian and I worked on three of my songs. Then it was time for me to return to the "song in waiting," "Mirror Mirror." In July 2015, the song "Free" emerged out of the blue and sidetracked my writing on "Mirror Mirror." A few months later, I was able to write a melody and an intro for "Mirror Mirror," and this was the first song Julian and I worked on. Ironically (and I don't know if this is the norm), the intro is always the last part of the songs I write. I deal with the "core" first (melodies for the verses and chorus), then I write lyrics according to the genre and feel of the song and then I add the "end pieces," like the intro and outro.

Julian and I collaborated by email, conference call and in person, and usually in that order. I'd email him my materials (instrumental melody, scratch vocal melody and lyric sheets), and then Julian would independently come up with chord arrangements, which he'd record in an MP3 file. That would be emailed to me, and we would schedule a call so I could give my first impressions and request any changes to the placement of the chords on the melody. To move forward with the final arrangement, I would meet with Julian at his home studio for 1-1/2 to 2 hours. In that time, seated at the keyboard, we'd run through a song, make adjustments, and at the tail end of a session, we'd discuss areas to edit. Within a couple of days, the final edited track was emailed to me.

In early 2016, we moved forward with two more songs, "Get Gone" and "Your Eyes on Me (Boy)." The process was the same as it had been with the first song we co-wrote, "Mirror Mirror," but paying attention to my lyrics and learning a bit about the characters for the musical, Julian gave more input. For example, when we were finishing up "Get Gone," he suggested an optional final verse that we may use if it works on stage.

"Your Eyes on Me (Boy)" was our final co-write piece. It's a challenging song, with four verses and no chorus, inspired by Alanis Morissette's song "Unsent" (five verses, no chorus), and made even more challenging by my unusual placement of the lyrics on the melody. Because of this, after adding the chords to the melody, Julian and I decided to meet in person to have a look at the lyrics. Maybe some words could be removed. It was very cluttered, very messy. We left it there, after the session, leaving the song with its original lyrics. At the end of the session, Julian remarked that the song needed to address who the boy in the fourth verse is, at the end of the song. Once that is known, things will become clearer. The good news was that this feedback made me think hard about the character in verse four and the future development of that character in the musical play. Eventually, that led to me writing the fifth verse of the song (many weeks later), which was needed to complete the story and the message of the song.

Time for a Pause

You gotta know when to take a break. And you shouldn't be hard on yourself for taking one. My mentor in screenwriting tells her students to take a break for a couple of weeks after receiving feedback or notes from readers on their screenplay drafts. A break helps you return to your writing with fresh eyes.

My break started in mid-February 2016. The instrumental tracks for three songs were completed by Julian by that time. But I was eager to hear the new songs recorded by a singer, so I reached out to one of my voice teacher's long-time students, Tricia Williams. The tracks and lyric sheets for "Get Gone" and "Mirror Mirror" were emailed to Tricia so she could learn the songs in advance of a recording session at a home studio. But soon after, I contacted Tricia and said the project was on hold (for now, anyway). I should listen to my own advice! My break had to be a complete break from the music of the play. Melodies for other new songs were sitting on my digital voice recorder, but they would have to wait, too.

ALL'S FAIR IN MUSIC SHARES

I might as well take a pause here, too, to discuss co-writing shares. As a writer of poetry, a few short stories and a few short film screenplays, I was not concerned about royalty shares. I'm unpublished and I write alone. With songwriting, you will likely have co-writers, especially if you want to create your best work. I learned that when two songwriters start from a blank slate in a session, they will sign a 50/50 share agreement up front, as one way to establish rapport and respect, get business out of the way and let creativity into the room. It's assumed they will equally participate in the writing of one song in the session, and if they have an ongoing collaboration, everything will even out over their catalogue of songs.

But in my case, I came into the room with melody and lyrics already written. So for my co-writers, Rebekah and Julian, our share split was based on another common 50/50 model, 50% for lyrics and 50% for music. I could share 25% of the 50% music share with Rebekah and with Julian on the songs they worked on. From the 50% music share, the split was 25% for melody and 25% for chord arrangement.

After there is consensus about songwriting shares among co-writers, a song can then be registered, noting all co-writers' names and their respective ownership (in percentages), with a national organization representing the performing rights of composers and musical publishers. In Canada, there's SOCAN, the Society of Composers, Authors and Music Publishers of Canada. In the United States, there are ASCAP, BMI and SESAC.

For musical plays, in addition to determining song splits, there's an opportunity to share recognition with your creative team collaborators in marketing and promotion for your stage production as well as future revenue sharing. This is a complex but important process that requires the guidance of an entertainment lawyer and preparation of legal agreements to ensure fairness for all parties. With compositions that comprise part of a theatrical performance like a musical or an opera, it's new territory. You're moving beyond "performing rights" into "grand rights," so it's wise to seek professional theatre industry and legal advice.

Writing the Book: The Script for a Musical Play

Now for the play part of a musical play! Taking a break from the music, I start to learn about the script, which is more commonly known as "the book." For example, on a playbill for a musical, you'll see something like, Book & Lyrics by John Roe; Music by Jane Doe.

It was now early spring. I was doing online research to find out more about writing the book for a musical play, and I bought a few publications on the topic. Reading these guides gave me a good start while I hunted for a local or Canadian online class to take, but I couldn't find one. A positive outcome of my ongoing search was that I was finding more and more professionals in musical theatre here in Canada and in New York City, home to Broadway musicals. Concluding that there was much more for me to learn about this art form beyond writing the book for a musical play, I decided to add a musical theatre section to this book to share these experts' words of wisdom with you in the interviews that precede this essay.

One of these interviews was with Elise Dewsberry, Artistic Director, New Musicals Inc. (NMI). NMI offers online courses for musical theatre writers. Just as I was reviewing my options for that and about to select the Book Lab, I noticed the Outlining Lab. I had a flashback to my screenwriting mentoring sessions with script consultant Stéphanie Joalland and the importance of creating a step outline before writing the first draft of a screenplay (*refer to p.320 to read the Mentor Me: Screenwriting essay*). So I registered in NMI's online Outlining Lab and I plan to take the online Book Lab in 2017.

Opportunity Didn't Knock (So I Did)

Once I found a course to help me with the writing of the musical play's book, I started to think about a professional studio recording for the song "Free." Of the four completed songs, "Free" might have the widest appeal. I assumed I would hire my co-writer Julian to engineer a session at my voice instructor's home studio and that I would be back in touch with the vocalist, Tricia, but there was an interesting step in between.

I created a new Twitter account and followed an initiative called Choir Nation. Choir Nation led me to the Toronto Songwriting School, and then I saw the affiliation of both initiatives to Murray Foster. Viewing Murray Foster's account and the account for his musical feature film, *The Cocksure Lads Movie*, I remembered his appearance on the venture capital reality TV show, *Dragon's Den*, through which he received funding from two "dragons."

The next day, the Toronto Songwriting School followed me back on Twitter, so I thought I would reach out to Murray to see if he would listen to "Free" and consider producing it. He had a listen, we met in person to discuss it and we set up my first session with a music producer.

Production Session One: Another Look at the Song

At the top of the session, I requested Murray's feedback on the composition itself, the songwriting. He suggested a redo of the chords in the bridge of the song. I contacted Rebekah (co-writer, who had done the original chord arrangement) and told her about Murray's recommended changes, and then we went ahead with them. Understanding that Murray had gone beyond the role of producer to that of songwriter as well, I discussed and cleared with Rebekah a 5% songwriting share to Murray on the song "Free," with 20% to Rebekah out of the total 25% share for chord arrangement.

445

The last half of the session was listening to the demo from beginning to end (again and again) to determine any additional instruments, which ones and where. I had mentioned wanting violins (which could be synthesized in, so we would just keep that in mind for later), bass and drums. Murray would write the bass and add that in a "bed track" (track underneath a piano track), along with the drums. I had no suggestions about the bass, but I requested that whatever drum beat he used, I wanted some tension—some authority to it, like a military march.

Murray created the bed track of bass and drums and then it was time to do a fresh piano track based on the newest and finalized version of the song's chords.

Getting Back to It

A few months passed since "taking a pause," and I got back in touch with Julian to hire him for the new piano track for the song "Free" but also to share with him short tracks (30 to 60 seconds each) consisting of one verse and one chorus for six new songs for the musical. Julian wrote the chords for these pieces and did instrumental tracks for each one. Admittedly, these songs are incomplete and will be until we return to them in 2017. At this time, they will become part of a five-minute medley that can be submitted to workshop or grant opportunities (along with the signature song, "Free"), while the musical is in its lengthy development phase. (*To learn about the development of musicals, from concept to stage, from my conversation with commercial producer Michael Rubinoff, see p.382.*)

Production Session Two: Recording Day

A couple of months before our scheduled recording session, I reconnected with Tricia Williams and hired her for the recording of the song "Free" and the medley at Murray's home studio. In advance, I shared my instrumental melody, scratch vocal tracks and lyric sheets and Julian's piano tracks (chord arrangements only), which would act as Tricia's vocal cues for the melody and on which Murray would place her vocals.

I was moved by Tricia's performances on her YouTube channel (www.youtube.com/user/tvwily), particularly her gospel/blues cover of the U2 song, "I Still Haven't Found What I'm Looking For" and the song, "Only Hope," from *A Walk to Remember*. Both of these performances were musically directed by our voice teacher, Ryan Luchuck, through his annual Own Your Voice performance workshops. Tricia's ability to master two completely different styles told me she could bring energy and inspiration to up-tempo pieces and softness and emotional connection to ballad pieces. I trusted that she would do a great job in the studio and she did. With her good instincts, she even made her way through the cluttered phrasing and lyrics of the song, "Your Eyes on Me (Boy)."

Post-Production

As I write this, we're in the midst of it! Murray will instruct me about next steps that will take place in the editing process, which I'm invited to be a part of, to make suggestions and provide feedback. It will be a collaborative process like the recording session, in which we (songwriter, session singer and producer) each share opinions about any improvements. Our edited, five-minute medley is now online at www.incommonthemusical.com.

AFTERWORD

Thank you to the readers of this guide!

Whether you are an aspiring writer, lifelong learner or just naturally curious, I wish you well in your personal and writing journey, as I do the grand prize winners of Aspiring Canadian Writers Contests (ACWC) who agreed to provide interviews and original poetry for publication.

When I conducted interviews across all areas of creative writing and mentoring covered in this guide, I was encouraged to find shared words of wisdom from interview subjects as well as many new insights. I hope the experience was the same for you as a reader, and that if you were drawn to this book to read a particular section, that you might have explored other sections too. Thanks as well to contributors who granted the reprint of interviews that they authored: Allyson Latta, Juliette Jagger and Amanda Clarke.

Many thanks to the acclaimed writers and industry experts who generously shared their time and knowledge in interviews and self-authored essays. You are an inspiration!

I'm so grateful to my one-on-one mentors (Janice Cunning, Shannon Bramer, Luther Mallory, Stéphanie Joalland, Julian Troiano and Murray Foster) for allowing me to share an inside view of our sessions together to benefit the reader experience. To celebrate the publication and release of *Mentor Me: Instruction and Advice for Aspiring*

HEIDI STOCK

Writers in 2017, there will be a list on our website with the names of mentors who may be hired for online mentoring in 2017. Visit www. aspiringcanadianwriters.org to view this list.*

All the best!
Heidi Stock, Founder
Aspiring Canadian Writers Contests

Please note that ACWC will determine if this list of mentors will be maintained and available on our website after 2017 just as mentors will determine their availability as online mentors throughout calendar year 2017 or later years (2018 onward), if applicable. The availability of any mentor is subject to change. All terms of the mentor/student relationship, mentoring sessions, and course or session fees are set by each individual mentor.

CPSIA information can be obtained
at www.ICGtesting.com
Printed in the USA
FFOW03n1325111217
44031145-43248FF